WHO'S AFRAID OF WEB PAGE DESIGN?

LIMITED WARRANTY AND DISCLAIMER OF LIABILITY

WHO'S AFRAID OF WEB PAGE DESIGN?

REBECCA TAPLEY

Morgan Kaufmann

AN IMPRINT OF ACADEMIC PRESS
A HARCOURT SCIENCE AND TECHNOLOGY COMPANY

San Diego   San Francisco   New York   Boston
London   Sydney   Tokyo

This book is printed on acid-free paper. ∞

ACADEMIC PRESS
A Harcourt Science and Technology Company
525 B Street, Suite 1900, San Diego, CA 92101-4495 USA
http://www.academicpress.com

Academic Press
24-28 Oval Road, London NW1 7DX United Kingdom
http://www.hbuk.co.uk/ap/

Morgan Kaufmann Publishers
340 Pine Street, Sixth Floor, San Francisco, CA 94104-3205 USA
http://www.mkp.com

Library of Congress Catalog Number: 99-62308
International Standard Book Number: 0-12-683620-5

Printed in the United States of America
99 00 01 02 03 IP 6 5 4 3 2 1

This book, as always, is dedicated to Steve.

Contents

Foreword

Why is this book different from other books on web page design? Because it uses the unique *Who's Afraid of?* system, which has one invaluable feature missing from other instructional books: It includes the feedback of someone who does not already know the material. I have found from years of experience that while it is necessary for an author to know a great deal about a subject to write about it successfully, that very same knowledge makes it virtually impossible for the author to understand which topics will be difficult for novices to follow. That is why the *Who's Afraid of?* books include the feedback of a real-life novice.

Of course, the idea of teaching via discussion with a novice dates to at least Socrates. The difference, however, between the Socratic method and the *Who's Afraid of?* method is profound. In the Socratic method, the author makes up questions that he or she thinks a novice might ask, but in the *Who's Afraid of?* method, the questions come from an actual novice. This provides a real test for the explanatory powers of the author, not just his or her own (possibly inaccurate) notion of what may or may not be difficult to understand for someone who does not already know the subject.

Judging by most of the mail I have received on my books using this approach, some of which is posted at http://www.koyote.com/users/stheller/wcppread.htm, it has made difficult topics such as C++ easier for those not previously acquainted with them. I hope that the other series books using the same approach meet with the same success. If you have comments on how it works for you, I hope you will tell the author, and also drop me a line at stheller@koyote.com. I am always looking for ways to improve my writing and the *Who's Afraid of?* approach!

Steve Heller
Series Editor

Titles in the *Who's Afraid of?* Series

Who's Afraid of C++? (June 1996) by Steve Heller,
ISBN 0-12-339097-4

Who's Afraid of Java? (July 1997) by Steve Heller,
ISBN 0-12-339101-6

Who's Afraid of More C++? (July 1998) by Steve Heller,
ISBN 0-12-339104-0

Who's Afraid of HTML? (April 1999) by Todd M. Howard,
ISBN 0-12-356915-X

Preface

Is This Book for You?

If you've got a decent grasp of the basics of HTML and want to learn how to build a better web site, the answer is yes. If you've never built a web site before, that's even better. This book will provide you with a place to begin, as most people who create web sites get hooked and stay hooked for a long, wonderful time.

(The World Wide Web, or just the Web as we'll call it, is a place of discovery, excitement, and imagination. It has quickly grown from its humble beginnings to become one of the fundamental and most important mediums of communication.) The downside of this explosive growth and all the attention, however, is the sense of mystique that surrounds many people's ideas about the Web. In the first book in this series, Steve Heller wrote that programming is commonly considered to be an extremely difficult, complex subject reserved for a "small number of specialists." He wrote his books about Java and C++ to prove that this attitude is dead wrong, and I believe that such elitist thinking about web page design is completely off the mark. It's easy to get the impression that the Web is out of reach when every large corporation has its own web site, and over

---

half the television ads you'll watch tonight will show you a URL just below the tag line.

The first goal of this book is to banish all such preconceptions. Anybody, with or without programming or design or high-end computer experience, can make a good web page and have fun doing it. Anyone. It's even easy to argue that the Web *should* be a place where all kinds of people with all kinds of skills and interests have all kinds of web pages. Part of the soul or spirit of the Web, and the Internet at large, always has been and always will be diversity.

The second goal of this book is to train your brain, so to speak. Web page design is as much a state of mind as it is a list of things to do or "rules" to follow, and it is a state of mind you can love to live in. So the second primary goal of this book is to make the work of constructing a web site not feel like work at all. You are laying the foundations for a new hobby, not a chore.

The tone of this book is chatty, informal, and exploratory. You will have to wrap your mind around some cutting-edge technologies like VRML and style sheets, but if you understand the larger picture of web page design, you will not feel lost or overwhelmed by your other choices. And *choice*, perhaps, is the key word to remember throughout the course of this book. Web page design is flexible, personal, and individual enough to accommodate people who just want to post their baby pictures, or people who want to advertise their business.

One important reason that this book is different from all the others is the presence and input of Amy Carpenter Leugs, the novice reader/tester/ guinea pig who worked on this book with me. I recommend that everyone read her account here at the beginning of the book before they dive in, so the nature of our "discussions" throughout the book will be clear. Amy's role in this project was to speak on behalf of the reader and the learner of web page design, while mine was to answer on behalf of more experienced web page designers. We both hope this dialogue yielded something valuable to you, beyond whatever facts and instructions we tossed around during discussion.

In the future, for information on updates, corrections, and other book-related matters, you can always access the web page I've constructed for this purpose at:

http://users.rcn.com/rtapley

You can also get in touch with me by writing to:

Rebecca Tapley
c/o Morgan Kaufmann Editorial Dept.
200 Wheeler Road, 6th Floor
Burlington, MA 01803

The "Letter from a Novice" is written by Amy. I hope you'll get as much out of her thoughts and participation as I have.

Rebecca Tapley

Letter from a Novice

Dear Reader,

If you are like me, you might be feeling a little defensive about picking up this book. After all, the World Wide Web is incredibly popular, and I am a fairly intelligent person with interests and ideas...so why haven't I already learned how to design a good web page?

The answers to that question are many. Learning web page design starts with the hurdle of learning HTML; though this is not a difficult language to learn, it still takes some time to familiarize yourself with the various tags, attributes and values. In my case, I learned HTML by reading *How to Use HTML 3.2* by Scott Arpagian and Robert Mullen, but the only pages I'd ever created were straight out of the book's exercises!

Even though you have HTML under your belt, you realize that you still don't know how to make a web page look good. Maybe you've even read a book such as David Siegel's *Creating Killer Web Sites,* but that, along with the tips you've gleaned from online primers and other sources, just isn't enough. You need to start at a slightly more basic level and work your way up to high-end design.

Consider also that web development is a time-consuming process, and that you probably have a life outside of web design. And you may have a different learning style than the people you know who took to web site design like a bear to the woods. You may need things laid out systematically, from the easy beginnings through to the fancy finishing touches. This book allows people like us to "begin at the beginning" and put together our bits and pieces of knowledge about good web page design into one complete and usable whole.

The reason that I really love this book is that it allows you to be smart; it goes way beyond the basics. *Who's Afraid of Web Page Design?* is about more than typing in lines of HTML. It teaches the novice universal concepts of design that have been adapted to the latest in technology. That means that you will be able to use much of what you read here long after VRML and style sheets are obsolete.

To ensure that our instructor/author Rebecca gives us enough, but not too much at any one time, I have read this book and asked questions or added comments along the way. I hope that they are the same kinds of questions and comments that you will be thinking as you read. Then you can see that it can be done; a novice who knows no more than you can become a full-fledged web page designer.

This brings me to a second point. As a soon-to-be web page designer, you have some serious issues to think about. Learning web page design makes you part of the Web community, which brings you into a worthy discussion that centers around this question: Now that we have the World Wide Web, what should we do with it?

What kind of content do you want to add to this global forum: educational materials, information about a political cause, your kids' pictures, or advertising and catalogs? What designs work best to inform, teach, or touch the people you want to reach?

Since the invention of the printing press, content, information, and stories have been partially defined by their limitations in text. Though I believe there will always be a place for reading text, whether from books or from archived files, I'm not the first to point out that a new age of literacy is dawning; the ability to present your ideas in an interactive medium of text, graphics and animation is what may set apart leaders in all areas of study.

Who's Afraid of Web Page Design? is a good way to get started being a leader in our global community. Fortunately, we have an interesting and fun author to show us what we need. Do the exercises, practice, and have fun. I'm sure I'll be checking out your site in the future.

Amy Carpenter Leugs

Thanks

First, thanks to my "Novice Reader," who turned out to be something closer to a coauthor, Amy Carpenter Leugs. Thanks for all your testing, your curiosity, your sharp questions, and the useful suggestions, even when we ended up adding new chapters. Similarly, thanks to Michael Leugs and Steve Mulder for excellent and expert technical editing above and beyond the call of duty. Your comments also helped a lot, and I am deeply indebted.

Thanks to Tom Stone, Thomas Park, Paige Whittaker, Julie Champagne, and Victor Curran for helping smooth the path at Morgan Kaufmann. Thanks to Steve Heller for his suggestions. And, last but certainly never least, thanks also to Benchmark and Morgan Kaufmann's production staff for making this book a book. Your hard work is greatly appreciated.

Thanks to Todd Howard and Ben K. DeLong for discussions of HTML, testing, and other commiserations (I owe you guys some dinner). Thanks also to the National Trust for Historic Preservation and Barbara Wuertz of SalemWEB for the pictures of the lovely old houses, and to Timothy Wallace, Elisabeth Parker Grace and Thomas Brattli for the scripts.

Last but never least, thanks to Chris Van Buren and the people at Waterside Productions for making it easier to do what I do.

Special Credits

We would like to extend special thanks to the designers, companies, and individuals whose web sites we have featured in this book. The URLs for these sites are distributed throughout the book where the sites are discussed in the text.

AdaWeb	HighFive.com
Abulafia/Dennett's Dream	Homewrecker.com
BoxTop SoftwareBRNR Labs	Mapquest
BRNR New Media	Margo Chase Design
Byte It!	Microsoft Inc.
Colony City	Mythopoeia
counterspace	Nationalgeographic.com
Cybertown	NetGrocer, Inc.
DeLiAs.com	The Official Riven Journals site
eBay	Salon magazine
FUSE98	Snapple
Gabocorp Imaging	TSDesign
Gamecenter.com	<typospace>
Guthrie Bowron	Virgin Records America
glassdog.com	Webmonkey
HealthRider	Wert & Co. (info@wert.com)

About the Author

Rebecca Tapley is an author, software tester, project developer, and web page designer. Her other publishing credits include *The GoLive Bible* (IDG Books), *The Web Authoring Desk Reference* (Hayden Books), *How to Use Netscape Communicator 4* (Ziff-Davis Press), and *HTML 4 One Step at a Time* (toExcel). She also teaches Internet-related courses at ZD University and consults on usability and ergonomics of web design. Rebecca lives in Boston with her husband and their two precocious cats.

CHAPTER 1

Prologue: An Introduction to Web Page Design

"Begin at the beginning," insists the King of Hearts in that famous magical adventure *Alice in Wonderland*. Only this adventure called web page design does not necessarily have a beginning, a middle, or an end. Part of the fun, and the challenge, of designing good web pages is taking a deep breath and sliding down the rabbit hole into a whole new, unknown world.

In this book, you will be introduced to the culture and environment of the Web as much as you will learn how to plan, organize, and design a good web site. You cannot design for the Web without being familiar with what's out there (the tour of Wonderland comes a little bit later), and you can't learn about what's out there without first having a general scheme in mind. So let's jump!

Starting with you, the reader, we are making a few assumptions. It's essential first of all that you own a computer and a modem or some other kind of Internet connection, and that you be fairly handy with HTML. This is not an introduction to writing HTML code, and it is not an introduction to the World Wide Web at large. In order to do the exercises and follow along with the conversations between Amy and me, you will have to know how to access the Internet and use a browser (preferably some version of Netscape Navigator or Microsoft Internet Explorer), and how to create a basic, simple web page in HTML.

> **Amy:** I should note that my experience in HTML is pretty basic. I've created a very simple page and used Internet Explorer to read it off of my own disk, but I've never uploaded a page to a server. This means, of course, that I've never tested any links that I've written into a page. And I've never made my own graphics for a page. Would you say I'm at the right level for this book?

> **Rebecca:** I'd say so. This book will teach you how to do all the things you mentioned: creating more complicated web pages, uploading them to a server, testing and evaluating links and pages, making graphics for the Web, and much more.

Before we move forward, however, we should agree on some simple definitions and terms. We'll begin with the actual system you're working on—the parts of your computer and how it's connected to other computers—and move on to more Web-specific ideas.

The Internet is, very simply, a huge network of computers all linked together (for now) through phone lines. When you send email, for example, you are on the Internet. If you visit an FTP site to download a game or a free demonstration version of some software, you are on the Internet. **The Web**, on the other hand, is common shorthand for the World Wide Web, and it refers to the one small part of the Internet where information can be relayed in words *and* pictures simultaneously.

> **Amy:** You write that the Internet is a network of computers linked together through phone lines, "for now." Is it only for now because they will soon be connected by a better system? If so, what will it be?

> **Rebecca:** Yes, soon there will be something much better for everyone that doesn't make use of regular phone wires. The problem with regular phone-based connections is that copper phone wire was never meant to transfer noise-sensitive data like the data you receive from the Internet (email, downloadable files, web

pages, and so on). The background scratches and crackles we hear when we talk on the phone don't bother us, but they can and do easily disrupt Internet connections. Also, regular phone wires are constantly victims to the elements: rain, wind, falling trees, and, according to some phone companies, even high humidity or heat. So now that the Internet is a time-tested, permanent fixture in our lives rather than just a passing fad, it makes no sense to keep using phone lines.

In fact, better technology is already in place for a select few Web users in the forms of cable modems (you receive the Internet through your cable TV connection) and T-type lines (the T1 and so forth). However, all the options mentioned in this paragraph are either very expensive or hard to get or both. It will very likely take 10 or 15 years or more before anybody living anywhere can get an Internet connection based on something other than a phone line. Obviously, people living in urban areas will have the advantage— those who live out in the suburbs and beyond will have to have more patience.

When we discuss **hardware**, we will be talking about the kind of machine you are working on, not just the individual pieces such as the keyboard, printer, and monitor. In Web design, two kinds of computers matter most—a **PC**, which is a computer that runs Windows software, and a **Macintosh**, which is a computer built by Apple that runs Macintosh software. We will explore the differences and features of these two systems in detail later on.

When we discuss **software**, we will be referring to programs that strictly involve creating and designing web pages. When we refer to image software, for example, we will be discussing specifically how to prepare photos and other graphics for the Web—not the word processing, spreadsheet, or email programs you may use at work.

A **browser** is a particular type of software specifically designed to translate HTML into a web page. The most popular browsers are Netscape Navigator and Microsoft Internet Explorer, and we will examine these two browsers in detail later on. A **plug-in** is an additional, smaller software creation designed to enhance browser performance (it cannot and does not stand on its own). Plug-ins are typically used to support the use and viewing of movies, sounds, Java applets, VRML, and other such advanced-technology web page elements. We will explore downloading and using plug-ins later on in the book when we talk about high-end web pages and web page design.

An **editor** is almost the opposite of a browser. It is also a kind of software, but it is a type of program you use to write your HTML code. The number and variety of editors available are increasing every day, and we will talk about what kind of editor is best for your personal needs and work style. We will also provide a short list of which editors (and other kinds of software) you should have installed on your computer before you begin web page design. Look for this discussion and these lists in the next chapter.

When we use the term **ISP**, we'll refer to your Internet Service Provider—the company that provides you with your Internet connection. We will cover how your choices affect your web page design, whether you're using America Online or a local ISP.

The terms **uploading** and **downloading** within the context of this book apply strictly to moving web page information off and onto the Web. Generally speaking, these terms can refer to moving anything to and from the Internet at large, but we are focusing on what you need to know to publish your pages.

A web page **author**, very simply, is the person who created a web page. The person who views this web page is sometimes called a **surfer** or a **visitor**, but we will not use these terms interchangeably. **Surfing** in this book suggests a style of using the Web that's much like watching television with a remote control—flying through all the channels too fast to really see what's on. While this way of experiencing the Web has its merits, as a web page designer you really hope to attract **visitors**, people who will happen upon your site and decide to stick around. By the same token, **visiting** in this book means getting onto the Web for the sole purpose of spending in-depth time at a few sites, rather than very little time at many sites as a **surfer**.

> **Amy:** I like the distinction between a Web surfer and visitor. I know that I usually visit a search engine right after I start up my browser, because I'm usually looking for some specific information

about doing my taxes or finding an art class or something. Would you call me a searcher instead of a visitor or a surfer?

Rebecca: I'd call you normal. Most people begin a search for something specific on the Web with the search engine of their choice—some of the most popular at this writing are Excite, HotBot, Lycos, and AltaVista—or an index such as Yahoo!. For the record, though, indexes and search engines are quite different. An index is a closed list of prepared and categorized sites that people usually search by moving from link to link. A search engine, on the other hand, is a type of program that scouts the entire Web for information that people specify by using a keyword. Indexes are better if you know the exact name or type of site you're looking for—vacation sites for a particular region or state, for example—but search engines are more helpful if you have a less specific idea, such as resorts in general.

An Introduction to Writing HTML

Now that we've covered some introductory information about the Web, let's delve specifically into writing HTML. (You probably know a lot of this information already, but consider this section a refresher course.)

HTML, which stands for Hypertext Markup Language, is a shorthand version of a much larger computer language called SGML. It's most important to understand the nature of HTML as a brief set of instructions rather than a whole, detailed vocabulary. Most people who use computers are accustomed to using word processing programs and other software in which they literally write as they read. Writing with HTML in an editor is more like writing in shorthand, with whole words, grammar, and punctuation—so it can take some time for web page authors to adjust their expectations.

Amy: I'm just curious; what does SGML stand for? Something something markup language, I presume. And how does it relate to HTML?

Rebecca: SGML stands for Standard Generalized Markup Language, the parent or base language of HTML. The difference between them is length and complexity. If you were writing in plain English and you wanted to begin a new paragraph in SGML, you'd have to write, "Please begin a new paragraph here, but add more space between paragraphs in Microsoft browsers and make the closing tag optional in Netscape and Microsoft browsers 3.0 or later." To do the same in HTML, you'd write, "Begin a new paragraph here; refer to SGML for the rest." Or, as we know it, <P>, for short.

In this book, the term **web page** will refer to one individual HTML document. Alternatively, the term **web site** will always refer to a linked collection of web pages, so that we can easily distinguish between HTML that affects one page or many. In other books on HTML design, and in popular Internet magazines, these two terms are used interchangeably to refer to web sites.

When we speak of individual pieces of HTML, we will be talking about **tags**, **attributes**, and **values**. Here's an example:

```
<FONT COLOR="blue">This is text that will be blue.</FONT>
```

The **tag** itself is the opening <FONT> *and* the closing </FONT>, including the all-essential brackets < and > on either side. <FONT> in this example represents a general instruction to a browser to change something about the font used in a particular area of a web page. COLOR, the **attribute**, gives a little more specific instruction: it tells the browser to customize the color of the font to something other than the default, black. Finally, the **value**, blue, provides the most detailed instruction of all—it tells the browser which particular customized color to display.

For the purposes of this book, tags and attributes will always be shown typed in all caps and values all in lower case. Although this might make the printed HTML code harder to read, it serves an important purpose: to lead your eye more easily down the line from tag to attribute to value, as you will most likely be making most of your changes to attributes and values rather than tags. This does not mean, however, that case makes a difference in how your HTML is interpreted; you can type <FONT> as <font> or even <fOnT> and it will always work.

Now let's define various elements of a web page, starting with the three most basic types: text, graphics, and links.

Text, Graphics, and Links

There are three primary elements of a web page: text, graphics, and links. When we speak of **text**, we will talk about words on a web page that are only there to be read, to be taken at face value. The amount of text you will want on your web page will depend upon your preferences and the page's purpose, as we will explore later on. Similarly, **graphics** will be discussed as nonmoving visual elements on a web page that also only exist to be taken at face value. Graphics can be pictures, photographs, backgrounds, icons, and other such things. **Links**, on the other hand, are selected text and graphics that take a visitor to another web page on your site. When we talk about links, we will be talking about where to place them, how they can appear on a page, and the particulars of the HTML used to construct them.

Now, let's move on to some of the more intermediate and advanced elements in web page design: forms, tables and lists; audio, video and animation; dynamic HTML; VRML; and style sheets.

Lists, Tables, and Forms

A **list** is a short lineup of brief items usually indicated by some kind of bullet or numbering system. A **table** is also relatively straightforward: it's a group of cells, or predefined areas, on a web page that may or may not contain something and may or may not be outlined.

A **form**, however, is a little more complicated. What you see here in these figures, and here in the HTML written out on the page, is really only half of what constitutes a form. In addition to these HTML instructions, which you write into your web page, you also need a CGI script or a second set of instructions stored on your ISP's server. The form HTML tells the visitor to your page what to type or what to do, and the CGI script interprets this response. (We will get into CGI scripts and other form-related issues in Chapter 9, "Positioning Text with HTML.")

Audio, Video, Animation, and VRML

Audio in this book will be defined as any way of adding sound to a web page—as a continuous soundtrack, as a sound effect, as a snippet of music, or spoken word such as a poem. **Video**, similarly, will refer to any way of adding motion pictures to a web page, such as a small portion of a movie or a homemade film of your cats rolling around the living room floor. The distinction here is that audio and video can always be controlled with a playbox, which is a tiny set of buttons that resemble the controls on a VCR or stereo player. You might elect to leave out the playbox so your sounds or video can play continuously, but the HTML you use will provide you with a choice.

Animation, however, will refer to a particular kind of special effect on a web page that moves continuously from the moment a web page loads up. Some business web pages, for example, have animated logos or other corporate identities meant to represent a business, just as its letterhead does. Other web pages use animated buttons, navigational bars, and horizontal rules just for fun. But in contrast to video, animation runs on its own and cannot be controlled by the person viewing your web page. For this reason, we will discuss how, when, and if animation can be used effectively in various web page scenarios.

> **Amy:** I'm pretty sure that we're going to talk more about how to create audio, video, and animation files. I'm hoping that we will also talk about the basics of writing HTML to include these elements, since I've never used them at all.

> **Rebecca:** We'll definitely cover more detail about adding audio, video, animation, and other more complicated elements. We'll also talk about how to provide contingencies for visitors/surfers using the different browsers on different platforms, as the HTML you have to

use to insert a movie in Explorer, for example, is very different from the HTML you have to use for Navigator. Don't worry, though! This is only the introduction; the details are on the way.

VRML is a slightly less common acronym and web page technology, but it is still somewhat misleading. VRML stands for Virtual Reality Markup Language, yet you can't really experience virtual reality via today's common personal computers. You need goggles, headsets, or a holodeck, to use Star Trek lingo. So instead, VRML at this moment refers to virtual reality "worlds," or three-dimensional sites, tours, and/or communities on the Web, which give the *appearance* of virtual reality. While this book does not teach you how to create these worlds, we will show you how to incorporate existing ones into a web page.

Amy: Wouldn't VRML sites take a long time to download? How well do existing ones work, in your opinion? Will we talk about ways to give a fairly 3-D feel without getting into VRML proper? The reason I ask is that I would eventually like to put up a site that is a "museum," in which people can visit different exhibits and (I hope) interact with them to some degree. Will this be possible?

Rebecca: Yes, VRML sites *and* VRML worlds do take a very long time to download if you're on the typical 28.8Kbps modem (if you're on a 14.4Kbps modem, you'd better bring a good book). They all require a set of plug-ins most people may or may not have installed, and some of them are poorly designed, so they crash your machine. And we're not going to get into how to actually *build* a 3-D VRML world, because that's as complicated and separate a topic as learning C++ or Perl. That's the bad news.

The good news is that the kind of museum site you envision is already possible to a limited but perhaps acceptable degree, with regular HTML, scripting, and a little excellence in preparing graphics. In fact, we'll look at a couple of sites like these in Chapter 4, "More Basics of Site Creation," and in the Gallery on the CD-ROM. Maybe you'll be inspired to try to design such a site anyway.

Dynamic HTML, Style Sheets, and JavaScript

Dynamic HTML is an enormous category that includes all kinds of things, and it's currently a hot topic in web page design, so it's a term that's being tossed around very casually. To put it briefly, dynamic HTML (or DHTML) is traditional HTML that can be made to move or be interactive after the page has loaded. Not much of a definition, if you think about it, so we will cut it down to a manageable size. Although dynamic HTML encompasses much more, in this book we will largely focus on incorporating JavaScript and other multimedia design elements such as style sheets. We will not cover how to write new JavaScripts, and so on, from scratch, and we will not even try to encompass dynamic HTML as a whole.

> **Amy:** Is animation a type of dynamic HTML, since it moves on a web page and is usually encoded in the HTML? I'm assuming there's a reason for the distinction between the two, but I can't quite figure it out.

> **Rebecca:** Good question. There are many kinds of animation you can include on a web page, one being DHTML. Let me use an example to describe the difference.

Imagine an animated ball bouncing on a web page. You see the ball drop in on the left side, bounce in the middle, and exit off the screen on the right side. One way to accomplish this effect is with a GIF animation, or a series of individual pictures showing the ball at every point in its movement across the page—like a cartoon, or a flip book you move with your thumb. Another kind of animation, which *is* DHTML, uses only a single graphic—an image of the ball—but it moves that one graphic along its bouncing path on the page using JavaScript.

We will cover how to create a GIF animation and how to incorporate JavaScript later on in the book, but I hope this sets the stage and answers your basic question.

Style sheets is actually a part of what's considered dynamic HTML in the strictest sense, but we are considering it separately. This is because style sheets is unlike other kinds of dynamic HTML such as JavaScript, and we will also be speaking of style sheets as a way to maintain and update your site over time.

Amy: If I'm correct, style sheets will basically be HTML but will have a section at the top in which you can define tags more specifically. For instance, you can make every <H3> (level 3 heading) in the document an italicized, dark burgundy and use 14-point font. Is this correct? (Though I think I know what a style sheet is, I have no idea how to write one.)

Rebecca: Yes, you're more or less correct. Style sheets do depend upon HTML tags, which makes them very easy to write, but there are many problems with support (at this writing, N4 doesn't support style sheets as well as IE4 does), and you can get into trouble with the "cascade," which is unwittingly writing conflicting instructions. We'll cover all of this later—it's one of the most exciting new aspects of HTML, in my humble opinion.

On with the Show

Now that we've defined some terms and focused in on what we want to discuss, let's move on to a general discussion about your computer. What kind of setup do you need? Should you upgrade your hardware? Which software packages should you get, and where can you find them? All these questions and more can be answered in the next chapter, "System Fundamentals."

CHAPTER 2

System Fundamentals

In this chapter, we will examine the hardware, software, and other system needs you will require in order to create your own web site.

As we mentioned in the last chapter, we will be speaking of your computer only in terms of web page design, not as the larger, more multifaceted machine it actually is. If you want (or need) more information on how your computer works, or if you are very new to computers and need to learn a computer's basic functions, you might look into a beginner-level book about your particular type of computer before getting into this one.

System Requirements

This section of the book might seem unrelated to web design and to the use of the Internet in general, but paying attention to this mundane stuff now may very well save you time and hassle in the future. With that in mind, then, here are some broad guidelines for the minimum system setup you should have:

Amy: I know this stuff is important, but you'll probably see that I'm not very knowledgeable about it. I think that could be true of a lot of people who are interested in web design; they can get a lot done on computers without knowing much about gigabytes and megahertz.

Rebecca: Most people don't know a lot about this stuff until they have to—that is, till they run out of room or get error messages saying they are low on memory and they don't know why. And while you're right about getting a lot done in terms of design without knowing these details, it's also true that distractions can prove very frustrating. So I'm taking the stance that a little forethought pays off.

Amy: You might mention that people who already know a lot about hardware and software can just flip through this chapter for reference and come back to it if and when they need it. However, for those of us who have not made our own purchasing decisions before (whether our company or our spouse or another family member has done so in the past), I really recommend working through this chapter; it's easy to read, which is more than can be said for most other chapters of its type.

Rebecca: I couldn't have phrased it better myself!

For the PC:

- A PC model with a Pentium chip or later

- 8MB free of RAM; 12MB or more is preferable

- 25MB or more free hard disk space

- A CD-ROM drive

- A 28.8Kbps or faster modem, an ISDN connection, or a network connection (T1, etc.)

- Windows 98 system software; Windows 95 or NT are also fine
For the Macintosh:

- A Macintosh model with a 68020 chip or later; a Power Macintosh or G3 is preferable

- 8MB of RAM; 12MB or more is preferable

- 25MB or more free hard disk space

- A CD-ROM drive

- A 28.8 or faster modem, an ISDN connection, or a network connection (T1, etc.)

- Mac OS version 7.1 system software; System 7.5.3 or later is preferable

Amy: Netscape Communicator 4 alone took up 16MB of hard disk space when I downloaded it. I know this isn't a book on how to use your PC, but you might mention how to look up your hard disk space and how to find out how much different browsers "cost" in terms of that space. I looked up my C: drive space by opening Windows Explorer, right-clicking on C:, and choosing Properties off the menu that appeared. I found I had about 460MB free, so I should be fine, right? On the Netscape site I looked at the Product Specs to figure out how much space the Communicator program would take. I don't know if this is too elementary for your readers, but I didn't know how to approach it at first.

Rebecca: No, I think keeping an eye on free hard disk space is a very good idea. We might as well encourage good habits now before readers begin downloading movies, sounds, VRML worlds, and other memory hogs. And it's always a good idea to skim the specs if only to be on the lookout for software conflicts and bug reports. You never know what two software packages can and will create havoc on your hard disk.

Here's a burning question you might want to ask: which kind of computer is better, a PC or a Macintosh? Welcome to the world of computer rivalry! Most people who have used both kinds of computers for any length of time will say they have a preference. Usually this preference is based on familiarity rather than performance or other logical reasons, just as many people say their first car was their favorite car because they learned to drive in it.

System Fundamentals

What does this favoritism have to do with web design? Many people in highly creative professions such as graphic and web design use a Macintosh. But PCs are more popular; that is, a larger number of people buy and own them in their homes, schools, and non-Web-related businesses. So at this moment in Internet time, most web sites are being created on Macintoshes, but most web sites are being viewed on PCs. We will explore the impact of this situation on actual web page design later on, though we will touch upon these platform issues here in a general way.

If you own or are planning to purchase a Macintosh computer, however, we will recommend that you invest in a Power Macintosh or "higher"-model Apple. Power Macs, and especially the G3, run much faster than any of the earlier Apple models, and they also read/translate PC files. This crossplatform support may become very valuable to you if you really embrace web page design, and you'll certainly appreciate the speed either way.

Why does *all* this technostuff really matter? That's the substance of the next section, which is a more thorough discussion of how your hardware can limit or frustrate your efforts to create and maintain a really good web site. So let's press ahead.

Hardware Requirements

When we speak of **hardware** in the context of this book, we are talking about monitors, computer boards (or just computers), CD-ROM drives, modems, and some other more specialized elements such as scanners and exterior storage peripherals. While you can certainly create, store, and maintain your web site on an "average" computer system, if web page creation is going to be part of your job or a large part of your life, you will eventually wish to upgrade your hardware. This section of the book, then, is designed to give you a general introduction to the system you've got and a long-range plan for when, why, and how to do an upgrade if you need it.

One final note, though: It is beyond the scope of this book to recommend or evaluate specific hardware brands and models aside from the general comment we just made about higher-level model Macintosh machines. We will restrict the reach of this section solely to web-design-related thoughts and concerns as they relate to your hardware.

Monitors

Many professional web page designers would say without hesitation that the monitor is the most important part of your computer. Why? Because the only way you can accurately view the work you're doing is on your monitor. So the more clearly and realistically you can view a web page in progress, the better.

It goes without saying that your monitor should have color capability. Black and white might be fine for word processing, spreadsheets, and other such tasks, but it won't work for web page design. You should also think about the size of your monitor if you're going to get into web page design with serious intentions, as the more web page surface you can fit on a screen when you're designing, the more quickly and efficiently you can work. Most computer systems, whether PC or Macintosh, feature a 16-inch monitor as standard issue. This means, by the way, that the monitor screen measures 16 inches diagonally, not horizontally or vertically.

Computers

The word *computer* has come to define the entire system that sits on your desk, from keyboard to printer, but in the strictest sense your computer is the rather nondescript, boxlike part that sits on top of or under your desk. With relation to web page design, your computer is important because of the system software you are running, the amount of RAM and hard disk space you have available, and the kinds of disk drives you have available.

The better—or more recent—your system software, the better your other software will run. Earlier versions of Windows and Mac OS system software are all right for web page design beginners, but as we've already said, if you really get into designing your own pages you will find these limitations frustrating.

RAM and **hard disk space** can also become a large headache. RAM, or random access memory, affects how well you can run multiple software programs simultaneously. If you don't have enough of it, you will be forced to wait for one task to finish before another can start, and that gets tiresome very quickly. Hard disk space, on the other hand, affects how much software you can install and whether or not you can also store your web pages on your computer. Having insufficient hard disk space is like not having enough space in your closet—you can't keep all the things you need in one convenient place, so you have to run all over the house just to get dressed.

Most computers sold today come with a 3 1/2" floppy disk and a CD-ROM drive as standard equipment. If you don't have a CD-ROM drive, however, you may want to make the investment. Installing software with CDs is easier, and many clip art and other design products only come on CD. However, neither a floppy disk nor a typical CD-ROM drive will be of much help to you in terms of real storage if you run out of hard disk space, because a single floppy disk cannot hold more than a handful of HTML documents or three or four graphics, and the standard issue CD-ROM drive only reads CDs—it can't write to them.

For these reasons, an external storage drive is the best investment you can make if you know you're going to get serious about web page design. Products such as the Zip drive by Iomega are relatively inexpensive, and just one Zip disk (just as an example) holds as much information as 100 floppies. Having this kind of external storage at your disposal will enable you to store your actual web pages, as well as all their graphics, sounds, video, and other doodads, in an alternative location, so you can fill up your hard drive with all the software you need.

Amy: How can a person who is not used doing her own computer shopping go about comparing prices on external storage drives, and such? Are the big electronics stores a good place to start, or should we look at an online or catalog source? This question really applies to all the equipment, of course.

Rebecca: Shopping for hardware is like shopping for any other large, expensive item; you need to look in all kinds of stores and catalogs, on web sites and in newspaper circulars. The Web is a particularly valuable resource for saving time, and for getting the *Consumer Reports*-type lowdown on hardware performance. Online magazines such as *MacWeek* and *PCWeek*, and sites such as ZDNet and clnet, are all places to search for user reports and reviews. Check a manufacturer's web site for FAQs, technical information, and specifications, and then decide what model and make (so to speak) you're after.

Other places to look for good deals on the web are the auction sites such as eBay and amazon.com. These online auction houses are just like the real thing—you view items up for sale, place a bid against other bidders, and try to win what you want for a price below what the item is worth. However, these are not shopping sites where computer hardware is concerned; you must know what you want and how much you are willing to pay *before* you jump in. As in the real world, a good price in a virtual auction does not always mean a good buy, so be careful.

Modems

If you are a typical web surfer, the modem sitting on your desk or installed in your computer can only reach a maximum connection speed of 14.4Kbps. While this may be fine for recreational sightseeing around the Web, it's almost guaranteed that you'll be frustrated with it if you design your own web pages. Why? The waiting game. At that connection speed, you may easily find yourself twiddling your thumbs as you download software, audio or video clips, as you try to upload your finished pages to your ISP, and/or as you try to manage your time efficiently.

The best, affordable option is a 28.8, 33.6, or even a 56Kbps speed modem, any of which will only cost a few hundred dollars. If you are really forward-thinking, or if you want to splurge, you might investigate a cable modem or an ISDN. These connections will cost you more money in hardware plus some sort of monthly surcharge, but for a residential-based web design system there is nothing yet their equal.

The best of the best in Internet connections are any of the dedicated lines: T1 or the ultratechy T3. But realistically, many of us have mortgages and kids to feed, so we can't afford them at current prices. In fact, don't expect such a connection to become affordable in the average home for another 10 or 15 years.

Amy: I am curious; what is the approximate current cost of a cable modem, ISDN, or T1 line? And where would one go to investigate these options further?

Rebecca: Hang on to your checkbook! To answer this question, I turned to my personal ISP and to our local telephone and cable TV companies here in the greater Boston metropolitan area where all these options are available. (This is definitely not the case in smaller cities or other parts of the world.) Let's go in ascending order according to speed.

An **ISDN** (or Integrated Services Digital Network) gives you up to 128K in speed, which can be up to four times faster than the fastest available regular modem in existence. The monthly fee range here in my area (according to both my ISP and our local phone company) is $34–$35 for 100 hours a month, the setup charge is $50–$67, and the hardware costs just under $450. The phone company also charges one cent per minute in special usage fees on top of regular telephone fees and services, and I would still have to find and pay for my own ISP that supports ISDN technology. Finally, neither option includes the required ISDN software, either, which may or not be free.

A **cable modem** is a direct feed off your cable television connection and provides an Internet connection speed about three to five times faster. As an example, the day I got my cable modem I went to download a software program that's just over 38MB. I couldn't afford to download it using my modem because it took almost three hours of waiting time. Performing the same download using the cable modem took ten minutes. Here in Boston, cable modems cost $39.95 per month and $99 to install, but of course there are a couple of catches. You must also have a compatible Ethernet card installed on your computer (this varies depending upon whoever is providing your cable modem service), and you must have a cable wire nearby, too. If you don't have the wire, the cable company will have to come out and install or extend one for you—don't make the mistake of doing it illegally yourself, or you'll have the additional cost of fines to pay!

Also, the long-term speed of a cable modem is directly proportional to the amount of online traffic. A cable modem will always be faster and less noisy than standard modem service, but as more and more people in your area and neighborhood get cable modems the overall speed of cable modem service will begin to decrease. Unfortunately, the only way to lower the price of non-modem cable services is for them to become more common and popular, so it's a trade-off.

Amy: You have mentioned to me that a cable modem gives you direct access to the Internet and eliminates the need for an ISP, yes? Where do you store web pages, then; do you become your own server? And I assume there is some interface software that you need, or is that what comes with the Ethernet card? Is the range on the cost of the Ethernet card something around $200 to $400?

Rebecca: A cable modem gives you direct access in that you never have to dial in and wait to get connected; your Internet service becomes like your television cable service, which is always on, twenty-four hours a day. However, you don't have to pay for an ISP the way you pay if you get an ISDN, because your cable modem provider *is* your Internet provider. So you don't keep your old ISP, but you do get a "new" one, which stores your email and web pages in the same fashion. As for the interface, the Ethernet card is all it takes. And I do believe your cost estimate is about right (there are Ethernet cards you can purchase for $20 or $30 but they lack decent lifespans) unless there's a sharp change over the next three months.

Last but hardly least, the highly coveted T1 is more a description of line speed than of line type—it clocks in at 1.54mHz. Per second, that is. My ISP sells fractional T1 service, which is a sliding scale in increments of 56K, 128K, 256K, 384K, and a perfectly acceptable

512K. However, the cost is incremental, too; fractional T1 service begins at $500 a month, startup costs begin at $1,500, and hardware costs begin around $2,000. A true T1 costs $1,500 to $2,500 per month, setup costs are around $2,500, and hardware starts at $3,000. You can see why usually only businesses, universities, and government offices have T1 lines—the rest of us can only dream of affording such speed in our home offices and family rooms at these prices.

On a positive note, the cost of all these services will decrease as demand for them—and our average communication technologies— increases. ISDNs are already nearly obsolete in larger cities and urban areas because of fiberoptics which make cable modems more affordable and accessible. And the advent of products such as WebTV signal the inevitable merger of televisions and computers. So who knows where this technology is headed and how long the current options will be viable?

My personal recommendation (because, like I mentioned, I did this myself) is to settle for the middle road and go with a cable modem if you need it, if you can get it, and if you can afford it. I have grown sick and tired of getting disconnected every time there's a stiff wind blowing against the phone pole in the street, and of waiting half an hour for a plug-in to download—but I work at home on the Internet at least eight or nine hours a day. For me, a cable modem is not some frivolous toy. So I guess the operative phrase in this paragraph—heck, for this entire sidebar!— is "if you need it."

Scanners and Such: The Christmas List

In my family, if there's something extra special you want but can't afford on your regular budget, you ask for it for Christmas. This section contains some wonderful, but highly specialized and pretty expensive, pieces of computer equipment.

A **scanner** is very likely the first thing you will crave if you get hooked on web page design. These flat, desktop machines hook up to your computer like a printer but work like a super-smart copier: whatever you lay under the flap, such as a photo, a newspaper article, or a map, gets translated into a web page–ready file. All you have to do is write the necessary HTML, and whatever you scanned becomes a part of your web page. A good scanner at this writing costs around three or four hundred dollars and requires a little experience to handle properly. (Are you thinking of your wealthy, eccentric, generous old aunt yet?)

Something else to ask Aunt Mildred for is a **digital camera**. These little wonders look and work like regular cameras, the kind that take film you get developed at the drugstore, but they save your pictures to a floppy disk instead. So all you have to do is put that disk in your computer, write some HTML, and you're all set. Digital cameras cost slightly more than a scanner, more like four to five hundred dollars, but they are much more likely to drop in price, as they are easier to use than scanners.

> **Amy:** You can get regular photos reprinted onto a CD at most photo-processing shops, which is an inexpensive way to load photos into an image editor. I'd like to see the information included, since it would save people scanning fees from places such as Kinko's until they can buy the equipment you mentioned.

> **Rebecca:** Good recommendation! I believe I'll start using this alternative myself as I don't have a scanner or a trust fund to finance my technological whims.

Software Requirements

In this section, we will discuss various kinds of software you will want to have at your disposal for creating web pages. The short list includes browsers, editors, graphics programs, and extraction/ compression programs. The good news about the majority of this software is that you can get it either for free or as shareware (for a small fee, usually less than $20) directly from somewhere on the Web.

Browsers

In the course of reading this book, you will see references to and screen shots taken from two browsers: Netscape Navigator and Microsoft Internet Explorer. Together, these two browsers dominate the Web with a whopping 90 to 95% of all designers and surfers using one or both of them. It is highly advisable, then, for serious web page designers to have both Navigator and Internet Explorer installed on their computers for testing, for comparison, and for good general reference.

However, in this particular case, restricting yourself to only the most recent versions of Navigator and Explorer is not necessarily a good idea. This is because the average, common web surfer uses older versions of these browsers, and the older versions do not necessarily support all the cutting-edge technology we will cover in this book. So if you download, install, and only refer to Navigator 4 and Explorer 4, you will be creating pages that thousands of people will not be able to appreciate.

The only way to compensate for this reality is also installing and/ or keeping version 3 of Navigator and Explorer, too. (The need for all that hard drive space is becoming evident now, isn't it?) Navigator 3 is still available on Netscape's web site as a free download, but Microsoft does not archive Explorer 3. And, unfortunately, Microsoft wasn't thinking of web page designers when they created IE4: it will completely and irrevocably overwrite IE3 when you install it, so IE3 becomes essentially nonfunctional.

To download Netscape Navigator 4, which is part of the suite of programs called Netscape Communicator, follow these instructions:

1. Log on to the Internet, launch whatever browser you're currently using, and go to http://home.netscape.com.

2. Look for the Netscape Downloads link.

3. On the Netscape Download page, you want to choose the entire Communicator program—in other words, you do NOT want to upgrade with the stand-alone version. This will overwrite Netscape

3 on your computer if you have it, and you want to leave Netscape 3 intact for testing purposes.

4. Choose the version appropriate to the platform you're running: Windows 3.1, Windows 95/NT, or Macintosh.

5. Skip any instructions that ask you to set Communicator as your default browser, or mention anything about uninstalling any version(s) of Internet Explorer. Remember: You also want to leave any version(s) of Internet Explorer untouched for testing purposes.

6. Download the Standard Edition, not the Professional Edition. The Standard Edition contains all the individual programs, support for JavaScript and Java, and other tools and features you'll need without anything extra. The Professional Edition is intended for use by system administrators and network types who run company Intranets and such—it will only eat up your hard drive space.

7. Select the Complete Install with Additional Components option. These components will support bitstream fonts and multimedia support with popular plug-ins, which you'll need later on in the book. You can also select to download U.S./Canada-only encryption if you're building a site to view or send credit card numbers, bank account information, or other sensitive data—you will have to fill out a questionnaire in this case, though, to verify your citizenship, address, and so forth.

8. If there's a connection available, a Save or Save As dialog box should appear. If all connections are busy, you should plan on returning during a time when there's less Internet traffic. This is not necessarily between nine and five, either; it's between 6:00 and 11:00 P.M. Eastern Standard Time.

   Amy: I don't know if you want to go one step further and let them know how to install the program. If you do so, you might want to point out again that during their first start-up they should look for a dialog box that offers to make Communicator their default browser: their answer should be no.

Rebecca: I wasn't given that option when I downloaded Communicator eons ago—thanks for that alert.

Reader, do *not* do anything to make Communicator automatically launch when you start up your computer. Generally speaking, don't *ever* give your computer the opportunity to favor one browser over another; chances are good you will write preference files and other such hidden documents that will inevitably, somehow, cause you trouble during page testing. This means paying close attention when you install browsers, and when you use Navigator and Explorer for the first few times.

Also, come to think of it, when I recently reinstalled Microsoft Office, the Installation Wizard asked if I wanted to make Explorer my default browser and FrontPage my default web page design software. Again, under similar circumstances, your answer should always be no.

To download Netscape Navigator 3, follow these instructions:

1. Log on to the Internet, launch your browser of choice, and go to http://home.netscape.com.

2. Click on Netscape Downloads.

3. Scroll down to the option called Netscape Communicator and find Navigator Archived Versions (2.02 to 3.04) and click it.

4. Find the heading "3.04—English" and choose an appropriate download location under "Navigator." Navigator Gold includes Netscape's old web page editor, the precursor to Netscape Composer, which you do not need.

5. Follow the installation instructions but do *not* make Navigator 3 your default or preferred browser.

Amy: I currently have Internet Explorer 3 on my machine. I am hesitant to download version 4 because I have heard that it will modify your Windows operating system when you install it. Is this true?

Rebecca: Yes and no. IE3 and IE4 do share certain .dll files, which makes it impossible to keep them both on the same computer even if you use two separate hard disks, such as the C: drive and a Zip or other external drive. (Bill Gates didn't win any fans among web page designers with this strategy.) I think you're referring to the subtle ways in which IE4 and other Microsoft products can infiltrate your default settings; we touched on this in our last conversation. The safest way to keep all your programs intact and pristine is to carefully monitor any Microsoft product installation, and to choose No if you're asked about creating default, preferred, or automatic start-up files. Even if you always open Explorer to check your email, every single morning, do not be tempted.

To download Microsoft Internet Explorer 4, follow these instructions:

1. Log on to the Internet, launch whatever browser you're currently using, and go to http://www.microsoft.com.

2. Find the Free Downloads page. Again, you want the demo, not the version you'd have to pay for.

3. On the Free Downloads page, look for the Web Browsers and Viewers link. Click Internet Explorer.

4. Choose the link that's appropriate to the platform you're using, and choose the version of IE you wish to download.

5. Now you've entered the Download area with instructions. Choose the platform and language of preference that's appropriate for you.

NOTE: If you are designing a web site for a bilingual or international audience, you may also wish to download browsers in the second or alternate language you'll be using. Netscape, for example, provides you with a long list of language choices when you go to download its software. This strategy is especially useful if the second language uses diacritical marks (slashes over vowels, the n with the tilde—ñ—in Spanish, and so forth) or if the second language is written using a non-Roman alphabet (such as Russian, Arabic, Chinese, or Hebrew). You will want to become as familiar with the way browsers display alternative languages and alphabets as you can, because certain unique design issues will pop up. For example, you may encounter additional spacing issues with these languages because the individual letters in some languages will be wider or taller than those used in English. You might also find yourself making different color and graphics decisions if you are working with a non-English alphabet. The appearance, curve, and overall shape of non-Roman characters can be very influential on your universal design choices.

6. Choose a download location that's closest to you geographically if possible. If the location you choose is busy, choose any location within a nation with the appropriate language. Again, the same Internet traffic rules apply, though: between 6:00 and 11:00 P.M. Eastern Standard Time, it will be more difficult to get through.

Installing these browsers should be easy if you know how to install other kinds of software on your computer. There is some technical help available on each of the sites listed above, however, if you run into any difficulties.

HTML Editors

There are a whole slew of HTML editors coming on the market as more and more software companies try to make creating web pages easier for the masses. Ironically, this particular kind of market growth has largely served to muddy the waters, as beginning and intermediate web page designers find themselves swamped with too many choices.

The good news is that you already have an HTML editor installed on your machine, regardless of the model or type of computer you own. NotePad on the PC and SimpleText on the Macintosh are perfectly wonderful, not to mention cost-free, HTML editors you can use without difficulty. You simply create a new document in SimpleText or NotePad, type in your HTML, and save your pages as .html or .htm documents. Period.

At the end of this chapter, we will make specific recommendations about the software packages you should seek out and install other than Navigator 3, Navigator 4, and Explorer 4. Don't mistakenly believe you have to download and install *all* the software mentioned here.

NOTE: Whether your HTML documents should end in .html or .htm can depend upon your preference, or perhaps your ISP's setup. Call or email your ISP technical support staff and ask if this is a concern for you; it's better to ask than to create a web page and not have it work simply for the presence or absence of one little letter!

If you are looking for a slightly more robust HTML editor with some tools and shortcuts, Bare Bones Software's BBEdit for the Macintosh and Allaire's HomeSite for the PC give you enough help without preventing you from writing efficient, accurate HTML.

The third category of HTML editor is by far the largest, and correspondingly the most difficult to sort out. These are the WYSIWYG editors that allow you to manipulate a web page as if it were a collage, moving and adding and deleting page elements using your mouse and keyboard shortcuts while the program writes the HTML for you behind the scenes. The most popular WYSIWYG is Microsoft FrontPage, with Adobe PageMill and/or GoLive, Macromedia DreamWeaver, and Netscape Composer also garnering a smaller market share.

Amy: What do you think of Microsoft Word's ability to save a document into HTML format? Apparently if you download Internet Assistant, Word will add all of the code to format the document in HTML as you had originally word-processed it. You can view the HTML source code by clicking that option under the View menu. Do you think that this creates the same problem that WYSIWYGs do?

Rebecca: Yes, I do believe any program that offers, however kindly, to write your HTML for you is only going to turn out to be a curse. (Well, I take that back: Macromedia DreamWeaver is an outstanding program that I rely upon very heavily, and Adobe GoLive is excellent also, but I wouldn't recommend either of them for the average reader of this book.) Even beginning web page designers need to understand why HTML works the way it does so they can fix problems and more easily increase their knowledge as time goes by. Besides, Word could never properly handle graphics, movies, sounds, VRML, JavaScripts, or style sheets—not to mention whatever hot new technology is just around the bend. The key word in your question is "word-processed." Web pages are moving away from looking like paper documents, rather than in the opposite direction.

While these editors are undoubtedly useful for saving time and creating the most basic, generic kinds of web pages, we are not recommending that you use them to accomplish what we show you in this book. This is because editing the actual HTML in these programs can be significantly more complicated than editing HTML in Notepad, SimpleText, BBEdit, or HomeSite—and we also take the stance that a web page designer should understand design from the foundation up. If you learn web page design the other way, from the top layers down, you are less likely to understand why certain problems and conflicts will arise and may be less able to fix what's wrong.

To download BBEdit Lite, go to Bare Bones Software's home page at http://www.barebones.com.

To download the HomeSite demo, go to Allaire's home page at http://www.allaire.com.

Image Software

Before we get into the subject of image software, it is important to remember how we are defining this type of software—they are programs that will help you optimize graphics specifically for use on web pages. We are not covering, exploring, or recommending graphics programs at large in the sense that you can use them to create original, fancy, or highly detailed art.

That said, the two king-of-the-hill image software packages for web design are still Adobe Photoshop and Equilibrium Debabelizer, but they are expensive and require a steep learning curve to use properly. If you've got the drive, the time, and Aunt Mildred willing to use her checkbook, you may want to learn to use them, but we are not requiring or assuming you will do so.

There are less powerful but still very suitable programs for preparing web page graphics that are less expensive and take less time to learn. Paint Shop Pro by JASC for the PC and GraphicConverter by Lemke Software for the Macintosh are the programs we recommend for simple graphics/image tasks, along with Adobe's Photoshop demo for those of you who are committed.

To download Paint Shop Pro, go to JASC's home site at http://www.jasc.com.

To download the GraphicConverter, go to Lemke Software's home site at http:/www.goldinc.com/lemke.

The Don't-Wait-for-Christmas List: Other Useful Utilities

There's one more kind of software we recommend you install on your system before you begin building web pages: a **compression utility.** This is a great little program you can use to compress, and then extract, entire folders of files to maximize your storage space. Sometimes these utilities can reduce a file size by as much as 50 to 75%, effectively doubling whatever hard drive space you have available. So if you cannot afford to buy a larger hard drive or an external storage device, you can use compression utilities to better keep your pages on disk or on your computer. Aladdin Systems's StuffIt for the PC and the Macintosh is available for a $15 shareware fee, and we recommend it for crossplatform use.

To download StuffIt, go to Aladdin Systems's home site at http://www.aladdinsys.com.

> **Amy:** I currently have WinZip for compressing and storing files. Until I see a need for a crossplatform compression software, I'm going to hold off on this and on paying the $15.

> **Rebecca:** WinZip is a wonderful PC compression utility. It should work just as well as StuffIt, but it's not available for the Mac.

We also recommend that you download GIF Construction Set for the PC and GIFBuilder for the Macintosh for use in Appendix A when we create GIF animations. You can and should use Paint Shop Pro or Photoshop to create your individual GIFs, but you'll need these freeware packages to put them into animations.

To download GIFBuilder and/or GIF Construction Set, visit the TUCOWS site at http://www.tucows.com. Follow the instruction to find a TUCOWS site near you, and then search for GIF Construction Set.

Plug-Ins

Even though both Navigator 4 and Explorer 4 come with a plentiful array of plug-ins for audio, video, VRML and other web page features, there are still a few others we recommend that you locate, download, and install up front. You can wait, of course, until you trip across a site where you need them, if you don't mind the interruption. In our experience, though, this can prove very frustrating if you're in the middle of a project and don't want the distraction.

RealPlayer is the audio and video player of choice, in our humble opinion, far superior to the ones that come standard with Navigator and Explorer. It plays both live and on-demand (or prerecorded) files, which is its specific advantage over the competition. You can download it for free for either your PC or your Macintosh from RealAudio's home site at http://www.realaudio.com. QuickTime is another popular plug-in for crossplatform multimedia all in one. Download version 3 for free from Apple's home site at http://www.apple.com/quicktime.

Shockwave by Macromedia is a web design favorite for creating all kinds of cool effects from simple animated buttons to movielike productions that fill the screen with sound, movement, and color. Download the Shockwave player for free for both PCs and Macintoshes at Macromedia's site, http://www.macromedia.com/shockwave.

WorldView by Intervista is one of many VRML viewers, but it is used by the VRML sites we will visit in the course of this book. Download it at http://www.intervista.com.

For the record, we are not presenting these three "extra" plug-ins as options among which you might pick and choose. We strongly recommend downloading and installing the correct version of all three, as RealPlayer will not necessarily read a file meant for QuickTime, and neither is capable of reading a Shockwave file.

Other Requirements

There is really only one other requirement you need to begin designing web pages, and that is an excellent Internet Service Provider. What makes a good ISP? It's not location, or even price. A good ISP provides you with web page support (this is not always a given), ample storage space, generous user access, and unlimited usage for a flat fee, and it is capable of supporting your advanced page design features such as forms and CGI scripts.

First and foremost, just because you have an email account with your ISP, this does not mean that you also have a web page account. Most basic email packages do not include space for web pages on your ISP's server, so call and ask whether you need to upgrade your account. Adding web page support can also add as much as $10 or $15 to your monthly fees, so take this cost into consideration as well. If you can't afford such an increase, it's entirely possible that your employers can give you web page space on their business server. Many companies nowadays can give their employees a small amount of server space, especially if the employees work in a computer, Internet, or support-oriented job. However, keep in mind that your employers may have rules about what you can and cannot put on your personal page if it's on their server, and how much space you can be allotted.

Storage space on your ISP's server, or main computer, is just as important as the amount of hard drive space you have on your computer. Again, your actual HTML documents may not take up a lot of space, but once you start adding graphics, movies, audio, and other space-consuming elements, you won't want to be restricted by your ISP's storage limitations. The average ISP gives you 10 to 15MB of storage space with an average web page–type account, but if you can find 20MB or more, you might appreciate it later.

User access can also become problematic if your web site becomes popular, and/or if you are designing some kind of corporate or business site. Some smaller ISPs do not offer round-the-clock access, or they might make you pay higher fees if your page advertises products or services for sale. Make sure your ISP knows the kind of page you want it to host, and make your expectations on user access very clear.

As you get into web page design, you will also want unlimited Internet access for a single flat fee. Do not settle for an ISP account that limits the number of hours you can surf by adding per-hour surcharges if you exceed a particular limit, even if that limit seems unreachable (100 hours is such a popular number). Think of it like this: If you spend a mere four hours a night surfing the web or testing your web pages online in the course of a 30-day month, that's 120 hours. And that doesn't include any marathon weekend sessions, or your kids, spouse, or roommate spending any time online, either. To put it briefly, time online adds up. Don't let it cost you more than it has to.

Finally, we will show you how to add elements to your web page that require a little cooperation from your ISP. Forms and CGI scripts, specifically, are one part HTML that you write into your pages, but they are also one-part script, and scripts must be hosted properly by your ISP. Always tell your ISP if you are planning to add forms, CGI scripts, or similar elements to your web site, and make certain your ISP has the server and software capacity to host them correctly. If it can't, you will have saved yourself lots of time and aggravation.

Review

As promised, here is a list of software/shareware/plug-ins we recommend that you download and install on your computer before you move ahead.

For the PC:

- Netscape Navigator 3 (14MB), Netscape Navigator 4 (20MB), and Microsoft Internet Explorer 4 (16MB)

- NotePad *or* HomeSite (4MB)

- Paint Shop Pro (17MB) (and the Adobe Photoshop demo if you'd like a challenge)

- StuffIt (WinZip is fine if you've already got it installed)

- GIF Construction Set

- RealPlayer, QuickTime, Shockwave and WorldView

    For the Macintosh:

- Netscape Navigator 3, Netscape Navigator 4, and Microsoft Internet Explorer 4

- SimpleText *or* BBEdit

- GraphicConverter (and the Adobe Photoshop demo if you'd like a challenge)

- StuffIt

- GIFBuilder

- RealPlayer, QuickTime, Shockwave and WorldView

This list looks very daunting, especially after you've probably spent so much time downloading these bloatware browsers! However, these other utilities and the plug-ins take literally no time at all to download and to install, so don't feel overwhelmed.

On with the Show

Now that we've explored the basics of your system, hardware, and software requirements—and, we hope, you've gone online and/or shopping to get all the things you want and need—it's time to dive into web page design. Let's get going!

CHAPTER 3

Basics of Site Creation

outfit 全套准在
全套2具

We've spent a little time discussing what this book will address, how you should outfit yourself with the right hardware and software, what constitutes a good ISP, and other generalities. Now it's time to get into the first phase of creating a web site—planning and executing your web site's framework.

Good web site design is half science, half art. There is a need for a little methodical planning and forethought before you sit down and begin writing HTML, so you know what you want to accomplish and how you want to accomplish it. The artistic part—the brainstorming, the inspiration, the aesthetic aspect—might already be forming in the back of your brain. But first, you owe it to yourself and the people who view your site to lay some good groundwork.

> **Amy:** I would mention here that novice web page designers such as myself may have considerable experience in evaluating the design of others' web pages. Many of us have surfed site upon site and have come to some conclusions about what we like and do not like. So if we're feeling overwhelmed as Rebecca starts in on the nuts and bolts of web page design, it can be helpful to realize that we do have some ideas and experience upon which to draw.

Definitions

Just for the record, let's define **web page** and **web site** again. In this book, the term "web page" will refer to one individual HTML document. Alternatively, the term "web site" will always refer to your entire collection of linked web pages, so that we can easily distinguish between HTML that affects one page and HTML that affects many pages. This is particularly important in the planning stages, as you will be making decisions about what affects your site *locally*—on one or a few pages only—or *universally,* on every single page in your whole site.

Similarly, when we talk about your entire site during planning, we will talk about its **framework**. This is not to be confused with a discussion of frames, which we will cover in Chapter 8, "Positioning Elements with HTML," in the midst of other design issues. Your site's framework will be either a literal map on paper or a visualization in your head—a flowchart, if you will—detailing how all your pages relate to one another. You can decide a little later whether you want to sketch out this framework with a pencil or try to see it relationally in your imagination.

> **Amy:** So all sites have a framework, or a structure, while only some sites have frames, which are minipages within pages? Frames is a technology that we'll discuss later, but framework is conceptualizing your overall site, and that's what we're doing now, right?
>
> **Rebecca:** All sites have a framework, and yes, we are creating one to conceptualize our web sites. Also, frames is a specific web design technique used only on some sites. (A page that uses frames is like a stained glass window, with solid unchangeable partitions dividing various content areas that load up like minipages.)

When we speak of **content**, we will be talking about material and information that will appear on your site—facts and figures, but also themes, ideas, and other less concrete elements. This chapter is not meant to encompass questions about **function** and **structure**, or how your site will actually display and behave. That will come as we move through the later chapters where we write actual HTML. You will also have to wait a little while longer for a discussion of **form**, which is the art of web page design and the subject of Chapter 4.

> **Amy:** This is a little unclear to me. How is form different from framework?

> **Rebecca:** For the purposes of this book, a web site's form encompasses all its aesthetic issues as addressed using the various web technologies. In Chapter 4, we'll take a tour of various web sites divided into "categories" depending on whether or not they use backgrounds, text, graphics, JavaScript, GIF animations, DHTML, style sheets, and other tools. I chose these sites because they use these technologies very well, so that the high-end design features accentuate the site's content instead of distract visitors from it.

> A framework, as we'll see very shortly, is little more than a graph or plan describing the number and purpose of each page on a web site and how, or if, they are linked together.

Objectives

Our objectives for this chapter are simple and complicated all at once: We are going to determine your site's content, its reason for being, its purpose, and other larger issues by narrowing down our options. (That's not a tall order, is it?) Let's take it one piece at a time.

The Five Ws

Who Is the Site For?

Because the Web is a diverse and generous place, there are no rules about who your web site should be designed to please or attract. At the same time, however, the content of your site will determine who visits and who surfs, who will be interested in what you offer, and whether or not someone will return.

So now is the time to ask yourself whether you want to create a personal site, a business site, or an interest site. As was already mentioned, we will be creating one of each kind.

A **personal site** is a web site that serves to introduce a person to the world on the Web. Common features of a personal site include:

- Information about the person's family, children, and/or pets

- What the person does for a living

- The person's hobbies, such as sports, home improvement, or other pastimes

- The person's interests, such as politics, UFOs, or cultural or social events

> **Rebecca:** There are purists who worry about whether or not everything on the Web is "useful" or "good," and they often complain about personal sites as a waste of the Web's resources. Many other people hold to the idea that the Web is a diversified space that's plenty large enough to accommodate every type of site, regardless of differing opinions on what the Web should contain.

> **Amy:** I agree. Though I have seen only a few personal sites that have really been enriching and enlightening to read, it is possible to be a presence on the Web that makes people think, laugh, and enjoy getting to know you—just as it's possible to develop that kind of personality. I would venture to say that the key to this is being interested in other people and in life itself; do you think the same is true for developing a personal web site?

> **Rebecca:** Here we go, waxing philosophical, and we haven't even gotten that far into the Ws!

> Yes, I think you've hit the nail on the head. It's true that a personal site won't have something for everyone, but it might have something for a person with a commonality to your life. Maybe you're both in the same profession, or you're both caring for an elderly parent, or you both collect antique spoons, or you both coach Little League. That's where the "value-added" content in a personal web page can be found, whether the Web snobs believe it or not.

A **business site** showcases a corporation with a product or service for sale, and everything needed to promote it. We distinguish business sites from all other types because they exist to make a profit. Here are some common elements of business sites:

- Corporate mission statements, company history, and other such material

- Sales facts and figures and marketing information

- Portfolios or pictorial catalogues showing or describing what is for sale

- Contact information and personnel pages

Strangely enough, some of the same people who criticize personal sites welcome all business sites, regardless of what they sell or promote. The theory here is that e-commerce will draw more funding and long-term investment in Web technology if companies see their profits growing as a result of web sites. Whether or not this ideology pans out in the near future still remains to be seen.

The third kind of site we will create will be an **informational site**, or a web site dedicated to a cause, movement, organization, or calling independent of one single person or an effort to make money. Sites that fall under this category can feature:

- The work and life of a popular performer, writer, or other artist

- Information for a group of people with one commonality, such as a chronic disease, the same national or ethnic heritage, or charitable goal

- Lists of resources for pastimes and hobbies such as genealogy, mountain climbing, or antiques and collectibles

One of the most interesting aspects of the Web's history is that everything originally on it was informational. Academic and government employees initially created the Web to share research, facts, and figures. Imagine—no online magazines, no CNN or weather, not even a search engine. Given its glittery appearance today, the Web's humble beginnings surely do boggle the mind.

Amy: Since this is the "Who" section, this is a good place to ask this question: How do we attract the audience that we want?

Rebecca: Yikes! If I *really* had the answer to that question, I'd be a billionaire!

No, seriously, one of the scariest (or most thrilling) aspects of the Web is its complete lack of context in these matters. When you talk about audience and demographics and appeal on the Web, you can't compare it with television or magazines or any other kinds of media that are not truly interactive. And I would hazard to guess that this is why traditional advertising/marketing people, and corporate bean counters everywhere, are so frustrated by the lack of substantial online revenue being generated by today's web sites—as well as site designers who just want their sites to get noticed.

So in my humble opinion, the only way to get and keep an audience is to recognize that your visitors are in total control and they are getting more Web-savvy every single day. Translation: Make, and keep, your site attractive, and they will come. Create pages that load quickly, look good, and have something to say. List your pages on search engines and use the <META> tag properly (we will cover how to do this later in the book). Utilize new or exciting technologies like JavaScript, DHTML, and style sheets when they're appropriate. And that's the best you can do.

What Belongs on Your Web Site?

Now that you've decided on the kind of site you want to build, it's time to make a list and/or begin to gather all the various elements you want to put on it. Take or find those cute pictures of your kids. Scan in your graphics or other graphical elements. Surf the Web a little to find links to pages that interest you and/or pertain to the kind of site you're going to build. It pays to collect all of this information now so you can assemble it later all at once without any delays.

With this in mind, you must also consider issues of copyright and ownership of any material you find on the Web. **Copyright** is a legal restriction placed on original material so only one person or group can distribute and collect profits from it. Most of the copyrighted material you find on the Web will be artistic, such as poems, paintings, film clips, and so on. **Ownership**, however, is a little bit different, as one person can possess the copyright to a famous sketch—one by Leonardo da Vinci from his notebooks, for example—but someone else can have ownership of the actual sketch when it comes to placing that image on the Web.

Amy: I'm a little confused by the example. Let's flesh it out. First of all, I understand that Leonardo's sketches themselves are no longer copyrighted because they're so old; they've exceeded any copyright time limits. So you seem to be saying that the publishers of an art book has the copyright to the particular Leonardo sketch they've printed. However, if Joey Smokes, a web page designer, got that same sketch from a general source, he has ownership of that particular graphic image. So you probably can't scan the sketch from the art book to your web page, but you could ask Joey for permission to use the image from his web page. Is this the distinction that you're making?

Rebecca: You've managed to touch on all issues involving copyright and the Web. It's true that the work of Leonardo da Vinci—and that of all artists dead for more than 99 years—is in the public domain, but to my knowledge no court has tested this law with regard to the Web. And it's true that the publishers of an art book of Leonardo sketches have or have obtained the copyright to whatever is in their book.

But designer Joey Smokes does *not* have ownership of that image if he gets it from a book or especially if he just "borrows" it from elsewhere on the Web. A museum, for example, with a page of Leonardo sketches on its web site would have ownership of those sketch images, but it would not possess the copyright. (Because, as you say, Leonardo is long gone, and the law of public domain applies.)

Yet if Joey wanted to go about getting permissions properly under these conditions, he would have to contact the museum, or the publishers of the book, and get permission to use the sketches on his web site. Obviously in some circumstances, using the originals just isn't a possibility.

Amy: Okay, I understand now. "Ownership" refers to the person or institution that has most recently purchased the work. How does that work with text: say, an excerpt from a popular work such as the novel *One Flew Over the Cuckoo's Nest*? I would say that ownership isn't really an issue (since something like six million people own a copy of the book), but that the work should be cited to avoid copyright problems. I'm assuming that I don't have to write Ken Kesey or the publisher to get permission to quote a few lines on my web page.

Rebecca: Nope. Text ownership and copyright issues are exactly the same, and they are even more hotly debated when it comes to the Web. Whether or not you have to get special permission to reproduce text on the Web depends entirely upon its publisher. All of Time Warner's magazines, for example, adamantly refuse to allow their articles to be reprinted in other places on the Web other than the Pathfinder web site (where the online versions of its magazines are located). Then again, there are unauthorized versions of poems, articles, excerpts, and other text all over the Web, mostly tagged with the line "Reproduced by John Doe without permission," and nobody's been prosecuted.

In recent notable memory, however, hundreds of people with unofficial *X-Files* web sites received letters from the FOX Network's legal department, telling them to remove their sites from the Web or face the consequences. This was the first time, to my knowledge, that a corporation or business has tried to enforce ownership/copyright of something abstract—the action had nothing to do with pictures, text, audio or video clips from the TV show, or any physical piece of information. It had to do with FOX wanting to protect its ownership of *X-Files* as a concept (and maybe to beef up the number of hits to its own official web site).

So it's hard to say where this issue is headed, but it's not so hard to avoid complications—that is, when in doubt, ASK.

So, what do you do if you want to put a picture of this da Vinci sketch on your web site? Do you have to have permission from the person or group that placed the sketch on the Web in the first place? At this writing, it depends on whom you ask. In an ideal world, the Web would be share-and-share-alike with no restrictions and no injured feelings, and for the most part this is the attitude you will come across among individuals, small groups, and even small businesses. However, large corporations such as Walt Disney, McDonald's, and Coca-Cola are notorious for saying no, and in some cases individuals have been sued or otherwise legally penalized for not listening.

With all this in mind, there is the middle-of-the-road plan we advocate. As you begin assembling the pieces and parts for your web site, keep a list of all the places you visit on the Web, what you download to borrow for your site, and the contact information for that site's creator. When you've finished your collection, email each creator individually; give your name, state your intentions, name any element you borrowed or say you want to create a link to that page, and ask permission. This procedure is not just intended to cover your, er, rear end, but it's also good "netiquette." If you are friendly and courteous to other people, chances are good that they will be friendly and courteous to you.

> **Amy:** Occasionally, a site clearly states that you may use anything from that site, sometimes with the stipulation that credit should be given. Do you still get explicit permission from the web site author?

> **Rebecca:** Absolutely; that site author might expect a copyright symbol and the author's name printed clearly on the image itself, rather than a written credit on the kind of Credits page I'm advocating here. This is the response I got from a museum in Texas when I emailed the directors to get permission to use a picture of an Arts and Crafts vase on my web site. They thanked me kindly for asking and told me exactly how they wanted the copyright line to read. I obliged quite willingly, though their vase is the only image on my entire site with such a byline, so it's not aesthetically pleasing. But the vase is gorgeous, and I really wanted it on my web page, so I had to compromise.

> What I'm really saying here is: Be nice! Always put yourself in the site author's shoes, and treat him or her the way you want to be treated.

> **Amy:** Now I understand. I hadn't considered that the site author might want the credit to be more visible than I had intended to make it. Good point.

If you want to borrow pictures, photos, film clips, or other copyrighted material, you should also add a Credits page to your site for good measure. Later on, we will explore the details of how to construct such a page. But if it's your intention now to create some sort of gallery of Impressionist paintings, a videography of the Rolling Stones, or some other borrowing-intensive collection, plan right now to put a Credits page on your web site.

When Do You Want to Launch Your Site?

Right now, you've got your web site taking shape in your mind, and you're getting all excited about showing it to the world. Your first inclination may be to create a few pages and immediately upload them to your service provider, but hang on for one moment and reconsider.

The timing of your **launch**, which is uploading a new site for the first time, is just as important as what your site contains and how it works. Remember the mindset behind surfing the Web; a person who is flitting around will only give your web site a few seconds to make a good first impression. So if you want to draw that surfer in and persuade him or her to stick around, you don't want to give off the idea that your site was hastily or haphazardly designed.

> **Amy:** I had not considered the timing of the launch before. It's a good point.

> **Rebecca:** Many, *many* people don't. Or perhaps I should say, web page designers do but their clients don't. Some companies toss up their web pages even before they work properly, just so they can meet a certain financial or coincidental marketing deadline. So the very people they built the site to attract get irritated and bewildered. Then the company wonders why their new web site gets lots of hits in the first few weeks but nobody comes back.

One common strategy is to create a temporary or "under-construction" page, especially if you are already locked into the look and content of your site before you even begin designing it. If you're creating a site for your business, for example, you can borrow elements from existing materials for a temporary page. Use the same logo or design scheme as your letterhead, brochures and pamphlets. This way, you can launch one web page that states your real site is under construction, using your logo or create a background resembling your letterhead. This gives people a taste of what your site will contain once it's up and running. Announce that you'll feature your catalogue of reproduction light fixtures, perhaps, or resources for feeding the hungry in your city. This preview will encourage interested visitors to bookmark your site or to check back later on when your site is finished, and you will have begun securing your audience without too much up-front effort.

> **Amy:** When I first began creating my UC page, I was not very impressed with my content. I was summarizing my personal life, although I wanted this page to eventually be full of information. I reread the paragraph about announcing what information I would be featuring in the future, and decided to make that announcement the main focus of my page. I feel much better about the first impression I will be making on the Web.

We will also be building a series of temporary pages as part of the three sample sites we'll create through the course of this book. Look for more information on how to create under-construction (UC) pages in Chapter 4.

Where Will Your Site Be Seen?

This question might sound like a no-brainer. There's only one World Wide Web, and your site will be on it, right?

The "where" in this question has to do with the exposure your site will get and the kind of person you hope to attract. If you're a web site designer by trade and you're creating your business site, you want to show off your skill by using the latest high-end technology. If you're a sculptor showcasing your work, maybe you want to pare down your site design to draw people's eyes only to images without words. If you're creating a site for children, you might want lots of bright colors, cartoonlike designs, and simple navigational capabilities. The point is that none of these approaches are interchangeable because the audience for each of these sites is so different.

So one of the most important questions you can ask yourself while you're planning your site is: Who are my ideal visitors? What are my visitors' expectations? How proficient are they with Web technologies? Will they appreciate an up-front and less subtle site design, or vice versa? What might please or frustrate these people the most?

> **Amy:** This seems like it might fit better in the "who" category. I had thought "where" might cover more about other pages that would have links to your page, and how search engines would find it, or how it could be included in search indexes (such as Yahoo!).

> **Rebecca:** Yes, but that is all beyond the scope of planning a web site if not utterly beyond your control, and this point in the process is all about you. You can't know at this point who will find your web site and create a link to it, or how a search engine will categorize or list your site, and the rest concerns HTML tags we'll cover in Chapter 8, "Positioning Elements with HTML."

> **Amy:** Okay. Still, I'd like to see more, though I understand it might be more appropriate later in the book. For example, how would you promote these different types of sites? What are some examples of sites that address highly "targeted" audiences? I think that this addresses the heart of the Web, the communities that we're seeking to build.

> **Rebecca:** I want to build up this discussion as we move throughout the book—this is supposed to be a practical, hands-on guide with a little theory, rather than a theoretical book with a couple of exercises. You're really asking about **information architecture**, too, which is rhetoric and marketing and design and communication all wrapped up together, and way beyond the scope of this book.

> So here's a short reading list of good books with more theory:

Clement Mok, *Designing Business*
Donald Norman, *The Design of Everyday Things*
David Siegel, *The Secrets of Successful Web Sites*
Edward Tufte, *Envisioning Information*
Richard Saul Wurman, *Information Architects*

And we'll have a look at how to promote sites and target audiences as we go. In the next chapter, actually, we'll visit several sites that cater to very specific groups or types of people. But let's finish the Ws first.

Why Create Your Site at All?

If you have the wherewithal to ask yourself this particular question, the big Why, we hope your first answer is, "Because I want to!" If you weren't interested in site design and you didn't want to create your own web site, you'd have bought yourself a nice paperback novel instead of this book.

Regardless of this philosophical stuff, you really should have a good reason for your page to be on the Web, because this good reason will keep you coming back. Do you have a passion for a particular artist, a historical event or period, or a leisure-time activity? Do you want to change a law, save the rain forest, or advocate women's rights? Do you have friends and loved ones all over the world with whom you want to keep in touch with letters, photographs, or even home movies? If you are interested in your site and what it offers, others will be interested, too.

Amy: This is my favorite question. I even wonder if it should be listed first, to get people to be clear about their purpose before they start on the rest.

I should add that the "why" is a large reason that I haven't yet really applied myself to getting a web page done. I tend to think in big strokes, and I really couldn't come up with a reason to do this page that was important enough. On one hand, I really just wanted to show off pictures of my infant son. On the other hand, I want to try to reach visitors other than my family and friends. Yet if I try to get too grandiose, the text just sounds too earnest and weird: "I want my son to know world peace, blah blah blah." So I've been avoiding dealing with content issues.

As I look at the issue more closely, though, I realize that as a writer and an English teacher, I'm used to working in text. Web page design is much different from writing plain text. Here I can create a texture of images, links, and text that will (I hope) be more subtle and yet powerful.

I write this because I wouldn't be surprised if many people experience the same kinds of feelings: "What could I possibly have to say that would be important enough to post for all the world to see?" Yet I'm coming to understand that the answer is: A lot. We each could have a lot to say that is that important, that is community-building, that will bring another person a smile. With the specialized medium of the Web and some knowledge of web page design, we might even hope to say it well.

Building the Framework

Now that you've asked all the questions, it's time to construct the framework. If you have the ability to keep your thoughts and objectives organized in your head, then perhaps you need not proceed as we have done—with good old-fashioned pencil and paper. In any case, you, the reader, are not psychic, so we had to put something down in print to make our point.

The "Under-Construction" (UC) Page

As you begin to think about how you want to construct your site and what you want to include on it, you might also begin thinking about creating an **under-construction** (**UC**) page. This temporary page will announce your web site and "hold" its place on the Web until you can finish the real thing.

You'll create a UC page in the next chapter, in the "Exercises" section, so for now let's go on with the framework.

The Entryway

Every thoughtfully designed web site should have an **entryway page**—the place where you present your visitors with the first glimpse of how your site is designed, where you establish the look and feel of your page, and some sort of hint at what your site contains. In your mind, or at the top or in the center of a piece of paper, if that's what you're using, represent this page with a square labeled "entry."

As an example, and to get your imagination going, Figure 3.1 shows the entryway to a personal web site, Steve Mulder's Sanctum Sanctorum.

What does this page suggest to you at a glance? The book looks like a medieval Bible with illuminated, or brightly colored, artwork. So this site will probably have rich and interesting graphics. And it's also probably well designed, because the author optimized this graphic very well—all the detail is here but the book image loads quickly—and because there are useful JavaScripts here. Notice the popup textbox that says "Do Come In," and the greeting written

FIGURE 3.1. The entryway to the Sanctum Sanctorum (http://www.tsdesign.com/mulder)

across the bottom edge of the browser window. Perhaps, then, this site will showcase some cutting-edge Web technology, too.

The site author could be a bookbinder, a librarian, an antiques dealer, or even a member of the clergy for all you can tell. This entryway suggests many things and effectively entices the visitor in. Click on the book to proceed.

The Home Page

In terms of your web site's basic content, everything mentioned or shown on your home page should somehow direct the visitor to another part of your site. Even if you go on to create a real menu, index, or list of other pages in your site, the home page's representational value is still very high. Remember that all-important first impression, and the very short attention span of surfers.

As a follow-up to the last section, Figure 3.2 shows the home page on the Sanctum Sanctorum site.

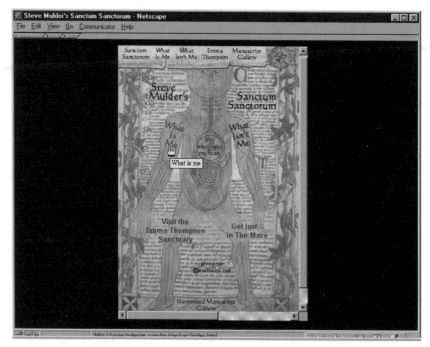

FIGURE 3.2. The main, home page for the Sanctum Sanctorum (http://www.tsdesign.com/mulder)

You do have to scroll down to get the full view of this medieval medical man (the study of anatomy has come a long way, hasn't it?), but it is still another beautifully optimized graphic. And it's on a background, too, which is even more impressive for a graphic this size. The grainy, leathery texture of the frame around the main image looks like the inside of an expensive book. If you continue to scroll around and roll around, you'll notice that the name of each link appears along the bottom of the browser window when the cursor touches its area of the body. Watch the eyes for a moment, too, and recognize an unobtrusive and completely fun use of a GIF animation.

The overall design of this page is worth mentioning as well—the page author recognized the completeness of the graphic as a background, an imagemap, and a design statement, so he added sparingly. The font, or style of lettering, he chose is well suited to the ornate look of the graphic but is still clearly readable. Also, its color blends in with the overall palette, yet it remains distinctive enough and easily visible.

The Secondary Pages

Secondary pages, also called subject pages, branch off the home page. On a personal page, for example, you might have one subject page each for your spouse, the kids, the pets, and your hobbies. Similarly, on an informational site you might have one subject page for an actor's theater roles, one for movies, one containing interviews and pictures, and one for multimedia samples such as radio interviews or performance recordings.

To round out our examples, Figure 3.3 shows a secondary or subject page from the Sanctum Sanctorum. Click the left arm of the figure on the main page to get here.

The goal of a secondary page is to present the viewer with information while still somehow tying it in to the home page and the rest of the web site in general. This secondary page does that very well. It presents a list of simple phrases that describe the web page author and point the visitor to a handful of interesting links, all against a faded manuscript flanked by lovely illustrated ornaments. (Note also the way all these links are presented—roll the cursor over

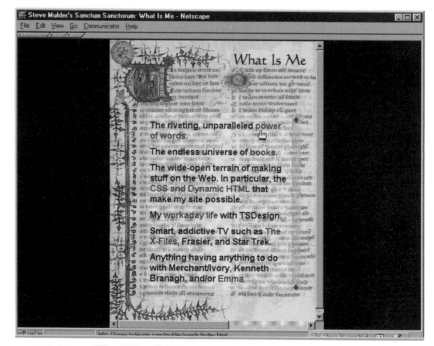

FIGURE 3.3. The What Is Me page, a secondary page from the Sanctum Sanctorum (http://www.tsdesign.com/mulder/yes)

an up or down arrow using Netscape Navigator and Internet Explorer for the PC, and the menu of links actually scrolls.)

In your framework, each of these subject pages should be represented by another box labeled according to its contents—kids, movies, multimedia, links, whatever—arranged around the home page box. Now you have before you (or in your mind's eye) the basic framework of your web site. It may seem pedantic or worthless to have done such a simple rendering now, but you will appreciate it later as things get more complicated.

The last subject page you should have is a page of links to other sites on the Web. This rounds out the idea that you have an In door and an Out door, and that you understand that everybody who visits your page is eventually just passing through. By giving visitors a page of your favorite links, or a list of links containing information related to what your site presents, you are also letting them leave your site without having to back up. So establishing a backdoor is not just good site planning; it's good "netiquette."

Navigation among Basic Pages

Now that you have more than one page in your framework, you should begin your first deliberations about **navigation**, which describes how a visitor will get from page to page within your web site. You definitely want the home page to link to all your subject pages, so draw arrows out from the home page pointing at each subject page. This indicates your intention to create, at minimum, one-way travel—a link from the home page to the subject page.

In the meantime, assume also that you want to have some way for visitors to return to the home page from each of your subject pages. Represent this intention by making the arrows two-directional, pointing to and away from the home page. Eventually you will add pages to your web site that do not require two-directional navigation, but you do want all the major pages in your site to be organized in this manner.

The Exit Page

If you have an In door, you should also have an Out door—an **exit** page of links that will allow visitors to continue on their journey across the Web. This is also a page where you can express your personality by showing people other things on the Web you like, if you haven't assembled a list of links related to whatever topics or interests you put on your other pages. The point of such a page is courtesy. Don't force visitors to back up to a page outside your web site that does have an exit, or make them go through the "hard" work of typing in a new URL.

> **Amy:** So the exit page might also have a link on every page, so that the visitor always has a chance to leave, right? Or you could try to lead the visitor through the site in a linear fashion and then the exit page would only have a link on your "second-to-last" page.
>
> **Rebecca:** The first option is more user-friendly and more easily accomplished designwise. If you use some sort of menu on every

page including links to all your secondary pages, then this always gives the visitor easy access to your exit page.

Then again, if you were creating a gallery (as you said you wanted to earlier), you might want to restrict the visitor's movement in the second way you describe. In that scenario, too, visitors would be more likely to understand having to use the Back button. They might even appreciate getting a second look at each piece of art.

Exercises

There's really only one goal to this chapter, and that is to get you, the reader, to organize and map out a framework for your web site. So this first exercise does not really have a ready-made answer in that regard—your framework will look unique, as it should. Draw lines denoting navigation among your home and secondary pages, and make quick notes stating generally what each of these pages will contain. In the "Answers" section of this chapter, we will present visual mockups of the three web sites we will be constructing throughout the course of the rest of this book: one personal site, one business site, and one informational site. You can "grade" or evaluate your framework by comparing it to ours, but keep in mind that there is no right or wrong here, except that you must be thorough.

Now for the second exercise, visit a web site you know is large and complicated—Netscape's site, Microsoft's site, the Amazon.com bookstore, McDonald's, Coca-Cola, or any other web site connected to a large megacorporation with lots of brand names or products that need to somehow be organized cohesively. Get out a clean (and *large*) sheet of paper and try to sketch out the site's framework. Assume right now, however, that you could cover the page with millions of lines denoting navigational directions, so try to find a notation that keeps this information simple. If there's a ubiquitous button bar or site menu that always gives the visitor the same basic options, for example, you could make a note of this by writing "menu" in the corners of the pages where it appears. Do your best, and pay attention to the details—but again, each of you will choose a different web site to evaluate, so there will be no clear-cut right answer to this exercise, either.

Amy: This was an interesting exercise, if a little confusing. Even when I simplified my sketch of the site's framework by using writing "menu" in the corner of each page as you suggested, there were still a lot of arrows back and forth and a lot of information in each box. For instance, on Microsoft's current home page, the visitor can choose any one of four feature articles, so I wrote in a note about that. I definitely learned a lot.

Rebecca: I confess, I deliberately suggested Microsoft's site *because* it's confusing—I don't even try to navigate it traditionally anymore, but head right for the Search feature instead. Sometimes I think you can learn more about how to do something by looking at examples of how you shouldn't do it.

Review

To recap what we discussed in this chapter, you should ask yourself five basic questions when you plan the content of your web site:

- Who is the site for?
- What belongs on this site?
- When do I want to launch it?
- Where will this site be seen?
- Why create this particular site at all?

Then, after you've thought through these considerations, begin to assemble the bits and pieces you want to include on your site, such as photos, backgrounds, audio and video clips, and so on. Make a permissions list if necessary, and begin to sketch out a basic framework.

Also, do a quick framework for a very complicated site on the Web. Use your results as a yardstick for how you want to organize the framework for your site, whether or not you feel this exercise was successful. After all, if you have difficulty following this complicated web site's navigational structure, you'd probably have a difficult time just meandering through it as a visitor, too. And what does that say about its overall design?

"Answers" to the Exercises

Figures 3.4, 3.5, and 3.6 show the three frameworks we have constructed for each of the web sites we'll design throughout the course of this book. These sketches merely list the number and general content of each page in these sites. They say nothing (yet) about how these pages will link to one another, what specifics they will contain, or where we will place examples of particular Web technologies such as forms, JavaScripts, VRML worlds, and the like.

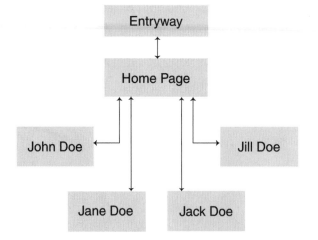

FIGURE 3.4. The personal site: Meet John Smith, Average Guy

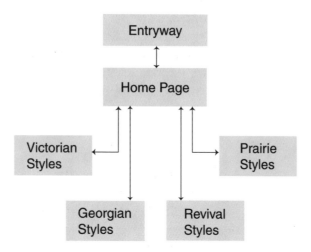

FIGURE 3.5. **The information site: Popular Historical House Styles, A Gallery**

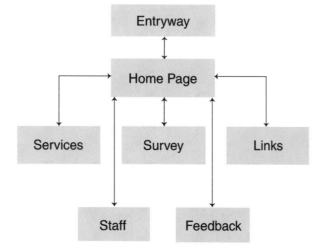

FIGURE 3.6. **The business site: Mula, Dinero and Cash, Accountants**

On with the Show

Now that we've planned out the rough idea of what our web sites will contain—and we've begun generating advance interest in these sites—it's time to talk and think about what they will look like, how they will work, and other questions about basic functionality. So turn the page, and let's move on.

CHAPTER 4

More Basics of Site Creation

If you've come directly from the last chapter, you are undoubtedly looking at a sheet of paper with boxes, lines, and arrows, and wondering how it will translate into the web page in your head.

Now it's time to set loose your imagination by discussing the art of building a web site—what you want your site to look like, what themes and ideas you want to convey, and how you can blend the function of your site's content with an interesting and creative form.

Definitions

In the last chapter, we discussed **content** and touched ever so briefly on questions of **function**, but now we will finally get around to discussing **form**. Within the context of our discussions, form will encompass everything about the way your web site is organized on the page. We spent the last chapter discussing and deciding how the individual pages of your site will hang together, but now we will think about how each page will be laid out. Do you want to convey your message primarily with words or with pictures? Do you like the segmented look of pages built with frames, or do you prefer a more open-looking space? These are the kinds of questions you'll ask yourself in the course of this chapter.

Objectives

The objective of this chapter is to pick themes, schemes, and presentational choices for your web site. We will be referring to various existing web sites to demonstrate how these choices can be made and how they work together.

The Lone H: How?

The best way to discuss and explore how a web site can be designed is to take a brief tour around various kinds of existing web sites. We will be looking at sites that are built around simple backgrounds, text, graphics, frames (this includes the "frameless" kind, which really do use frames) and sites that use technologies such as GIF animations, JavaScript, Java applets, and style sheets.

How Do You Want Your Pages Constructed?

The special appeal of the Web is its fluidity, its ability to create more from a three-dimensional space compared with the flat text-based appearance of other parts of the Internet. So now is the time in the web page design process to react with your emotions, not your brain. When you look at web pages within the context of this chapter, don't ask yourself, "Can I learn to design a page like that?" Ask yourself instead if you like (or dislike) the page in front of you, then ask yourself why, and take the rest from there.

It's worth mentioning here that there are as many ways to define good web page design as there are web sites. There are "authorities" on "good" web sites—David Siegel, Lynda Weinman, and Clement Mok all leap to mind—but if you asked them to name their top three favorite sites, chances are very good that they'd name nine different ones. You could sit down with three programmers, also, or three Fortune 500 CEOs (or better yet, the web- or sitemasters for those Fortune 500 companies' sites), ask the same question, and again get completely different answers.

➤ Why? Because different kinds of web designers qualify "good" very differently. Siegel, Weinman, and Mok come from a traditional graphic design-oriented background. They are focused on color, texture, and visual criteria as much as good usability, loading time, and other concerns specific to the Web medium. A programmer, on the other hand, would have much less to say about a site's aesthetics, as he or she would about how well the site is scripted; that is, the programmer would know the kinds of programs used to run the site and how elegantly, easily, and/or intelligently they work. On yet another hand, someone with a strictly business-oriented background approaches good site design from the standpoint of economics or marketing or even sales. A good site for someone with fingers on a calculator is a site that gets a lot of hits, a site that resembles or otherwise falls in line with the corporate logo or identity, or a site customers use often to make purchases. The code that makes this site work, along with its artistic merits, is merely a means to a concrete, dollar-based end.

➤ Arguably, a good web site looks good, works well, and generates lots of hits (or sales, if it's a business web site). Again, it's a given that people will be less likely to come back to, or stay with, an ugly site or a site that's hard to use because the programming doesn't work or is too complicated. In either case, getting a high number of hits or a high number of sales from such a site is unlikely, so the definition of "good" under these circumstances is both clear and vague. This is a question of form, of function, and of content, the Big Three we'll keep mentioning over and over. Somehow, a good site must please all three kinds of people and address all three concerns—ideally, that is. How ideal does it get? We'll find out.

> **Amy:** This is a really helpful explanation of what makes a good site. It seems that this book can help us figure out how to come up with a web site that has pleasing form and functions well, but the content is up to us. Or will there be tips about that along the way as well?

Rebecca: No, there will be no tips, criteria, or parameters for evaluating content. I really do think that everything on the Web can be interesting, even though not everybody on the Web may be interested in it.

Be aware, though, that you can lose your ISP account if you put content on your page that generates too much traffic. Pictures of naked celebrities will do the trick, for example—or instructions on how to build a bomb. Even though there's no law or legal provision for censorship on the Web at this writing, your ISP can make an issue about server capacity and accessibility. You can also get fired from your job for putting such pages on your employer's server (yes, it's happened) so use a *little* common sense.

NOTE: You can always further your HTML education by having a look at the source, or HTML, of a web page on the Internet. In Netscape Navigator 4 (for either the PC or the Mac), open the main View pulldown menu and select Page Source. In Internet Explorer 4 (for either the PC or the Mac) open the View pulldown menu and select Source.

Before we begin our tour, you should launch both Netscape Navigator 4 and Microsoft Internet Explorer 4; you should enable Java, JavaScript, and cookies if you've disabled these browser functions; and you should be prepared to encounter sites that use many different plug-ins, such as RealAudio and Shockwave. If you don't have the plug-in you need, both NN4 and IE4 will tell you and ask if you want to download it—your machine won't crash or otherwise freak out—but this will temporarily interrupt your progress.

The "Rating" System

As you flip through this chapter, you'll see web sites that look very different and behave in sometimes drastically different ways. Some of them have won design awards from various "authorities"; others are simply web sites that, in our estimation, work. The whys and wherefores of our choices will be explained as we go.

Still, keep these key questions in mind:

- What kind of site is it—personal, informational, or business? Or is the site some combination of these three types?

- Who is the intended audience for this site, based on first impressions?

- Does the site deliver on its promises to its intended audience? Why or why not, in our humble opinion?

- Was this site launched prematurely? Is it complete, or does it leave the visitor wanting more?

- Do we like the aesthetics—the tone, the style, the colors, the type? Does the site seem cluttered, or too spare?

- Does the page appear complete on our screen or does the visitor have to scroll down to get to an important feature?

- Does it load quickly? Did we wait impatiently, and if we chose to wait, was it worth our time?

Now, let's get on with it!

Common Site Design Styles

Sites Using Effective Backgrounds: The VF

One of the most ubiquitous backgrounds used on web sites is the **vertical form**, which we call the **VF** for short (there's no cool tech-lingo term for it). This background simply consists of a vertical stripe of color, with or without links and buttons, designed to run down the browser screen. Once you recognize it, you'll begin to see it everywhere. The sites we have chosen here use basic VF format for decorative, navigational, and many other purposes, and they use them well.

What does "well" mean? The vertical slash of color, buttons, links, or patterns on a web page can be said to do two things, no matter how they slice up a page. The VF adds a bit of tone or style to a web page while still leaving a blank field for content, and/or it draws the viewer's gaze down the page to whatever else is featured below eye level. It can link secondary or tertiary pages to the home page and the main design without really drawing attention to itself. And it can provoke viewers to scroll down, even if what they see at first glance does not suit or match their expectations—which might just give your page a precious second chance.

> **NOTE:** Since this is a section on backgrounds, you might wonder why we don't advocate or even mention web sites that use a full background pattern. In a word, it's function. The first and primary goal of a web site is to convey its content effectively, and most background patterns are too busy or distracting to make this possible. Plain text is harder to read when it's placed against a pattern, and links tend to disappear or stand out too much. Also, it's too difficult to combine graphics, movies, photos, or any other kind of picture effectively with a background pattern—you have too many other colors and patterns going on to make any sort of decent design statement. So for many reasons, we do not recommend background patterns that span the entire web page.

Most VFs are on the left because we Western web page designers are culturally biased—that is, we read from left to right, so our eyes instinctively start on the left side of whatever's in front of us. (See Figure 4.1.) This is reason enough for many prominent and noteworthy web design authorities to wrinkle their noses at the VF (remember, the "ideal" design should be unique and globally aware), but you can incorporate the left VF style and still have a well-designed page.

> **Amy:** The use of lots of yellow in MapQuest tells me this is a site that means business. Though I probably wouldn't use this color scheme in my own page, I think it's pretty effective for what MapQuest is doing. The yellow gets your attention and gives a "construction" feel; it's road related and taking care of business.

> **Rebecca:** It's true, come to think of it, that I've rarely come across a personal site that uses yellow. Do you think most adults make that yellow-construction connection because of yellow road signs? I wonder what children think of when they look at it.

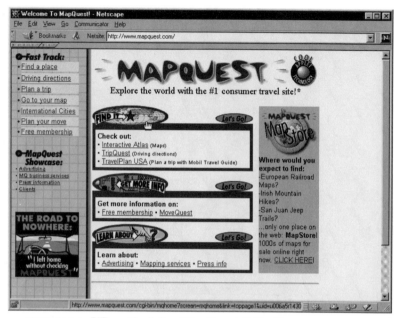

FIGURE 4.1. VF on the left—MapQuest (http://www.mapquest.com)

As for general color theory, there's a lack of consensus on what yellow (or any color) definitively means. Psychologists say that young children get more anxious and/or excitable in a room painted yellow, for example. But the medieval scholars thought yellow represented rebirth and spirituality. Even modern-day color associations vary from culture to culture, if not from person to person. Traditional Chinese brides wear red, whereas Western brides wear white, which is the traditional color of mourning in Muslim countries. So Muslims might think Western weddings resemble funerals, and Westerners might think a Chinese wedding gown looks like something for a Christmas party.

Here's an excellent example of a left VF: that yellow gridded vertical bar running behind the site menu down the left-hand side of the page. Its subtle background pattern helps draw the eye to the individual menu items, while its bright bold color highlights the graphics and other features elsewhere on the page. Let's click on Find A Place and look at a secondary page on this web site (see Figure 4.2).

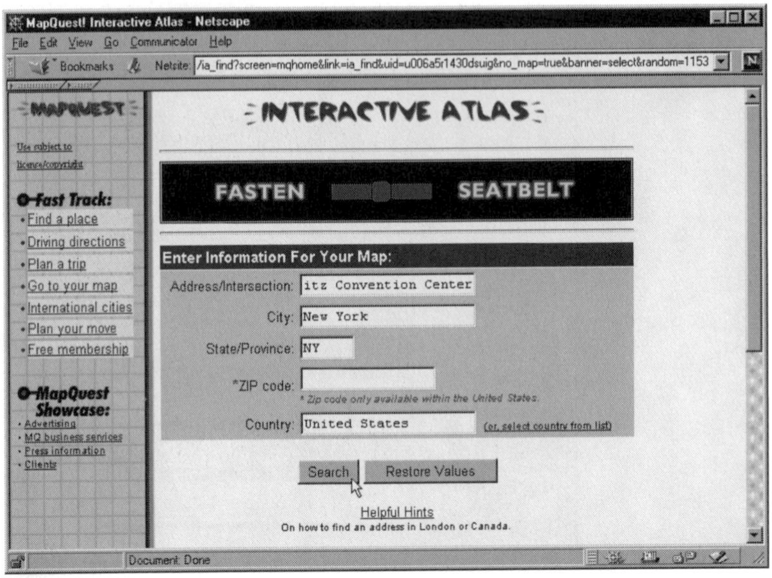

FIGURE 4.2. A secondary page on the MapQuest site

Notice that the basic menu items have not changed. Let's look up the Jacob J. Javitz Convention Center in New York City. Type in "Jacob J. Javitz Convention Center" in the Address/Intersection text box, then "New York" in the City box, and "NY" in the State/Province box. Click Search to go to the next page, then click the New York, NY, option. (See Figure 4.3.)

Here's the same color palette, the same basic page design, but even more detailed information. Notice here how maintaining the simple left VF serves to emphasize what's on the rest of the page—lots of information you probably want to read quite thoroughly if you've come this far into the site. The left VF and the information it contains is there if you need it, but functionally invisible if you don't. That's the beauty of this design strategy; don't let its popularity distract you from its appeal.

Sometimes a designer will go against the cultural grain and arrange a VF on the right, as in Figure 4.4.

Where did your eyes go when this page first loaded up? They probably skirted across the entire field of the page, starting left and

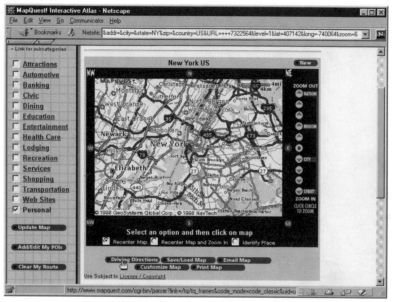

FIGURE 4.3. More VF on the left—a tertiary page on the MapQuest site

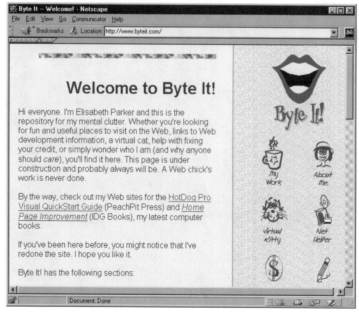

FIGURE 4.4. A VF on the right—Byte It! (http://www.byteit.com)

ending right, subconsciously taking in an overview of what the page offers. That's the subtle benefit of the right-sided single VF.

On this site, the right VF menu also remains constant throughout the secondary and tertiary pages. Notice, though, that the menu items represent the variety of what's available on this site—the author's personal information, her portfolio/résumé, personal interests, and more. This is a clever way to tie disparate personal and business pages together in one cohesive design. (See Figures 4.5 and 4.6.)

A double- or multi-VF approach can also play positive psychological tricks on the eyes. Take Gamecenter.com, for example. The vivid mustard-yellow stripes with just the slightest drop shadow on the edges cause the white field in between, and everything on it, to pop toward the viewer. (See Figure 4.7.)

Amy: Looks like a piece of paper laid on a surface. Neat illusion, though I'm surprised that such a tech-centered company would use this particular illusion. I guess this raises a question for designers: Just because I *can* create a certain illusion or use a certain technology,

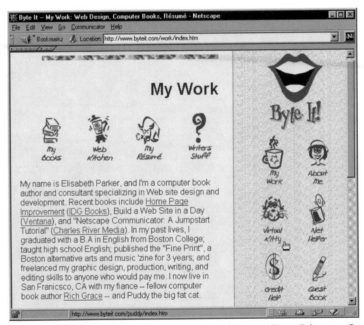

FIGURE 4.5. The VF remains on the right—a Byte It! secondary page

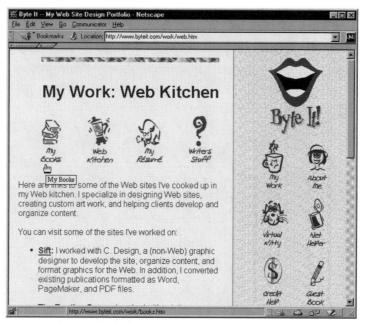

FIGURE 4.6. "Right" to the end—a Byte It! tertiary page

should I do it? Is this the best way to display my particular content? I'm not saying that this is a bad form choice for Gamecenter's content; I just think it illustrates the form/content design question.

Also consider Snapple's web site, even though it's under construction. (See Figure 4.8.)

This page is purely vertical, incorporating a simple scheme of primary colors, pulldown menus, and nifty JavaScripts called **rollovers**—in other words, you roll the mouse over the unassuming bits of text, such as "Snapple Info" on the red stripe, and the text becomes a graphic. Be on the lookout for other rollover effects, as they are a common and simple way to spice up a web page. Also look for more sites using JavaScript later on in this chapter.

Amy: Love the colors! I first visited this site using IE4 and couldn't figure out what you were talking about; the rollovers didn't work. I switched to NN4 and was pleasantly surprised.

**FIGURE 4.7. The double VF—Gamecenter.com (http://
www.gamecenter.com). Reprinted with permission from CNET, Inc.
© Copyright 1995–8. www.cnet.com.**

Rebecca: That's my fault. I should have mentioned right here that
rollovers are JavaScript-based features, which means rollover
effects don't always work reliably in IE4. At this writing, people are
still getting their first glimpse of IE5 so it's hard to say if this
version is an improvement. But there are ways to compensate or to
design alternatives to JavaScript rollovers. We'll create rollovers
and alternatives for one of the sample web sites later on in the book.

Now that you've got a good idea how backgrounds can enhance
and facilitate web site design, let's see how other site elements can
help or hinder this process.

Sites Built around Text

As the Web grows more sophisticated—or, perhaps, as the Web
catches up to the media-savvy expectations of the people who use
it—text is arguably more of a bother than a benefit. Take television,

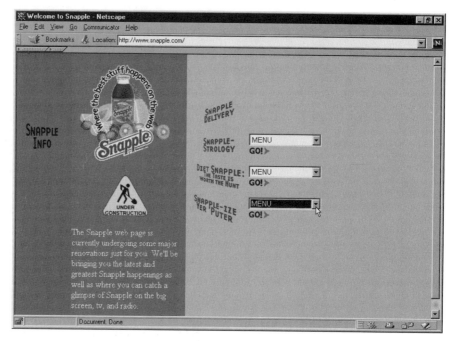

FIGURE 4.8. Only VFs—Snapple (http://www.snapple.com)

the Web's closest cousin; nobody expects to read very much of what they see on the TV screen. Maybe we're supposed to notice the label on a food jar or the number on somebody's apartment door if there's a mystery to be solved. Naturally, advertisers would like to believe we see and remember their product names, but that's marketing. We're really talking about entertainment.

However, what do you do if your product or service is text-oriented? This section explores web sites that rely on text to sell or grab their audience, and manage to do so through well-executed design.

eBay, an online auction house, uses columns and tables of text descriptions to catch the eye of prospective bidders. First, visitors select a category of items from the main list, after scrolling through any number of "hot" deals (designed to encourage impulse bidding, undoubtedly). Then visitors arrive at the category listings, a group of links that seems more like an impressive inviting selection than an overabundance of information purely because of content. (See Figures 4.9 and 4.10.)

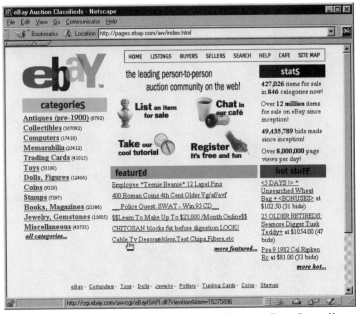

FIGURE 4.9. A home page of lists and links—eBay (http://www.ebay.com)

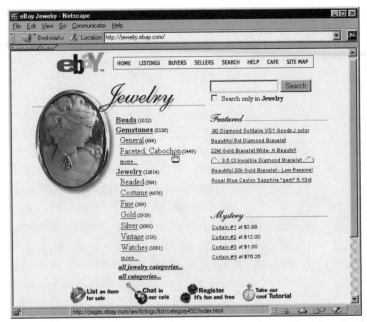

FIGURE 4.10. A secondary page on eBay—increasing detail without adding clutter

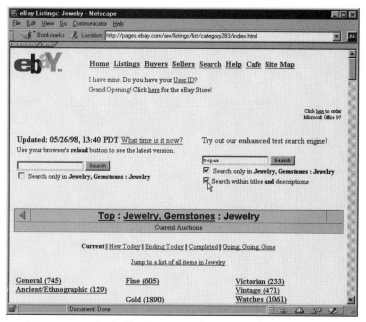

FIGURE 4.11. A tertiary page on eBay—even more detail but still just the facts

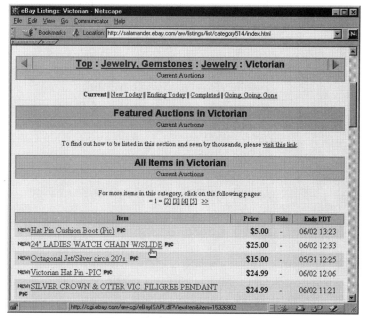

FIGURE 4.12. Minute details in text, and (finally!) a graphic

The reason that eBay's site design works, after all, is because its subject and/or purpose lends itself to increasing text-based detail. You are drawn in by the phrase-link descriptions, so you click on something to read all about it.

> **Amy:** "Drawn in" is right! I just spent 30 minutes checking out some of the items. I'm not sure I should thank you for introducing me to this site!

> **Rebecca:** Well, people, Amy Sez put your money out of reach before you go any further. (Guess the site design works, though, right?)

If there are graphics at all, they are here on the individual auction item pages, but for once on the Web, you only want to see a graphic if you've read all its associated text and decided it's worthwhile.

> **Amy:** Actually I went to the picture of the item first and then looked at the description and other information. Since I'm looking for certain styles of things (for instance, Art Nouveau or Art Deco), I wanted to see the item to see if the seller's and my definitions of Art Nouveau matched.

> **Rebecca:** This brings up a good point about search engines on web sites. In my humble opinion, it is rarely useful or worth the effort to put a search engine on your web site unless you have an extremely complicated or large site framework. calling for lots of pages that contain large amounts of text-based information—such as a site like eBay or Microsoft's site, which we discussed in Chapter 3, "Basics of Site Creation." Why do I recommend against them? Because keyword searching in a small or limiting environment can be a big hassle if you don't know the exact word to use. And you don't want to make life on your site difficult for your visitors; you want to make them feel at ease.

Online magazines and other periodicals also rely on lots of text, ideally without crowding the screen space or giving the viewer too much to absorb at a glance. Salon magazine offers reviews, columns, and other features of the traditional print medium scaled down for the Web. (See Figure 4.13.)

Notice particularly that the background is clean and white, which neatly emphasizes the simple font and text colors denoting plain text,

FIGURE 4.13. Readable text—Salon magazine (http://www.salonmagazine.com). (This artwork by Christian Clayton first appeared in SALON, an online magazine, at http://www.salonmagazine.com. An online version remains in the SALON archives. Reprinted with permission.)

links, subtitles, and other choices. And the secondary pages are just as pleasingly spare. (See Figure 4.14.)

Details worth mentioning on this secondary page are the Entertainment index, represented at the top of the page with lowercase, uppercase, and italicized text, and the site index, running unobtrusively as a solid red bar along the bottom of the screen window.

The Salon Bookcase is still quite severe, with the merest dash of color even against the presence of these book covers. If the Salon site design strikes you as a little too spartan, remember also that a sparing use of primary colors makes the browser/platform color problem less obvious. Less is often more for a variety of reasons. (See Figure 4.15.)

Now, here's a tricky proposition for a web site, even one that would use plenty of graphics: Convince viewers to do their grocery shopping on the Internet. Few other things go so much against basic human nature—who doesn't want to inspect the eggs or thump a cantaloupe to

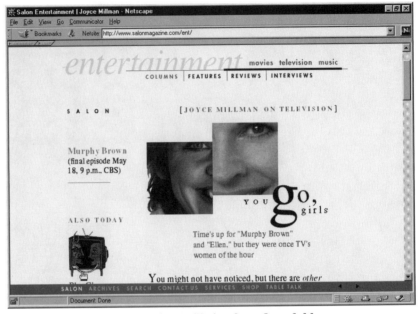

FIGURE 4.14. A Salon review, still simple and readable

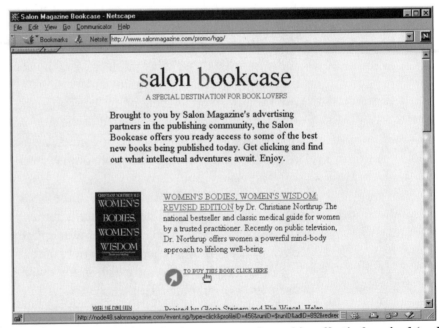

FIGURE 4.15. The Salon Bookcase, text and graphics effectively paired (and pared)

make sure it's whole and fresh? Can't do that on the Web. But a smart shopping service could emphasize, and eliminate, the hassles of an actual grocery store visit. Enter NetGrocer. (See Figure 4.16.)

This home page quickly presents the casual cynic with answers to his or her immediate questions: How's the selection? Are the prices cheaper? How can I see what's in my cart and how much I've spent? How does delivery work? If this first page passes muster, the visitor can click on the Grocery link on the store menu at the top, which will bring you to the Breakfast and Cereal aisle. There you will see submenu along the top of the page featuring easily recognized categories with previews of common breakfast foods with prices in the main window.

If anything, the images on this site can be a drawback as much as they are a benefit. Most people can't list their favorite foods by name, so they need to see an image to choose the right brand, but even these tiny graphics (Figure 4.17) make the shelf pages load up a little more slowly. Still, this site makes the most of its dependence upon text and numbers.

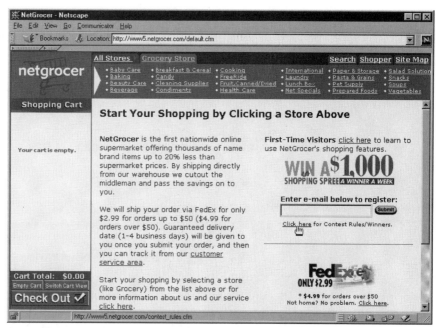

FIGURE 4.16. All text, all shopping—NetGrocer (http://www.netgrocer.com). Copyright 1998, Net Grocer, Inc.

FIGURE 4.17. A tertiary page, the Cereal Flakes shelf. Copyright 1998, Net Grocer, Inc.

If your web page in the making has to be text-intensive, take this lesson from these pages: Keep it simple. Use text that is short, pointed, and informational, both in meaning and in appearance. Even a poem or a bit of lyrics from a song can remain simple if you use fonts, colors, and page placement effectively.

Amy: Good point. Keep text abbreviated and simple. Got it.

Rebecca: Okay!

Sites Using Effective Graphics

Now let's swing around to the other side of site design and look at web pages that rely heavily, or even exclusively, on graphics. First, the contradictions: Yes, as we already said in the last section, too much text or even any text at all is considered somewhat passé and looks too far backward to other, nonweb media. If you follow any of the sites or design "authorities" that grant web design awards such as David Siegel's High Five, you will see a conspicuous preference for sites without words. Such is the current climate among the highbrow Web designers.

But then again, people—ordinary, Web-surfing common people— still need landmarks to orient themselves on a web page. They are accustomed to "bad" design that makes use of underlined text links, labeled buttons, and other text-based page elements, and they do tend to get nervous or feel lost if they don't see any road signs, so to speak. (You wouldn't think this is the case, given our earlier discussion regarding text and television, but there it is.)

So is it possible to make a graphic more compelling and understandable than a written actual word? Can you create a relationship between a graphic and the mouse in the mind of a web page viewer without writing "Click Me"? Absolutely. Let's look at some sites that accomplish exactly that.

First, here's Figure 4.18—Mythopoeia, the Making of Myths.

Whereas Salon magazine uses white to completely emphasize text, this site uses black to focus the viewer's eye on these extraordinary graphics. The colors, textures, and subject matter invite curiosity and speculation without too much text up front. But the text that's here distinctly serves the purpose of the graphics, rather than the other way around.

The bit of text on the page shown in Figure 4.19 is a prose poem, not a list of items for sale or a news article, with keywords links to other images. The plain text is a sort of frame with the links standing out almost as their own pictures, though they do lead to more, related graphics.

Amy: The graphics actually are meant (I think) to make you think how they might relate to their text link—the relationship is not obvious at first click.

Rebecca: Yes, I think the site designer took a bit of a gamble in that respect. It's difficult to get people to pause when surfing around at warp speed, and this site does make the relationship between the

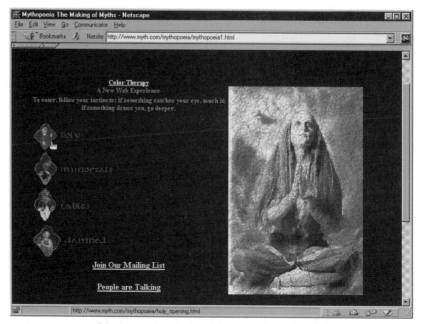

FIGURE 4.18. Mythopoeia, the Making of Myths (http://www.myth.com)

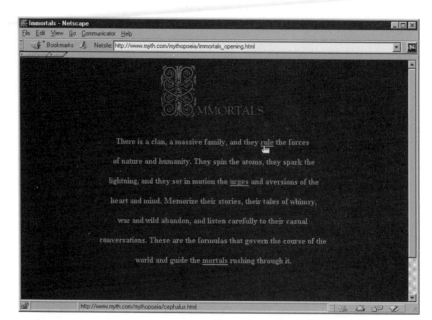

FIGURE 4.19. A secondary page, The Immortals

text and graphics a little obscure. Is it a mistake, or a technique? Reader, you decide.

On the tertiary page shown in Figure 4.20, there are even fewer link-words, and they are contrastingly simple. The purpose or feeling of this page might take a bit of adjustment after the three strongly practical web sites we examined in the last section, but that's the Web. Would these images evoke the same response if they were presented in the same way as eBay's auctions? Would you bid on a secondhand blender posed in Mythopoeia's highly presentational style? The answer to either question is very likely no, because content and form are inextricably connected. That will remain true no matter what design style a good web site utilizes.

Now for a different kind of mind trip: Homewrecker (see Figure 4.21).

Never mind the multi-VF background; let's concentrate on that retro montage in the upper right corner. Getting a clue as to this site's contents? (There's a plainer clue in the innocuous dark blue text down the left side, though it's probably deliberately obscured by the bright blue background.) Then go down the checklist. Let's click the big orange button and enter.

> **Amy:**   Okay, for those of you who haven't downloaded Shockwave yet: *You can't get in without it.* How do you think I found out? Yes, I was a bad reader. Shockwave was one of the only things I didn't take the time to download in Chapter 2. Silly me. Oh well, it took all of four minutes to download, install, and restart my browser.
>
> Let your browser give you the dialogue box and go get it now; it's worth it. This site will blow your mind and give you some great inspiration for your own site. I love the color choices (well-placed simple shapes of blue and orange) and the animation choices.

If you can tear your eyes from the cool Shockwave Flash movie shown in Figure 4.22, the more mundane stuff is scrolling across the bottom of the browser window.

Look at the clothes, place your order, and so on. (Bet you didn't see any text except the menu items at the top; these graphics are so

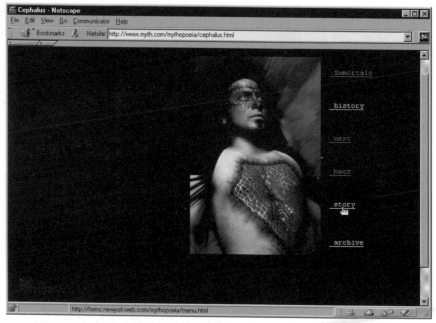

FIGURE 4.20. A tertiary page, An Immortal

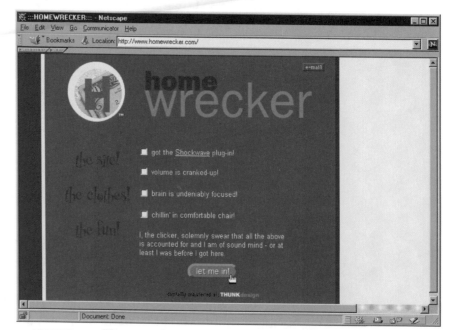

FIGURE 4.21. Homewrecker (http://www.homewrecker.com)

FIGURE 4.22. A sample of the Homewrecker effect

mesmerizing.) Click on The Store to look at the secondary page shown in the screen shot shown in Figure 4.23, and take the audio effects into consideration, too.

As on the other web sites we've considered in this chapter, the use of black, white, and gray deliberately offsets the crazy colors and movement of these graphics. The store menu is no exception; click when it says Come On In! and choose your next destination from the five available items. (See Figure 4.24.)

This site design evokes an eclectic mix of influences: a little Japanese animation, and possibly a dash of the Brady Bunch. Or Speed Racer. This strange nostalgic reverie certainly isn't provoked because of the text—it's in the graphics, and even just the colors of the graphics. The words are just function; the graphics make the form.

To shift gears again, let's visit part of a web site that uses no words whatsoever, just so we can examine the extreme use of graphics as communication. Here is the official web site for Riven, the sequel to Bröderbund's incredibly popular CD-ROM game, Myst.

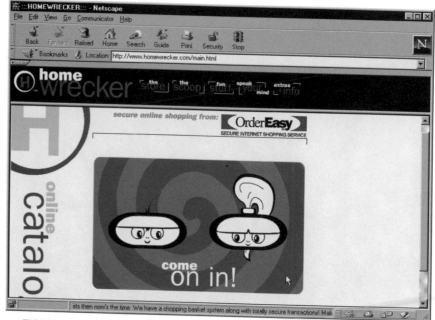

FIGURE 4.23. A secondary page, The Store

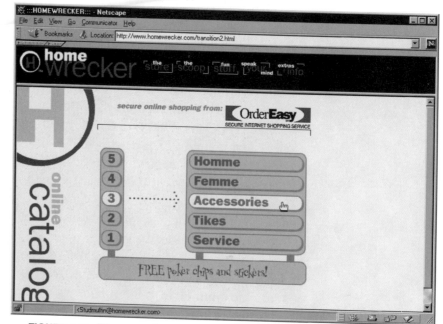

FIGURE 4.24. The secondary page menu—groovy, man!

Who's Afraid of Web Page Design?

The main home page is fairly straightforward, listing different resources for playing the game, including background on Myst and the inhabitants of the Riven world. You can browse these links if you like, but we want to proceed to the Riven Journals themselves; nothing else on this page will provide more detail about the game. (See Figures 4.25 and 4.26.)

So here we are on a page without words. If you're feeling anxious, you can click that promising piece of parchment on the wall, but clearly you as the visitor to this page are supposed to choose a journal. The very title of this web site—The Riven Journals— suggests that somebody wrote something in these books in the way of clues or instructions, so we should look for comforting, purposeful words there. Roll the cursor over the tables and read the helpful hints at the bottom of the browser window; have a look at Journal One.

This is probably my favorite site ever; it educates and promotes problem-solving and thinking in its visitors; it creates an intriguing and believable virtual world; and it draws the visitor into some rather

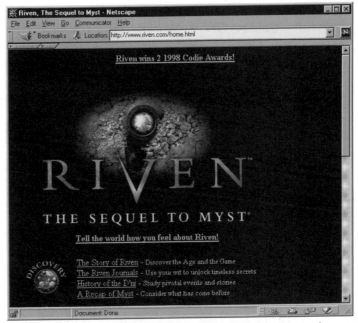

FIGURE 4.25. The official Riven web site (http://www.riven.com)

FIGURE 4.26. The real home page, The Hall of Journals

difficult (and time-consuming!) puzzles, which ensures some return hits. The colors are rich and subtle. It does take some time to load, so I used to keep a magazine handy before I got a cable modem. But I think it's well worth the wait.

If you spend some time exploring this site, you will find that it takes more than one click to open a journal and that there's more to these journal pages than meets the eye. (See Figure 4.27.) Impatient viewers might find this frustrating, but these graphics are meant to force you to notice details—the kind of binding on these books, the images or glyphs on the cover, the condition of the journals and what might have caused them to become distressed. Also remember that this is an extremely sophisticated advertisement for an equally sophisticated game. You are intended to take away a desire to buy Riven as well as whatever bits of tantalizing information you can glean about the game itself.

> **Amy:** This is a good point about the frame of mind that the visitor will take away from the site. I hadn't realized that this site was designed to be a sales tool as well as a fun site; it's very subtle.

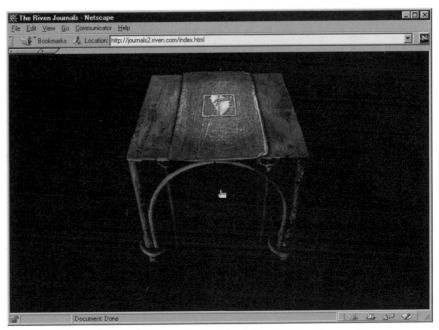

FIGURE 4.27. A secondary page, approaching the first journal

It's also fairly effective—I own the Riven game. (And no, I haven't solved it yet.)

Those of you seeking an ultra-graphics-intensive experience can go right on to Journal Five as an experiment. (See Figure 4.28.) You can tell at a glance from this screen shot that just opening the book is a riddle—you'll have to swing the middle part around to the front somehow to be able to read it. (Here's a helpful hint, though: You do have to read all the other journals in order first to find the actual "key.") The point, though, is that this particular journal relies heavily on Java applets and individual graphics to keep the viewer interested. No words, except for the simplest of navigational instructions, are necessary or apparent.

We've had a look at sites that use a particular kind of background, the VF; we've glanced over some sites that make the most of text and of graphics. Now let's look at sites that make excellent use of GIF animations, JavaScript, Java applets, style sheets, and other high-end features that we will be incorporating in this book's sample pages.

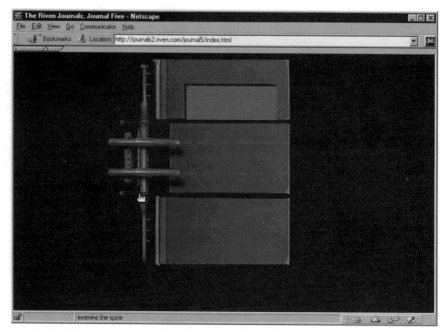

FIGURE 4.28. Another secondary page, Journal Five

Sites Using Effective GIF Animations, JavaScripts, and Other Cool Stuff

The web page designer's toolbox can be a full one, with all the various technologies, plug-ins, and recent newcomers such as DHTML. In this section, we will show you web sites that use one or more of these tools together for a cohesive effect.

First, just to whet the appetite, let's look at two pages using single noteworthy elements to good effect. The first is Webmonkey. (See Figure 4.29.)

At a glance this site might look a little dizzying, with all the bright colors against the stark black background. Also, there's more than one GIF animation in motion on this page, which gives it an unfortunate but all too common twitching effect, as the animations run slightly out of synch. We want to focus, however, on that innocuous little vertical blue bar, which turns red-and-green striped, and then slides out. Click anywhere on the bar to close the menu, and then open it again. (See Figure 4.30.)

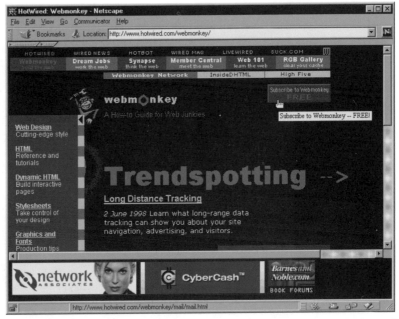

FIGURE 4.29. The retractable site menu using JavaScript—Webmonkey (http://www.webmonkey.com). Here, it's shown open.

Notice first how the design of this page works regardless of whether or not this menu is open. The corner and edge of the open menu do not cover the text, and they intersect precisely with the Webmonkey brandishing his wrench. Similarly, when the menu is closed, its presence is indicated only by the narrow striped bar, which does not distract the user from the other items on the page. Pretty cool, huh?

Amy: Yeah, I guess it is. Maybe I'm just a little tired of the ubiquitous menu bar (though I realize they're often necessary). This didn't wow me as much as it was supposed to.

Rebecca: I agree that it's hard to get enthusiastic about a menu bar, but this is an innovative solution for the ubiquity you just mentioned. Another drawback to this JavaScript (since we're talking about the negatives) is that many people might not realize what it is. The strip with the triangle mechanism would have to become a universal symbol for a retractable menu bar, and there are very, *very* few universalities on the Web.

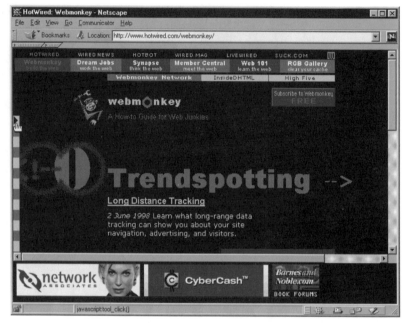

FIGURE 4.30. The Webmonkey retractable site menu, here shown closed.

It gets cooler. There's a particular kind of JavaScript that many pages, including Webmonkey's, use to get around HTML problems between Navigator and Explorer. A "browser detect" JavaScript actually communicates with your browser to recognize its make and version number when you first locate a URL. Then the JavaScript retrieves a customized page designed specifically for the browser you're using and loads it up. This means that all the text you see is lined up correctly with the graphics, the margins always look neat and clean, and you'd never know the JavaScript did its job.

Now let's look at sites that pair JavaScripts and GIF animations with a little more grace and style. Figure 4.31 shows a good example, the web site for BoxTop Software.

This page uses GIF animations and JavaScript literally from top to bottom. That Bela Lugosi–type guy with the shifty eyes, in the top frame, is a GIF animation—nine separate GIFs assembled in a sequence. If you watch this sequence a couple of times, you can see why a GIF animation works for this concept. The movements are simple and the message is

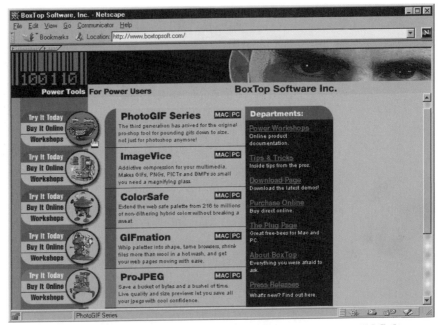

FIGURE 4.31. BoxTop Software (http://www.boxtopsoft.com). Ed Sultan, designer (invisible ink, http://www.invisibleink.com).

direct, but simplicity and straightforwardness are part of this banner's overall content as well as its function.

There's another GIF animation used with the vertical button bar down the left side of the page (do you see the left VF behind all these features, by the way?). Roll the mouse over the fantastic-looking machines, and the background color changes. Also, at the same time, a brief description of that button's link appears on the bottom edge of the browser window. That's a JavaScript prompted by the same mouse action but not otherwise related to the color-change GIF animation. See how these two technologies can work together?

Amy: That is interesting. I suppose the color change gets visitors to take notice, and then their eye might catch the text at the bottom of the screen. Since I usually notice link descriptions without the help of a background color change on a graphic, I guess I'm thinking that this again begs the question "Just because you *can* do, does it mean you *should*?" The more laid-back side of me, though, asks, "Why not?"

Rebecca: Well, the *worst* you can do if you overdo is annoy someone. But then, your choice of background color could annoy someone too, so there's the subjective element of good content popping up again. (I sense a theme here....)

These questions also touch on knowing one's audience. Remember that in Chapter 3 we said that people who design sites to show off their technological prowess will be more inclined to include all the bells and whistles they can. (BoxTop falls into this category, perhaps.) If casual surfers or people in a different profession happen upon their site and wrinkle their noses, it's unfortunate but not such a big deal. Obviously balance is better, but they are logically going to lean toward satisfying their largest audience.

On the PhotoGIF series page shown in Figure 4.32, the GIF animations and JavaScript rollovers maintain the functionality and the feel of this web site. The menus still use the simple rollover animation, while a JavaScript fires off a short description along the bottom of the frame. The moving machine in the upper left is pretty cool, too, isn't it? Another excellent use of animation.

The tertiary page shown in Figure 4.33 is a culmination of all the other elements we've seen on previous pages, along with another feature. The rollover, the JavaScript description, and the moving machine are all here, but now we have the vertical marquee, too. This particular marquee is a Java applet, though you can add similar marquees to a web page using JavaScripts. We'll explore inserting, but not creating, JavaScripts and Java applets in Appendix A, "Adding DHTML: JavaScript, Style Sheets, and More." For now, let's look at another example site.

Amy: Here's a tip: You may have to wait a minute for everything to load before the applet begins. At first I didn't see what vertical marquee Rebecca was talking about. I don't think that the load time is a bad thing, because people who go to this page not just to check out the

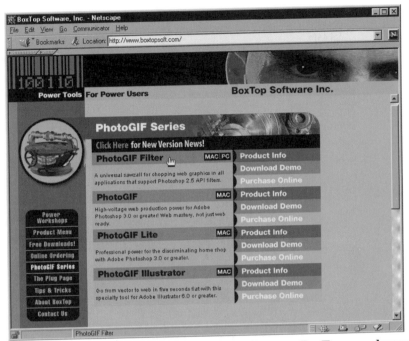

FIGURE 4.32. More GIF animations and rollovers, a BoxTop secondary page. Ed Sultan, designer (invisible ink, http://www.invisibleink.com).

design but to read the information will, of course, stay around long enough for things to load while they're reading the text.

The Fantastic Forest is part of National Geographic's web site, and it incorporates all kinds of nifty web site technology—JavaScripts, Macromedia Shockwave, QuickTime VR, all within an excellent use of the "frameless" frames approach. This site is geared toward children about 11 or 12 years old, so it is topically simple and not as visually elegant or hip as others you might see. Click on the leaf to proceed. (See Figure 4.34.)

The JavaScript that launches this new, unresizable window is particularly useful under these circumstances. (See Figure 4.35.) The forest view and the visual map in the left-hand frame are exactly the size you see them here, so it helps the ambiance and usability of this site to keep the window as it is. Yet the instructions in the right-hand

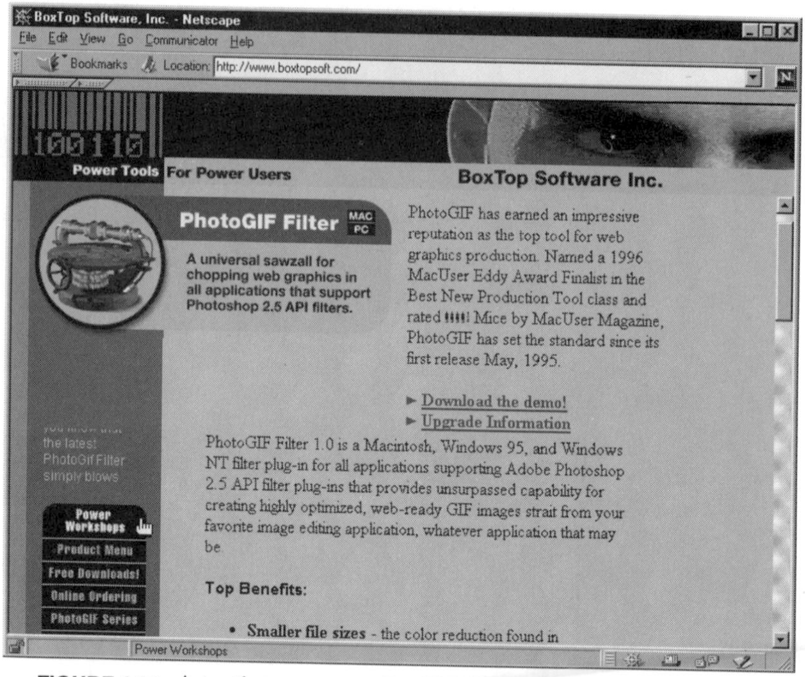

FIGURE 4.33. A tertiary page on BoxTop Software's web site—the PhotoGIF page. Ed Sultan, designer (invisible ink, http://www.invisibleink.com).

frame are scrollable, so the directions and other helpful information are not restricted in quantity because of the window's set size. Follow the instructions on the map (Enter) to continue.

Amy: I can see how useful this unresizable window is to make sure everyone is seeing the same thing, but I find that I want the forest views and the QuickTime view to be bigger so I can get into it more. The Riven pages created a whole world, while the smaller window here interferes with that illusion. Of course, the smaller window also makes for shorter download time, so it's a toss-up.

Rebecca: You hit the nail(s) on the head. These site designers sacrificed image quality for usability, probably hoping the content would be compelling enough to override the interface constraints. Did they accomplish their first goal? Again, Reader, you decide.

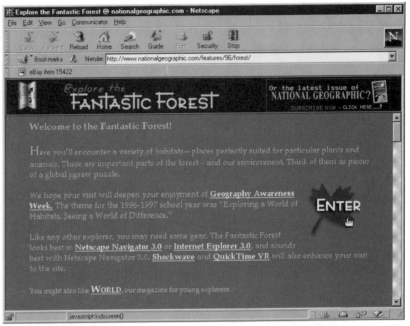

FIGURE 4.34. The Fantastic Forest (http://www.nationalgeographic.com/features/96/forest)

FIGURE 4.35. Beginning the exploration—the entrance to the Fantastic Forest

Education is the purpose of this site, so the user is supposed to search the forest for various plants and animals while tallying points or leaves on the Forest Finds chart. Roll the cursor around the forest till the arrow becomes a pointing hand, click, and you'll probably discover something you're supposed to find—a corresponding description appears in the right-hand frame. (See Figures 4.36, 4.37, and 4.38.)

This site is noteworthy not only for its appropriate and savvy use of various web technologies, but also for its graphics. We have briefly touched upon the idea of how to prepare graphics for the Web, and how colors and color palettes work, but before we tackle this subject in the next chapter, take another look at these forest illustrations. For their size and audience, these drawings are beautifully rendered and optimized to load quickly and look good, as still images and as panoramic QuickTime movies (particularly the Night Forest images, in my opinion). Though as Amy said, they might not be as impressive as the Riven pages, but they're well above mediocre.

Sites Using Style Sheets

Ideally, a web site design technology should be so ingenious and so well integrated that you shouldn't be able to tell it's there. And when cascading style sheets in particular work well within a web page design, you won't really know it, unlike the very popular JavaScript button rollover or the telltale multicolored Q that appears when a QuickTime movie loads up.

On the other hand, when style sheets doesn't work well, you will definitely know it. You won't get an error, as you would with a badly executed Java applet, and you won't get a request to download a plug-in you're missing. The web page will simply look like garbage. In webdesignspeak this means that the web site you're viewing doesn't **degrade** well—in other words, it has not been designed for the possibility of viewers' using older browsers or browsers that don't support style sheets at all.

So in order to show the truly proper use of style sheets and its **properties**, or the individual little tricks that style sheets enables you to use, we will have to do this part of the tour a little differently. First

FIGURE 4.36. The graphics-based Left, Center, and Right views...

FIGURE 4.37. ...compared with the Panoramic QuickTime view

we'll show you web pages in Microsoft Internet Explorer 4 for the PC, the kind and version number browser with the most style sheets support. But then we'll show you the same web pages in Netscape Navigator 4 for the PC, and in both these browsers for the Macintosh,

FIGURE 4.38. Finding treasures in the forest using links, graphics, and JavaScript

knowing all the while that none of these latter options support style sheets reliably or even at all. (Once we get into the discussion of each of these sample sites, the reasons for this will become more clear.) Figure 4.39 shows the first example.

In Internet Explorer 4 for the PC, this title piece looks gorgeous. However, compare it with the same web page loaded up in Netscape Navigator 4 for the PC. (See Figure 4.40.)

Amy: I think they've got a JavaScript pulling up a different page if you access it in NN4 now; check it out yourself.

Rebecca: Yes; after looking at the source code for this page, I agree. This is one way to get around platform-based design issues, but it's twice the overall work. It's ultimately less time-consuming and more elegant to have one site for everyone. (Reader, rely on these screen shots for my point, and not what you might see on the screen.)

Here's the first lesson to be learned about using style sheets: Either you must design alternate pages without style sheets for

FIGURE 4.39. First sample from the style sheets Microsoft Gallery sample (http://www.microsoft.com/workshop/c-frame.htm#/gallery/stylesheets/ default.asp)—looks great in IE4 for the PC

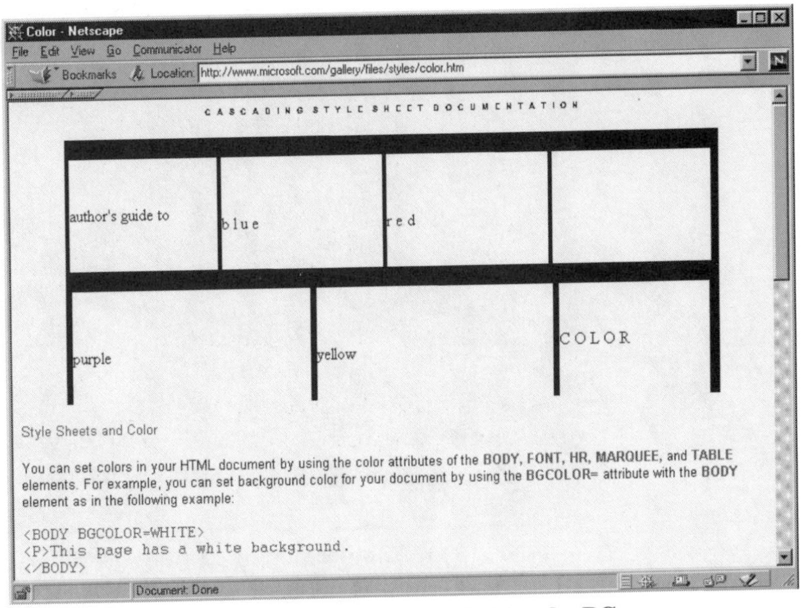

FIGURE 4.40. Looks very different in NN4 for the PC

Netscape Navigator, or you must design your pages with style sheets in a nonessential fashion. Everybody using any kind of browser should be able to view and use your web pages effectively, period. That's rule number one.

Now let's check a different style sheets web page only in Internet Explorer 4, but on each platform, to illustrate rule number two. (See Figures 4.41 and 4.42.)

You *might* be able to get away with calling the Macintosh version of this page an ultrahip grungelike design choice.

However, these two pages ably illustrate rule number two: You must check and recheck style sheets–based web pages on both platforms, even though Internet Explorer 4 for both platforms supports style sheets. This is because not all style sheets features and properties supported on the PC are supported on the Macintosh. And in this particular instance, these differences mean that the background graphics overlap, that some of the type is unreadably small and dark, and that the first line of text is missing from the top of the page.

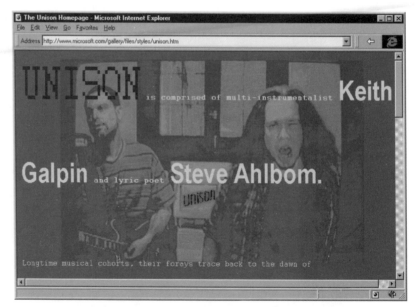

FIGURE 4.41. Another sample style sheets web page from the Microsoft Gallery (http://www.microsoft.com/gallery/stylesheets/unison.asp) in Internet Explorer 4 for PC...

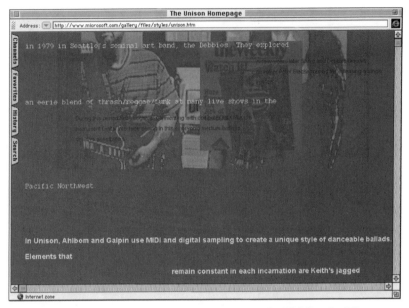

FIGURE 4.42. ...and here, the same web page in IE4 for the Mac

Amy: Since I currently do not own a Macintosh, nor do I know anyone whose machine I could use, should I just cross my fingers and hope for the best when it comes to crossplatform issues?

Rebecca: Now here's where I transform into a double personality; the designer part of me says, "Never! Search out a Macintosh as if it were the Holy Grail!" but the average person part of me says, "Well, we do have other things to do in life; now, don't we?"

You can cover your bases two ways. First, always aim for the safe middle. Choose moderate-sized fonts and graphics, never deviate from the browser-safe list of colors, and be very careful with margins and spacing around graphics and text. Also, learn your HTML attributes, tags, and values thoroughly—some work on a Mac but not a PC, some work in Explorer and not in Navigator, or even in Navigator for the Mac but not Navigator for the PC. Nothing beats true crossplatform and cross-browser testing, but these two rules will help you avoid most glaring problems.

Now let's look at how a web page using style sheets might degrade properly, in terms of both browser support and platform issues. We are using examples from Day Five in Steve Mulder's style sheets tutorial on Webmonkey.

In this example, the font and font color should be customized, and the text and graphics should overlap in a staggered, horizontal spread from left to right. Look at Figures 4.43, 4.44, and 4.45 to see which browser on which platform translated the style sheets correctly.

Amy: I can see that these style sheets sites look different than other sites, but I can't quite put my finger on how it's done. The use of color (lots of colors), the horizontal layout, the varied texts—is that what style sheets does?

Rebecca: These things and more. Style sheets gives you more control over the detail of these page elements, letting you place and arrange elements more precisely, and letting you assign particular

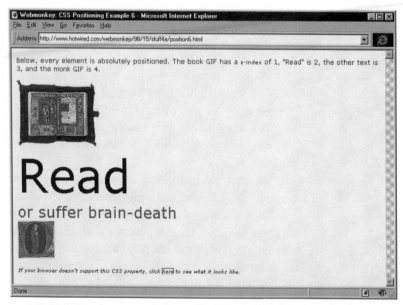

FIGURE 4.43. An example from Day Five of Mulder's style sheets tutorial on Webmonkey (http://www.hotwired.com/webmonkey/98/15/stuff4a/position6.html) using Internet Explorer 4 for the PC—the positioning properties don't work, but it looks okay.

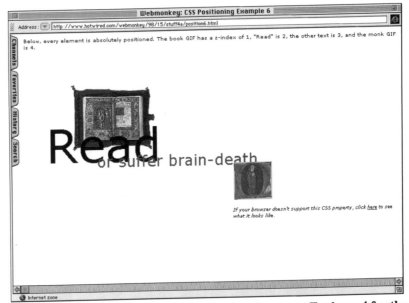

FIGURE 4.44. The same example viewed in Internet Explorer 4 for the Mac—the positioning works correctly, too.

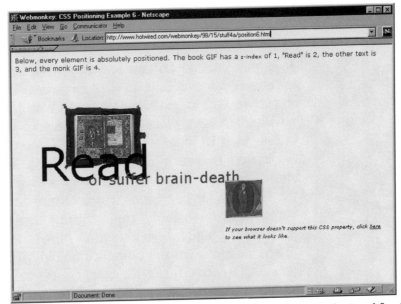

FIGURE 4.45. The same example viewed in Netscape Navigator 4 for the PC—surprise! everything works in Communicator!

colors to particular elements. We'll get into the details of style sheets in Appendix A.

There's a corollary to rule number two: Sometimes you can check style sheets on a browser where you think nothing will work, yet it does! We will delve into the mysteries and details of which style sheets properties work under which conditions in Appendix A, "Adding DHTML: JavaScript, Style Sheets, and More."

Exercise

Now that we've taken some time to tour the Web and get an idea of everything that's out there, you might have some clearer ideas about what you want your own web site to look like. We hope you've been taking note, or even taking notes, as we've seen backgrounds, menus, buttons, graphics, and other elements you may or may not like. (Sometimes it's just as valuable to see something you don't like, as long as you can clearly identify your reasons for disliking it.)

So now, for this exercise, it's time to build an optional temporary or under-construction (UC) page. Remember, this is a simple web page you can upload immediately as a teaser or placeholder to advertise your web site as "coming soon!" Figures 4.46 and 4.47 show two UC pages taken from the Web to illustrate some of the possibilities (also, glance back at Chapter 3 to refresh your memory of Snapple's UC site).

There's not much to these pages, really. The Modern Times page shows the logo above the ubiquitous yellow-and-black UC bar, and the HealthRider page shows a picture of the product along with a verbal description of the page as being temporary. Both convey the same idea at a glance, neither must be scrolled down or manipulated to see the message, and both load quickly. These are the three goals you should strive for in the creation of your own temporary pages: simplicity, brevity, and speed.

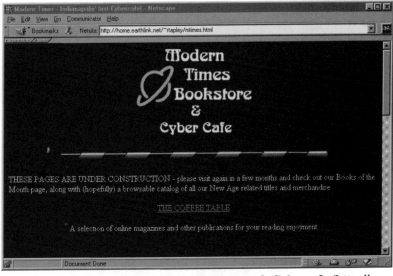

FIGURE 4.46. The Modern Times Bookstore & Cybercafe (http://home.earthlink.net/~rtapley/mtimes.html)

FIGURE 4.47. HealthRider (http://www.healthrider.com)

This exercise can actually serve as a crash course in total site design, as you should ask yourself all the same questions we reviewed in Chapter 3, as they apply to this single page, which will be your first impression. If you're so inclined, make a rough sketch of what your UC page will look like: the graphics you'll use, the text you'll add, any logos or identities, any backgrounds or other artistic renderings. Then translate this sketch into basic (repeat, *basic*) HTML and test it on each of the three browsers you downloaded in the previous chapter. If you like how your page looks, upload it to your ISP and view it on the Web.

Some of you may feel this step is a bit preliminary. We haven't discussed how to use any intermediate or advanced HTML, which is the reason (probably) that you bought this book in the first place. And now we're asking you to create a web page anyway. Seems like the wrong idea, perhaps?

The answer is no. Do the best you can with this UC page, even if you're dissatisfied with the results. Why? Because you'll be giving yourself an actual page to work from in the chapters ahead; up to this point, we've been talking and thinking and sketching but not coding. And you have to start somewhere, both to establish the limits of what you already know and to give yourself a place to implement the improvements and new skills you'll learn later. Right? Of course.

> **Amy:** I found this exercise very valuable, since it did force me to practice my HTML skills and to start thinking about how I want my site to look. My UC page features a lot of text because that was faster and simpler to create for now. I decided on a fairly conversational feel to my page, and I tried to entice the visitor by give a sneak preview of what would be coming soon. I really encourage readers to give this a try; it takes some work, but you learn a lot in the process.

Review

To recap this chapter, we flitted around various web sites looking at how various elements, color and pattern schemes, and web technologies can make or break overall web site design. We moved from the simplest design statement made by a VF background (single or multiple, left or right) to complex, high-end pages using GIF animations, JavaScript, Java applets, and even QuickTime movies. We hope you also had fun!

"Answers" to the Exercise

Obviously your own completed UC page is the answer to this exercise. But for further reference, here are the finished UC pages for the three sample sites we'll begin creating in Chapter 6, "Advanced Graphics Techniques." (See Figures 4.48, 4.49, and 4.50.)

Also, here's Amy's UC page, to help illustrate her progress. (See Figure 4.51.)

Note that all these UC pages are simple and use relatively uncomplicated HTML—the Gallery/information page is the most complex because it uses the <TABLE> tag to position the house photos. (If you don't know how to do this yourself, don't worry. We'll cover tables and graphic placement in Chapter 8.) The important thing is that these pages are substantial enough to give a visitor the flavor and tone of the real page(s) to come.

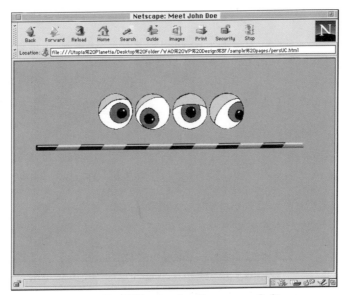

FIGURE 4.48. The UC page for the personal site

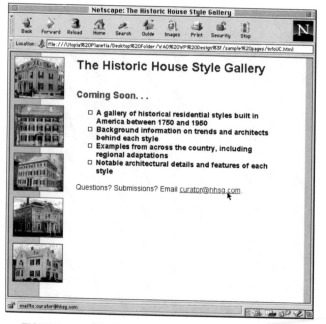

FIGURE 4.49. The UC page for the information site

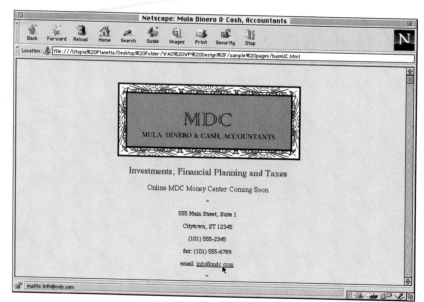

FIGURE 4.50. The UC page for the business site

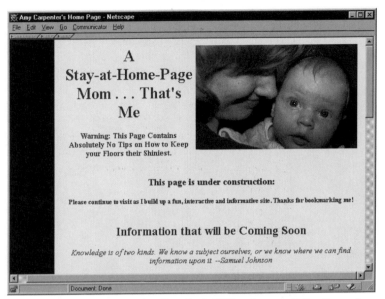

FIGURE 4.51. The Novice Reader's UC web page (http://members.aol.com/
arcarpenter/home/ucpage1.htm)

On with the Show

We're done discussing pure theory and ideas, and we've finished our preliminary research into what else is out there on the Web. We've also created simple UC or under-construction pages to announce the location and style of our polished sites to come. So now it's time to get to work on our finished product(s), starting with the most important skill you can learn to improve the usability and design of your web pages: optimizing graphics. Turn the page, and we'll begin.

CHAPTER 5

Preparing Web Graphics

Now that we've taken some time to cruise the Web and establish the form, the function, and the content of our fledgling web site(s), we need to finesse some of the various elements we will include. The first task, and one of the most important, is preparing web graphics.

In this chapter, we will do our best to condense and explain the unique challenges of creating and/or customizing pictures, photographs, drawings, and other graphics for display on a web page. However, this topic is huge and highly debated; entire books have been written about preparing graphics and the particular challenges that accompany the procedures and the software. But because this book is meant as a primer for all kinds of web page designers—not just the traditional kind who may have worked in ad agencies or in print, or who went to art school—we won't dwell on the details. We want to teach you what you need to know and get on to the next job at hand.

One more note worth mentioning: This is not a color book, so all of us are working at a disadvantage. It's impossible to show you the difference between certain graphics at different bit settings, for example, though we will do our best to provide the settings and describe the differences in the hopes that you will follow along. Just try to read and understand the logic behind the various tasks, decisions, and exercises in this chapter, and do your best with your own color monitor, graphics software package, and browser.

Definitions

When we speak of preparing graphics for the Web, we say we are **optimizing** them. Optimization refers specifically to this process—it is not the same process as preparing a photo to be printed in a magazine or broadcast on TV—and also to the task of altering the file size and the number of colors in a graphic. Traditionally, file size and color reduction don't need to be done in other areas of media such as print and television. But when it comes to putting graphics on the Web, not much else is more important or more challenging.

We will also speak peripherally about **bandwidth**, which is the whole reason that optimization is necessary. Bandwidth is both an idea and a reality; the term is used to express the maximum amount of available "space" on the Internet. Think of a pipeline and the flow of water through it to visualize bandwidth properly.

> **Amy:** So bandwidth is the amount of "space" (which translates into uploading time) that a page's information takes up, correct? The pipeline metaphor is used because only so much water can fit through the pipeline at a time; in the same way, only so much information can fit through our modem connection at a time. Is that right?

> **Rebecca:** Yes—bandwidth is used to describe both the capacity of the entire Internet (as in "This ugly page is a waste of bandwidth!") *and* the capacity of an Internet connection (as in the example of the pipeline.)

> **Amy:** Is there a unit measure for bandwidth, so instead of saying, "This graphic takes up too much bandwidth," you could say, "This graphic takes up six million (fill in unit name here) of bandwidth, and I need to reduce that number to 300"? Or do we just speak of the file size in kilobytes instead?

Rebecca: You can speak of bandwidth in concrete numerical terms, but this does not account for the difference in people's connection speeds. As we already discussed, most people have a 14.4 or 28.8 modem, but others have much faster connections, such as a 33.6 or cable modem or even a T1 line. This affects the way you have to think of optimizing graphics, because you *must* design for the lowest common denominator. As long as so many people have so many different connection speeds, you have to try to reduce the overall size of your graphic as much as you can without destroying its aesthetic appeal.

In practical terms, you can figure out that a graphic takes up too much bandwidth just by clocking it on an "average" modem. It doesn't really matter how many kilobytes the graphic takes up; if it's slow to load up (I have patience for about six seconds tops) then it's too large. These criteria are somewhat ambiguous, but it's really about context.

A photograph that has been scanned in and uploaded to a web page without any optimization takes much longer to load up on a browser, in which case we would say that it has, or creates, a bandwidth problem. The graphic can look good and load up correctly, but if it takes too much time, few people visiting your web page will wait for it.

Resolution is a related topic you will also need to understand, both in terms of your hardware and in terms of web-ready graphics. **Screen resolution** is an expression of pixel size as it is displayed on your monitor, while **file resolution** or file size is an expression of the amount of detail and/or colors a graphic contains. A **pixel** is the basic unit of a graphic just as an atom is the basic unit of matter; it is made up of the tiny dots of light a monitor displays. Similarly, a greater number of pixels translates to more **K**, or kilobytes, because more pixels take up more file space. We'll discuss resolution in greater detail later on in this chapter, and throughout the rest of the book as needed.

Compression is another important term we'll explore; perhaps you've heard the term used before with regard to regular text documents. When you want to send a file over the Internet, you use a program like StuffIt on the Macintosh or WinZip on the PC to reduce its overall size and speed up the transfer. The same logic applies to compressing graphics you want to include on a web page; compression removes some of the "extra" information and makes the graphic smaller. This process is a little more complicated with graphics, though, so we will save the details for later on in the chapter.

> **Amy:**   Please remind readers of the overall difference between the way colors display on a PC versus the way they display on a Macintosh.

> **Rebecca:**   Good idea. As a general rule, the same color (whether it's browser-safe or not) will look darker on a PC than it does on a Macintosh. And as we already mentioned, this is a *hardware* thing—it has nothing to do with the software you're using or your skill in preparing web graphics. You should keep this situation in mind during this chapter and the two that follow on advanced graphics prep and web color. (But we'll remind you again in case you forget.)

Objectives

The objectives of this chapter are at the same time simple and very complicated. You are about to take a crash course in adjusting graphics size and file format, even though this is not a skill you can develop or acquire in one sitting. It's also important to remember that the needs and wants of a particular graphic will change, depending upon many variables. We will try to touch on these variables throughout the chapter, but don't expect to understand or process all this stuff right away.

Resolution, Color Values, and Other Scientific Stuff

Ready for a little math, optics, electronics, and chemistry? We promise this won't hurt your brain a bit.

Let's explore the terms we mentioned earlier in the definitions, paying special attention to how your monitor displays and processes color, as this obviously defines the way your web page is viewed. To get started, open your HTML editor and your browser of choice (you don't need to log on to the Internet, though). When we get to the part where you need other software, we'll let you know.

Resolution

Resolution is both a monitor thing and a graphics thing. First we'll discuss your monitor.

A monitor does its work by shooting electrons onto the phosphor dots spread across the backside of your screen in red, blue, or green. These dots glow at a rate of brightness established by whatever pattern and whichever colors they are trying to portray: documents, photographs, web pages, and so forth. Pixels are the basic units of measurement for an image on a monitor screen, composed of these combinations of red, blue, or green dots. Most monitors are 480 by 640 or 600 by 800 pixels, though with some you can change the setting to increase or decrease pixel density (which, as you may already realize, will significantly affect the way graphics appear). That's the electronics lesson; here's where we get back to graphics.

Part of the optimization process is trying to allow for all these resolution variables as you reduce the number of colors. To a certain extent, you and your web site are held hostage to the visitor's monitor, which is likely to display in 256 colors but may display in more—this is one technology standard that's evolving quickly. So you want to reduce the number of colors in your graphics to improve their size and portability, but not so much as to render them ugly in a higher-color environment. It's a tricky balance that takes practice, but for now just remember that web graphics should be 72 **dpi** (or **dots per inch**, as in those red, blue, and green dots mentioned above). We will discuss the way to guarantee this later on, in the exercises.

> **Amy:** We haven't specifically discussed the unit of dpi before. Does this refer to pixels per inch? We jumped from discussing the need to balance the color scheme between good looks and

manageable file size, to this hard-and-fast rule that all web graphics should be 72 dpi. I feel like we're missing a step or two in between.

Rebecca: Sorry—I was trying not to bore everybody with a detailed description of how a monitor works! Dots are those red, blue, and green phosphor spheres on the backside of your monitor screen that determine the color of what you're looking at, and they are always the same size. Pixels are actually composed of these dots; although a pixel on a PC and a pixel on a Macintosh are different sizes. This is why you want to save all your graphics at 72 dpi rather than at a pixel-based measurement.

Amy: Why the magic number of 72 dpi? And do most graphics programs allow you to control the dpi when you save an image?

Rebecca: The magic number is 72 dpi because most people's monitors display graphics at that size. So if you save graphics at 72 dpi, you eliminate the difference in pixel size between PCs and Macintoshes, for one thing—you ensure that 1 dpi will equal 1 pixel. (Try saving an image at 300 dpi and opening it in your browser, for example, to see the difference.)

Most graphics programs do give you different dpi settings, but they don't necessarily have the web-proper default setting. So you can't let the dpi setting options fly by when you optimize graphics for use on the Web—always check to make sure it's 72.

For the web page designer, establishing the right resolution for a graphic is a tightrope walk between what an individual graphic needs and what a monitor can do. (To say nothing of how long that graphic will take to download at different resolutions—but we'll get into that in the exercises.)

√*Palettes and RGB Color*

Palettes are simply groups of colors used to design graphics for the Web and used by browsers to display web pages. However, just because the *definition* of palette under these circumstances sounds the same, this doesn't mean that the *colors* on all designers' and browsers' palettes are the same. Remember that as we go ahead with this part of the chapter.

Both Netscape and Microsoft encountered the same problem with color palettes when they developed their browsers: Early Web users owned monitors that displayed pages only at 256 colors. (Undoubtedly they preferred to add a few more features elsewhere, like email, rather than take designers' needs into account!) Therefore, both Netscape and Microsoft "solved" this problem by reducing their palettes. What's the catch? There are two different palettes, one for the PC and one for the Macintosh. So graphics that look good or accurate on a PC might very likely look awful on a Macintosh—and vice versa.

Enter the "browser-safe" color palette, a group of 216 colors present on both the Navigator and the Explorer default palettes. Designers can import this palette into their graphics programs for use when they customize web graphics, create backgrounds, and choose solid colors for links and text. The consequences of not using browser-safe colors can be extreme if you're a perfectionist; your lovely graphics may look pixellated or grainy, or Navigator and/or Explorer may substitute a shade or color you don't like.

We will show you how to use the browser-safe color palette (which is included on the CD in the back of this book), and how to incorporate individual browser-safe colors, in the next chapter, "Advanced Graphics Techniques." For now, it's simply important to understand that graphics programs use color reduction or elimination to reduce overall size.

Available Graphics Formats

There are three graphic formats that are more or less available as choices for use on a web page: the GIF, the JPEG, and the PNG. In this section, we'll explore them one by one, along with their merits and drawbacks, their strengths and weaknesses, and any related technical or design issues.

The GIF

GIFs (Graphic Interchange format, pronounced "giff," not "jiff") were first developed by CompuServe back in the early 1980s. This "long" history gives the GIF wide support among all the traditional and popular browsers such as Netscape and Microsoft products.

However, the GIF was created at a time in technological history when most people had very slow modems and low-end monitors with a very limited, 256-color palette. So turning a graphic into a GIF means settling for an equally limited color palette; this does reduce the size of your graphics by as much as one third, but it greatly reduces quality and vibrancy, too.

On the plus side, the GIF process automatically compresses a graphic without your having to do lots of additional thinking or work. Also, the GIF format lets you easily create a simple **transparency** by selecting certain pixels or colors in a graphic that will not display, allowing a web page's background pattern or color to show through behind them. Last but certainly not least, you can create simple animated GIFs to add basic movement to your web page without writing scripts or otherwise complicating your HTML. We will show you how to do this later in the book.

The JPEG/JFIF

The **JPEG** (Joint Photographic Experts Group, pronounced "jay-peg") was created specifically with the needs of photographs and other full-color files in mind. The JPEG process is unbeaten when it comes to compressing photos, reducing file size, and allowing more than 256 colors without dramatically sacrificing quality. In other words, if you scan in a picture of your dog Rover and its file size is 194K, you can use the JPEG process to easily and beautifully reduce it to a mere 44K.

The other benefit of the JPEG format is **progressive display**. Some, but not all, JPEGs can be built in place on a web page gradually, as the information is downloaded, rather than making the web page visitor wait till the download is complete. Progressive display works as a sort of preview, enabling visitors to get a brief glimpse of what's on your site and move on if they choose. Its primary attraction, though, is speed and visibility that cannot be matched by either of the other two formats we mention here.

The PNG

The **PNG** (Portable Network Graphic, pronounced "ping") is unquestionably the best of all these formats. It was created by graphics tools developers for the Web as it exists today, a melange of all platforms, browsers, system software, and connection speeds. What's the catch, you might ask? PNGs are not widely supported— that is, both Microsoft and the W3 (World Wide Web Consortium) have embraced the PNG format with both hands, but Netscape (to extend the metaphor) is dragging its feet. And as long as Netscape Navigator is the most popular browser software, you as a web page designer should not get too enthusiastic about PNGs. Yet.

> **Amy:** I haven't heard of PNGs before. Are they also supported by most graphics software, such as Paint Shop Pro?

> **Rebecca:** PNGs are supported by some graphics programs such as Photoshop, and there are freeware/shareware utilities that will transform other file types into PNGs. But the limited support for PNGs on the Web makes for limited support among software developers, too.

> I would recommend waiting for another six to eight months to begin experimenting with PNGs, and I wouldn't advise incorporating them into a web page without an alternative GIF. The version 5 browsers might say they support PNGs, but even if they do, the majority of people on the Internet will still be using earlier versions that do not.

The benefits of PNG far outstrip those of both the GIF and the JPEG. You can create a PNG in full color (like a JPEG), in indexed color (like a GIF), or as a grayscale file, rather than having to switch color formats every time you want to optimize. PNG compression is superior to GIF compression, creating even smaller graphics for even easier downloading. Also, PNG easily beats the GIF format when it comes to creating higher quality transparencies, for adjusting brightness, and for interlacing.

As a side note, Netscape has promised PNG support in the forthcoming Netscape Navigator 5. So keep PNG and all it promises for web graphics in the back of your mind for now, as we use GIFs and JPEGs to accomplish our goals in this chapter.

Tricks of the Trade: Optimization Techniques

Now that we've touched on the colors you should use, let's talk about using these colors for all they're worth. In other words, how do browsers compensate for the 216-color palette when they encounter a nonoptimized graphic, and how can you anticipate these changes with workable solutions? Web design technology presents us with tricks to help us do the best we can: dithering, interlacing, and progressive JPEG display.

> **Amy:**   It doesn't seem that interlacing or progressive JPEGs fit in this category: they deal with making up for long download time instead of dealing with the limitations of the browsers' color palettes. Or is there something I'm missing?

> **Rebecca:**   No; you're correct. Dithering and antialiasing involve making physical changes to the graphic itself, while interlacing and progressive JPEG display don't. I presented these options this way to create a logical progression of techniques if you have a graphic you don't want to optimize to death.

Dithering

Because this isn't a color book, you'll have to do a few exercises using your graphics program, Internet Explorer 4, and a file on the CD-ROM. So open GraphicConverter, Paint Shop Pro, and/or Photoshop, depending upon which program you chose to install in Chapter 2, and pop in the CD-ROM. The file you're looking for is called *rainbow.tif.* Open it in your graphics program.

In your graphics program, this rainbow is still a thing of beauty if your monitor displays more than 256 colors—your graphics program, after all, is not limited to a specific list of a few hundred colors. Now open it in Microsoft Internet Explorer 4. The gradient tones between the major colors are gone, and the graduated blend between the stripes looks grainy. What happened?

Dithering is the name of this unfortunate effect—the browser took the unoptimized graphic and substituted all those subtle colors with the closest shades available on its default palette. There's nothing really wrong with the graphic itself or the way your browsers are working. But now you see what most of your visitors will see if you don't learn to optimize graphics properly.

> **Amy:** In the introduction to this section you asked, "How do browsers compensate for the 216-color palette when they encounter a nonoptimized graphic?" They do it by dithering, by substituting colors, correct?

> **Rebecca:** You can deliberately dither an image in your graphics program by forcibly reducing the number of colors yourself, and indeed this is the most popular way to prepare graphics for the Web. This technique takes a great deal of practice, though, as you can inadvertently create something ugly, like what you've just seen with the rainbow TIFF file. It is almost always better to use one of the other techniques described in this section, and we certainly recommend another route at this point in your Web education.

Interlacing

Sometimes you just can't bear to mess with a particularly beautiful graphic for fear of ruining its colors or appearance. In that event, depending upon what kind of graphic you're enamored with, consider **interlacing**. This technique creates the illusion of smaller graphic size by gradually displaying an image in small, successive pieces. Interlacing (more properly called GIF interlacing, since it works only with GIFs) causes images to fold in by pixel row, sort of like opening a set of blinds. Visitors to your page gets a peek at the general shape and appearance of the graphic, so you can both convince them to stick around and preserve the overall design of your page.

The downside of interlacing is still speed. You should not use interlacing with essential graphics such as imagemaps or logos—anything your visitors need to see immediately for "brand" recognition, navigation, and so on.

We'll cover how to interlace a graphic in the exercises at the end of the chapter, but we'll cover a more advanced technique called progressive JPEG display in the next chapter. So if you're dissatisfied with interlacing, hang on for progressive JPEG display.

Compression

We've saved the best for last. **Compression**, as we said before, is a lot like using WinZip or StuffIt to archive a bunch of files—all the blank spaces and other "extraneous" information is removed, reducing the file's overall size. Each of the web file formats we've introduced here (GIF, JPEG, and PNG) takes compression a little differently, so we'll discuss them in separate sections.

For the record, though, there are two ways to compress graphics. **Lossless compression** reduces the size of a graphic without re-arranging its pixels; the finished product is not altered in any way. **Lossy compression**, however, is based on the idea that subtle details can be permanently removed from a graphic without compromising its overall appearance. To learn about each method, let's compare the way GIFs and JPEGs are compressed.

GIFs can be reduced by using a method called LZW compression. (The rest is complicated math; let's skip the long irrelevant definition and stick to how it works.) This method reduces a GIF by horizontally "stacking up" strings of similar color values. In other words, if a piece of a graphic looks like "red red red blue blue green," LZW compression makes it smaller by compressing it to "3 red 2 blue green."

The important thing to remember here is that LZW compression only works well when there are pixels of the same color to "stack up." A string of colors that reads "black orange blue yellow white," for example, cannot be compressed, so the overall image size will not be that much smaller. For this reason, the GIF format is better for drawings, text, and other graphics that are simple at the basic pixel level.

By contrast, JPEGs are compressed via another complicated mathematical process called discrete cosine transform. (Again, we'll forgo the advanced math and stick to web page design.) This method doesn't really abbreviate anything, but instead decides to throw away certain small details the human eye supposedly cannot see. This reduces the overall number of colors used to display the graphic, which in turn reduces its file size.

The key word in that last paragraph is *supposedly.* If you take a finely detailed photograph, such as the sample cat.psd on the CD, you can play with it in your graphics program and see the difference those "invisible" details make.

Before you begin playing with this photo, take a good close look at it. Take note of all the different tans, browns, and oranges in this cat's striped fur. These are the details that will become less apparent or may even disappear as you reduce the number of colors in this photograph using the JPEG process. This is one of the main reasons that photographs should always be transformed into JPEGs, not GIFs. Although lossy compression can ultimately ruin the finer details in a photo, it does give you more control than the GIF process.

Keep in mind, then, that you have to trust your eyes as you prepare JPEGs using this process. What matters most, paradoxically, is how the end result looks, and not how big the file is, if you want to make a good impression. We'll compare and contrast different resolutions later on in the exercises, but for now use your graphics programs to play with these files.

Amy: You mention that we should trust our eyes as we prepare JPEGs. How much control do we normally have over the amount of detail included, or over which detail is lost? I didn't realize we had any control over that.

Rebecca: You only have control over the difference between bit settings. Open a photo in Paint Shop Pro and choose Decrease Color Depth from the Colors pulldown menu; as you move back and forth between these options, you'll see the difference the higher and lower settings make. The difficulty is that sometimes a lower setting is too drastic (it removes too many colors), and the higher setting isn't reductive enough (the file size remains too large). This is the situation in which you must trust your eyes—if you choose the lower setting, your graphics will load more quickly, but they will look bad. In this case, it's better to err on the side of larger file size rather than sacrificing visual quality.

If you are forced to make this kind of choice, you can always design a warning into the entryway to your web site. Alert visitors that they are entering a high-quality graphics page ahead of time, or you can even design two versions of your site: one that's "low-res" containing smaller graphics that look less than perfect but load up quickly, and one that uses the best resolution and takes more download time. This gives visitors a choice without letting them stumble into a high-quality graphics page unaware.

There's a freeware utility that will help you decide how much compression your image can comfortably handle—it's the Browser Preview filter from Furbo Filters, and it does two handy things. It previews your compression choices and shows you the difference between the way the graphic will look on a PC and the way it will look on a Mac. This utility is available only for the Macintosh, but the site says the PC version is "coming soon." Also, Furbo Filters are fully compliant with Photoshop 5 and are built into Adobe ImageReady. The URL for the site is http://www.furbo-filters.com. Keep an eye out for this one; it will save you lots of time and trouble.

For now, the rules are simple: photographs should be JPEGs, and everything else (line drawings, logos, sketches, and so on) should be a GIF. The exercises will help to show you the reasons for this.

Exercises

To carry out the two exercises in this chapter, you'll need to open your graphics programs and use some of the files on the CD-ROM. We will first turn the logo from the business site into a GIF, and a photograph from the informational site into a JPEG. Then we'll show you how to make GIF backgrounds transparent, using the best of the optimization techniques we discussed earlier in the book.

> **NOTE:** Ordinarily, I'd do all the exercises myself and give them to Amy to try. However, because we have two platforms to consider and several graphics programs to use, Amy will be working with the PC tools and I (Rebecca, that is) will be working with those for the Mac. This way we hope to cover the needs and questions of everybody reading this book, no matter what programs or computer types you're using.

Before we get started, let's import the browser-safe color palette from the CD-ROM.

To import the palette into Paint Shop Pro:

1. Open Paint Shop Pro and choose Load Palette from the Colors pulldown menu. The Load Palette File dialog box will open.

2. Select the file PSPCLUT.pal from the CD-ROM. At the bottom of the Load Palette File dialog box, choose the Nearest Color option from the Apply Palette to Image Using menu.

3. The new palette will open in its own window as a square of tiny swatches. You can change the order of these swatches with the Sort By pulldown menu at the top. (We will sort colors by hue throughout the book, but you can choose your own setting.)

4. Click OK.

Creating GIFs

Let's work with the logo (busnlogo.tif) for the business site to demonstrate optimizing GIFs.

For these exercises, you want to open Paint Shop Pro or Photoshop if you're using a PC, and GIFConverter or Photoshop if you're using a Macintosh.

Creating GIFs with Paint Shop Pro

1. Open busnlogo.tif by opening the File pulldown menu and choosing Open. Choose busnlogo.tif from the CD-ROM and click OK.

2. Choose Save As from the File pulldown menu. The Save As dialog box will open. (See Figure 5.1.)

3. Choose GIF from the file type pulldown menu along the bottom of the dialog box and Click OK. Paint Shop Pro will open a dialog or warning window that asks you if it is your desire to reduce the number of colors in the image to 256. Click OK.

4. When the process is complete, you'll see at the top of your screen that the file name has changed from busnlogo.tif to busnlogo.gif.

> **Amy:** This seems like a simple exercise in using the Save As button. But what we're really doing is reducing a file from a

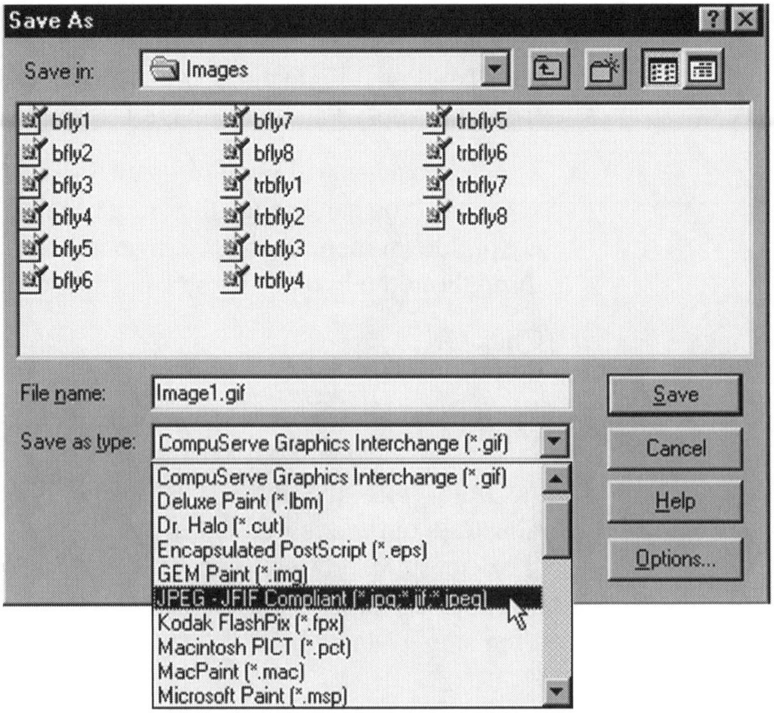

FIGURE 5.1. The Save As dialog box in Paint Shop Pro

whopping 300.6 K to a reasonable 51.3 K by reducing the colors used, correct? (I got those numbers on the bottom right-hand side of my Paint Shop Pro window when I passed the cursor over each first the TIF and then the GIF.) In terms of disk space, the file went from 154 K to 8 K as shown on Windows Explorer.

Also, I think I've read that you can have some control over the colors in an image that are emphasized when the number of colors is reduced. Can't you select some areas of the image to try to influence a limited palette?

Rebecca: Yes, this is a simple exercise, but I wanted readers to take a look at the color reduction options box. This is an important step in the saving process that readers shouldn't gloss over too quickly, given our discussions of color earlier in the chapter.

As for the second part of your question, you certainly can manually attempt to reduce colors (or, actually, choose only browser-safe colors) in certain parts of an image. However, this is an advanced graphics task, and Paint Shop Pro does not permit users to do this. Also, the danger of doing area-specific color reduction is very similar to the dangers of hand-dithering. You really, *really* have to know what you're doing with browser-safe color and even with overall graphic design, and I don't think the average reader of this book is going to have that kind of deep experience. (You can develop it over time, but not within the context and timeframe of this book.)

Creating GIFs with GIFConverter

1. Open busnlogo.tif by opening the File pulldown menu and choosing Open. Choose busnlogo.tif from the CD-ROM and click OK.

2. Choose Save As from the File pulldown menu. The Save As dialog box will open. (See Figure 5.2.)

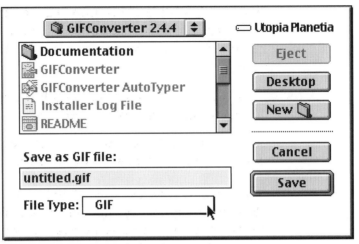

FIGURE 5.2. The Save As dialog box in GIFConverter

3. Choose GIF from the file type pulldown menu along the bottom of the dialog box and Click OK. GIFConverter will show you the conversion process as a bar graph.

4. When the process is complete, you'll see the TIFF information at the top of the graphic has changed to GIF information. That's all there is to it.

JPEGs

For these exercises, you can still use the same graphics programs, but we're going to be working with one of the photographs from the informational site UC page: salem1.tif.

Creating JPEGs with Paint Shop Pro

1. Open salem1.tif by opening the File pulldown menu and choosing Open. Choose salem1.tif from the CD-ROM and click OK.

2. Choose Save As from the File pulldown menu. The same Save As dialog box will open.

3. Choose JPG - JPEG - JFIF Compliant from the file type pulldown menu along the bottom of the dialog box and Click OK. (Notice all the different choices you have in this pulldown menu, just for future reference.)

4. When the process is complete, you'll see that the file name has changed from salem1.tif to salem1.jpg.

   Amy: As with the GIF conversion exercise, I can see that the file size has reduced, which was the point, right?

   Rebecca: Yes and no—with a JPEG, especially, file conversion is about preserving quality. This goes back to the earlier part of this chapter, where I encouraged readers to play with the bit depth of a photograph in Paint Shop Pro. I'm glad you made this comment at this point, though, so I can remind readers that while it's easy to save or convert a file to the GIF or JPEG format, there's more to it than that. I hope we've covered the "more" part of that statement in enough detail so that readers got it.

Creating JPEGs with GIFConverter

1. Open salem1.tif by opening the File pulldown menu and choosing Open. Choose salem1.tif from the CD-ROM and click OK.

2. Choose Save As from the File pulldown menu. The same Save As dialog box will open.

3. Choose JPEG from the file type pulldown menu along the bottom of the dialog box and Click OK. GIFConverter will show you the conversion process as a bar graph.

4. When the process is complete, you'll see that the TIFF information at the top of the graphic has changed to JPEG information. That's all there is to it.

Creating Transparent GIFs

In this exercise, we'll use Paint Shop Pro, Clip2GIF, and the GIF89 plug-in for Photoshop to make part of eye2.gif transparent.

Creating Transparent GIFs with Paint Shop Pro

1. Open eye2.gif in Paint Shop Pro.

2. Double-click on the background-color sample square on the right-hand side of your screen (above the RGB numbers and partially behind the foreground-color square). When the palette comes up, choose the same green as the background color. Now Paint Shop Pro recognizes your background color as the one you want to "drop out," or make transparent.

3. Pull down the File menu and click the Save As option. On the bottom right of the Save As dialog box, you will see and click an Options button. (See Figure 5.3.)

4. Choose "Set the transparency value to the background color" and click OK.

5. Click the Save button, and then click Yes when the warning window comes up to ask you if you want to replace the existing eye2.gif file. You're done!

Creating Transparent GIFs with Clip2GIF

1. Open the File pulldown menu and choose Open. Select eye2.gif from the CD-ROM and click OK.

2. Now open the Options pulldown menu; select Transparent Background, and then Based on First Pixel. The first pixel in this

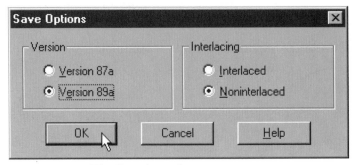

FIGURE 5.3. The Save As options

GIF is in the upper left corner and is lime green, which is the color we want to make translucent.

3. Clip2GIF saves your changes automatically, so you can Close the application via the File pulldown menu or by pressing Cntrl+W.

NOTE: For the record, these eyeball graphics originally came on a white background, but I changed it to green using Photoshop to make transparency easier. If I hadn't done this, it would have been impossible to select just the white outside the eyeball. In both the GIF89 plug-in for Photoshop and Clip2GIF, you must select pixels for transparency by their color. So I could not have left the white of the eyeball alone and just selected the white background.

Also, you want to select a background color for transparency that occurs nowhere else in the graphic, for the same reason. If I had chosen a background color matching one of the purples in the eye, for example, there would be speckles in the iris where the background color dropped out.

Interlacing a Graphic

For these exercises, you'll want to open your browser. The interlacing effect cannot be seen in Paint Shop Pro or in any other graphics program; it's an uploading thing.

Interlacing in Paint Shop Pro

1. Open Paint Shop Pro and choose Open. Select blogo1.gif from the CD-ROM and choose Save As from the File pulldown menu.

2. Choose Options in the lower right corner, and the Save Options dialog box will appear.

3. Choose Interlaced and click OK. Then rename blogo1.gif as test.gif (You're going to experiment with interlacing with this graphic because it has lots of detail, but you don't want to alter the original).

4. Open test.gif in your browser and have a look. Return to Paint Shop Pro switch back and forth between Interlaced and Noninterlaced, applying the changes by clicking OK as you prefer.

5. When you're satisfied, save test.gif if necessary by choosing Save from the File pulldown menu or by pressing Ctrl+S.

Interlacing in GIFConverter

1. Open GIFConverter and choose Open from the File pulldown menu. Select blogo1.gif from the CD-ROM and save it as test.gif. (You're going to experiment with interlacing with this graphic because it has lots of detail, but you don't want to alter the original.)

2. Choose File Settings from the Special pulldown menu. A dialog box with several options will appear.

3. Interlaced is an option on the left side of the box. You can click and unclick the box, and then apply the changes by clicking OK. As long as you don't save test.gif, you won't actually make the interlacing permanent, so feel free to switch back and forth.

4. View the interlaced and noninterlaced test.gif in your browser to see the difference. When you're satisfied, save test.gif if you like by choosing Save from the File pulldown menu, or pressing Apple+S.

Review

To recap what we've learned in this chapter, here are the highlights:

- Optimizing graphics is the process of preparing them for display on a web page. This is necessary because of bandwidth, file size (or resolution), and color palette limitations.

- Each graphic is comprised of pixels, tiny square points of light displayed by the monitor in red, green, or blue. GIFs are optimized by reducing or removing certain colors, thereby reducing the number of pixels, which in turn reduces the graphic's file size.

- There are two universally acceptable graphics formats, the GIF and the JPEG. (The PNG is far superior, but it isn't supported by many browsers yet.) The JPEG format is best for photos or photo-realistic graphics, and the GIF is best for everything else.

- The ultimate goal in preparing graphics for the Web is to make each graphic as small as possible without sacrificing overall sharpness, brilliance, and quality. Sometimes this means leaving a graphic (particularly a JPEG) larger than you may like, but this can be better than saving it at a smaller file size and making it look ugly.

- Never make an important graphic too large, period. You have some leeway over the size of non-essential graphics, but image maps, menus, logos, and other crucial elements should load quickly and easily if your visitors cannot navigate or understand your site without them. You are better off changing the overall design of such a graphic to make it simpler or less colorful (and therefore smaller) than leaving it too large.

"Answers" to the Exercises

If you completed the exercises successfully and your end results match the graphics we already showed you, then you've arrived at the correct answers.

It might be worth your while to repeat the exercises if they don't feel intuitive—if you really get into web design, you'll be making dozens if not hundreds of GIFs and JPEGs.

> **Amy:** I'm sure I'm not the only reader who would appreciate a quick explanation of the way you made the graphics used for the exercises in this chapter. I feel that I now know something about optimizing graphics, but I still am not sure where or how to get them.

> **Rebecca:** As for the files for this chapter, I borrowed some of the files for this chapter with permission from the Web (remember that "netiquette"), but I also got some of them from a CD-ROM

collection of royalty-free clip art I got at a trade show. The operative word in that last sentence is *royalty-free*, which you should look for very diligently in the fine print if you're going to go out and purchase such CDs for yourself.

On with the Show

From this point in the book, you can choose two paths. If you want more information on how to find and prepare original graphics for use on the Web, along with other advanced graphics topics, turn to the next chapter. But if you move directly on to Chapter 7, "Preparing Web Colors," you won't be behind and you won't have missed anything vital to the creation of our sample web sites.

If you want to proceed directly with the design of a web site, skip to Chapter 8. We will begin diving into positioning web page elements with HTML, including using tables and frames, by building various web pages that belong in the informational, the business, and the personal sites we've been crafting all along.

So choose your next move, and let's keep going.

CHAPTER 6

Advanced Graphics Techniques

In the last chapter we talked about optimizing graphics for the Web and briefly introduced many core concepts such as browser-safe color, various graphics formats, and optimizing with software such as Paint Shop Pro. However, we only showed you how to take an existing graphic and prepare it for display on a web page. How would you create and prepare original artwork, or make a sketch into a graphics file by using a scanner? These are the kinds of questions we'll answer here.

This chapter is for people who want to learn more about graphics preparation, beyond the basics needed to create our three sample sites. Amy and I added this chapter into the book at a late date because she felt readers would eventually want more direction and insight into graphics prep than Chapter 5 provides. So we decided to combine both these subjects here, with a quick taste of Adobe Photoshop 5.

Definitions

There are no real new definitions for this chapter, as we covered all the terms you'll need to know in Chapter 5. However, we don't want to toss you into the deep end of the Photoshop pool without a life preserver, so here's a general yet succinct introduction to that software.

If you are indeed a graphic designer or someone who's had occasion to work in Photoshop before, you will understand just how ridiculously brief, even deceptive, this introduction is. Most full-length 400-page books about Photoshop merely scratch the surface of this remarkable software product, so this handful of paragraphs cannot truly familiarize you with its use; however, this section will give you a topographic understanding so you can find your way around. First, for general reference, Figure 6.1 shows you Photoshop's main toolbar with all the tools and other popular features listed by name. We will explain how some of these individual tools and functions work as you use them in the exercises.

You should also understand how **layers** and **filters** work if you're going to make your way successfully through this chapter, as Photoshop's overall logic can be demonstrated by these two features.

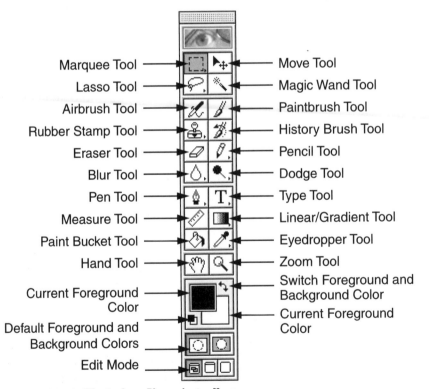

Marquee Tool — Move Tool
Lasso Tool — Magic Wand Tool
Airbrush Tool — Paintbrush Tool
Rubber Stamp Tool — History Brush Tool
Eraser Tool — Pencil Tool
Blur Tool — Dodge Tool
Pen Tool — Type Tool
Measure Tool — Linear/Gradient Tool
Paint Bucket Tool — Eyedropper Tool
Hand Tool — Zoom Tool
Current Foreground Color — Switch Foreground and Background Color
Default Foreground and Background Colors — Current Foreground Color
Edit Mode

FIGURE 6.1. Photoshop 5's main toolbar

If you want to create something totally new in Photoshop, begin by opening a New file and at the same time creating a new **layer**. In other words, if you draw a circle, a square, and a rectangle that sit next to each other in your new file, Photoshop is actually remembering each shape on its own temporary canvas. This allows you to edit, add color, erase, or otherwise change one shape without disturbing or altering another.

If you're opening an existing graphic in Photoshop, you want to transform it somehow by using Photoshop's various tools, settings, measurements, and so on. A **filter** is a pre-established handful of these specifications that create a certain effect. Photoshop has dozens of them listed on the Filter pulldown menu, and you can purchase and import many more, though we will only touch on a few.

If you like what you see in this chapter and you want a full introduction to the Photoshop program, consider *Photoshop Studio Skills* or anything from the *Photoshop Magic* series, both published by Hayden Books.

Objectives

The goal of this chapter is to pique your interest in advanced web graphics preparation. We will use the best of Paint Shop Pro to show you text and graphics effects you can fold into your web design work. Use them to imagine all kinds of new buttons, image maps, GIF animations, and much more—what you already know how to do, and what we're going to teach you.

This chapter also shows you an advanced graphics program like Photoshop. We will take the effects work further by making use of Photoshop's plentiful supply of filters, and we will show you how to use Photoshop to create graphics from scratch.

> **NOTE:** Undoubtedly, some of the effects and techniques discussed in this first section about Photoshop can be duplicated in Paint Shop Pro if you take some time and noodle around. One of the goals of this chapter is to introduce the curious reader to more robust graphics

programs, so if you're flipping through this chapter and you see something you want to try but you only have Paint Shop Pro, do take an hour or two and try to translate these exercises. No matter what happens, you'll learn something.

Exercises: Creating Web Artwork from Scratch

In this section, we're going to have lots of fun. How's that for an introduction?

Most of the techniques we'll show you here can be applied to text or to graphics, either for a masthead or some sort of writing on a graphic, or for a button, a background, or some other sort of object. We hope these exercises will also serve as a springboard for your imagination, so you can take these basic ideas and develop them into something unique.

First, if you've got Photoshop 5, open it. You will not need any additional plug-ins or other software to do these exercises, though you may have to select your own fonts and find your own backgrounds and photos. You should also put in the CD-ROM that accompanies this book. We will be using some of the exercise files to demonstrate the techniques in this chapter, so you should have the CD handy. Take a moment now, also, and install the browser-safe color palette.

Amy: Here's how I found the browser-safe color palette for Photoshop and installed it: I went to http://www.lynda.com—Lynda Weinman's excellent site on web design, per Rebecca's instructions—and downloaded the Photoshop CLUT. Then in Photoshop, I chose show Swatches from the Window pulldown menu. I clicked the arrow at the top right-hand corner of the Swatches window and then clicked on Replace Swatches. From that dialog box I found the file, selected it, and clicked OK. Done!

NOTE: You should also take the time to download and install the Browser Preview utility from Furbo Filters if you didn't do it in the last chapter. This filter lets you compare the way a graphic looks on a PC with the way it looks on a Macintosh, and it lets you preview different graphic compression settings. The URL where you can find it is http://www.furbo-filters.com. It is currently available for the Macintosh, and the PC version is "coming soon," so keep an eye out. This utility will save you lots of time and trouble.

Drop Shadows

We'll start by adding drop shadows, which are extremely useful and popular.

To add a simple drop shadow, first create a text file to which we can add our effects.

1. Create a new file by pressing Control+N or choosing New from the File pulldown menu. The New dialog box will appear. (See Figure 6.2.)

   Name this new Photoshop file text.psd (the .psd stands for Photoshop Document). Its height should be 75 pixels and its width 225 pixels, and its resolution should be 72 pixels/inch. Also, choose RGB from the Mode pulldown menu, and choose Background Color in the Contents area. Click OK.

2. Open the Layers dialog box by choosing Show Layers from the Window pulldown menu. Here, you can see that Photoshop automatically created a primary or background layer as soon as

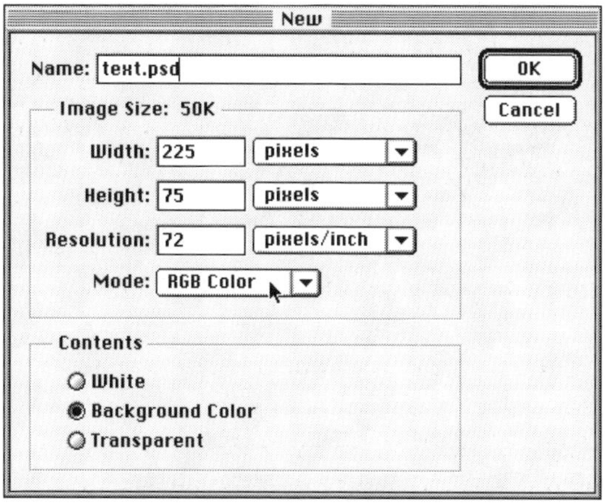

FIGURE 6.2. **Photoshop's New dialog box**

you created text.psd. From this point forward, everything we add or do to this file will have its own layer displayed here complete with a tiny preview. (See Figure 6.3.)

3. Open the browser-safe color palette by choosing Show Swatches from the Window pulldown menu. Click once on the Eyedropper tool, and then click on the top square in the palette to choose a new foreground color—you'll see the foreground color square on the main toolbar change accordingly. We stayed with black in our example because this is a black-and-white book, but you can select whichever color you prefer *as long as it's dark.*

4. Next, add a word to work with. Choose New, Layer from the Layer pulldown menu, and the New Layer dialog box will appear. (See Figure 6.4.) Name this new layer Text and click OK.

5. Click once on the Type tool icon on the main toolbar, and click once anywhere in text.psd. Photoshop will take a moment to create its font list, but then the Type Tool dialog box will appear. (See Figure 6.5.)

6. You want to choose a simple, readable font (like Arial, the font we used in the next few figures) and you should also leave it in Regular style. We also chose a size of 32 points so there would be

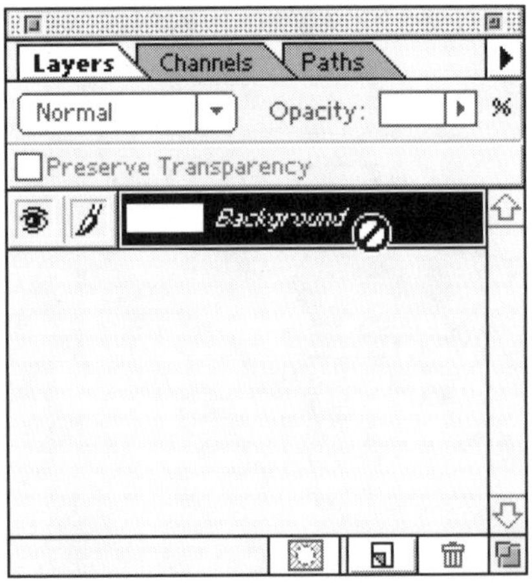

FIGURE 6.3. Photoshop's Layers palette

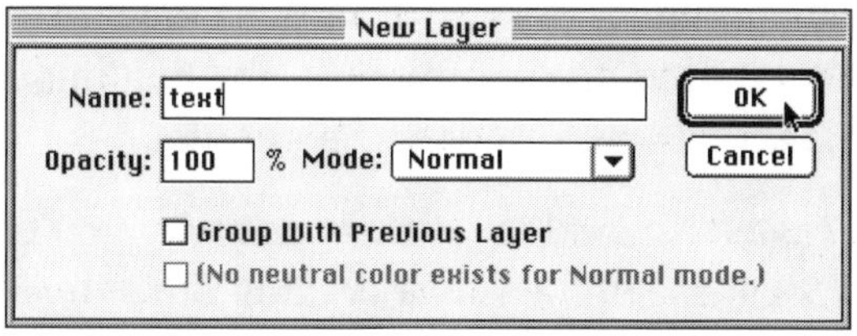

FIGURE 6.4. Photoshop's New Layer dialog box

sufficient white space all around the text. Now type a word in the box at the bottom of the dialog window. The word we used, *backgammon,* might seem a little weird, but notice that it uses angular, curved, wide, and tall letters all together. This type of word using all these letter shapes will give you a good idea of how an effect will look overall. Click OK.

7. You'll have to reposition the word in the middle of the text box, as it will initially appear off the page. Click once on the Move tool and grab your word by holding down the left mouse key. When you've got the word where you want it, release the mouse key and click once on the Marquee tool to "reset" the cursor.

8. Notice that you now have three layers in the Layer dialog box. Before we create our shadow, the word *backgammon* has to be on

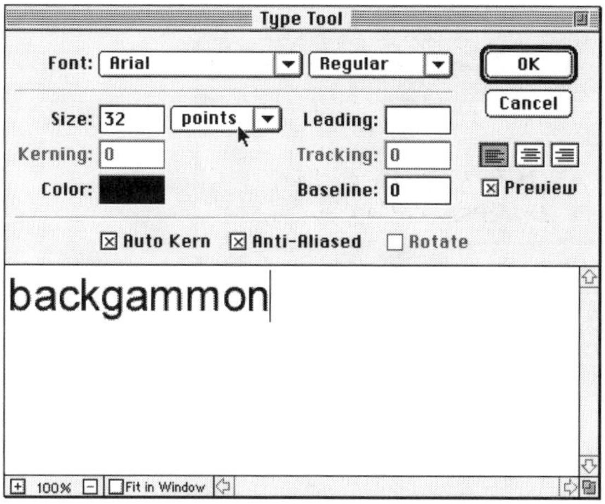

FIGURE 6.5. Photoshop's Type Tool dialog box

the text layer, so choose Merge Down from the Layer dialog box. This will flatten, or compact, the floating word *backgammon*, and the text layer, into one. (See Figure 6.6.)

9. Create a second layer the same way you created the first and call it Shadow. In the Layers dialog box, click and drag the shadow layer down between the text and background layers—the pointing hand will close in a fist when you've grabbed it successfully—releasing the mouse key when you're finished. (If you mess up and it appears last, press Control+Z to undo and try again.) Now click on the little eye in the box to the left of the text layer to temporarily hide it, and the word *backgammon* will disappear from the file window. (See Figure 6.7.)

10. Click once on the shadow layer in the Layers dialog box. Now select a new background color, lighter than the first. This is the foundation of the actual shadow, so the color you choose here must be noticeably lighter than and different from the one you chose for the text layer. We used the browser-safe medium gray #99999.

11. Click once on the Type Tool and add the same word to this layer that you did in the text layer—the same font, the same size, the same letters—and click OK. Here, the word *backgammon* appears in the lighter gray. Center it with the Move tool, and

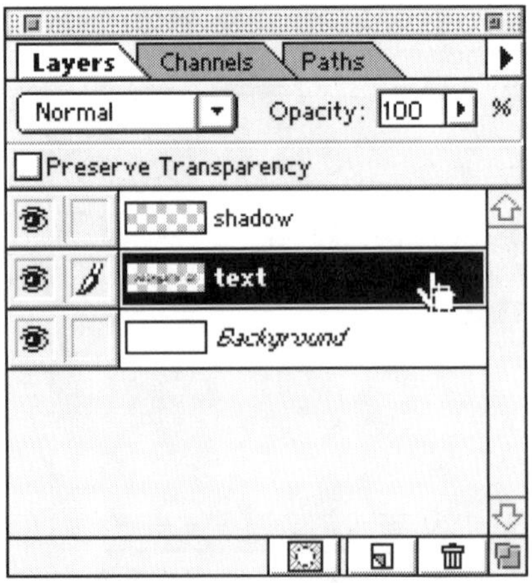

FIGURE 6.6. Merge Down—the word and the text layer become one

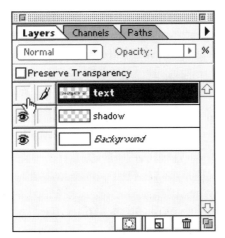

FIGURE 6.7. **The layers are rearranged properly, and the text layer is temporarily hidden**

choose Merge Down from the Layer pulldown menu again to compress the second word with the shadow layer. Don't worry if you can't see the lighter-colored word in the shadow layer preview on the Layers dialog box; it's still there. (See Figure 6.8.)

12. Now let's make the shadow look like a shadow. Click once on the shadow layer in the Layers dialog box to make sure you're working with the lighter-colored word. Now choose All from the

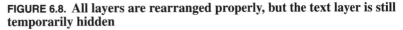

FIGURE 6.8. **All layers are rearranged properly, but the text layer is still temporarily hidden**

Select pulldown menu, or press Control+A, and choose Blur, Gaussian Blur from the Filters pulldown menu. Now the edges of the lighter-colored word are blurred and soft. (See Figure 6.9.)

Amy: What's the difference between a normal Blur and a Gaussian Blur? As I look through the exercises, it seems that Gaussian Blur is the only type we use. Why?

Rebecca: I believe the term *Gaussian* refers to the math behind this kind of blur. We use the Gaussian Blur filter first because I like it best. It produces that fine shading of color between the darker, inner part of the circle and the lighter, faded edge in such a way that none of the other Blur options can manage. This effect is very important on the web page, because a blur needs to be exaggerated but well executed to look good. In other words, there have to be many shades of blue between the center and edge of your button for it to be recognizably blurred on the pixel-scaled surface of a monitor screen. If you print something onto paper, you can work at a much tinier and more subtle scale.

Also, with Blur or More Blur, for example, you don't get any manual control. Some of the Photoshop filters are like that; you choose them from the pulldown menu, and they are automatically applied. Most of the ones I like are those with sliders, scaling, and other controls that let you fine-tune your work. This is the difference between a robust graphics program like Photoshop and other graphics programs.

13. To see the final product, go back to the Layers menu and click on the spot in the text layer where the eye should be. Now the darker, top word will appear again, but you can see the lighter shadow beneath. Use the Move tool once more to position the darker word where you

FIGURE 6.9. The finished shadow layer—soft and blurry

want it against its shadow. Remember, shadows can fall up, down, from an angle, or from either side; it's your choice. Once you've moved the top word, click on the Marquee tool once and anywhere else in the image to deselect. Want to move the word again? Control+Z will undo your deselect for you—or, in simpler terms, it will reselect the word for you. (See Figure 6.10.)

text.psd @ 100% (shadow,l

backgammon

100%

FIGURE 6.10. The finished product

Applying Textures and Filters

The basic steps for this exercise are the same as above, but we're importing a texture and adding the power of Photoshop's filters so the drop shadow effect can be more pronounced.

1. Create a new file by pressing Control+N or choosing New from the File pulldown menu. The New dialog box will appear.

2. Name this new Photoshop file object.psd. Its height and width should both be 100 pixels so it's square, and its resolution should be 72 pixels/inch. Leave the rest of the settings as they are and click OK.

3. Now open the file blue1.pic from the CD-ROM. We are going to use this blue-beige background to create the button pattern.

4. Open the Layers dialog box by choosing Show Layers from the Window pulldown menu, and open the browser-safe color palette by choosing Show Swatches from the Window pulldown menu.

5. Choose New, Layer from the Layer pulldown menu, and the New Layer dialog box will appear. Name your first layer Sphere and click OK.

6. Next, click once on the blue1 window to bring it forward (that is, to start working in it). You want to use the elliptical marquee

rather than the default square marquee, so hold the left mouse key down on the Marquee tool, drag it right to the circle icon, and release. (See Figure 6.11.)

Rectangular Marquee Tool ——————————— Single Row Marquee Tool

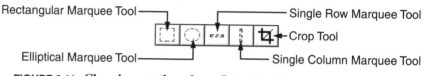

Elliptical Marquee Tool ———————————— Single Column Marquee Tool

———— Crop Tool

FIGURE 6.11. Choosing another shape from the Marquee tool selections

7. The pointer-shaped cursor has become a set of crosshairs, and you can now draw a circle. Position the crosshairs in the upper left corner of blue1, hold down the left mouse key, and drag down and right. When you've made the correct-sized circle, release the mouse key—keep it relatively small, about an inch in diameter.

8. Now let's shop around blue1 for the right pattern. You can move the circle you just created by placing the cursor on its edge; when it changes to a small triangle, hold down the left mouse key and move the mouse. Use the circle as a target finder, to select a nicely marbled area of blue1. (See Figure 6.12.)

9. Select Copy Merged from the edit menu (or press Shift+Control+C) to grab your area of choice.

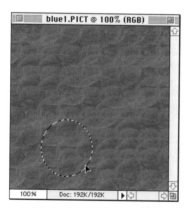

FIGURE 6.12. Pick an area with a nice overall pattern and as many colors as possible

10. To add a little curvature to make this circle look like a marble, press Control+A to select everything on this layer, and then choose Distort, Spherize on the Filter pulldown menu. The Spherize dialog box will appear. (See Figure 6.13.)

    Play with the slider and watch the percentages change if you like, but leave the Mode selection at Normal. Click OK when you're satisfied. Note that the circle within object.psd enlarges—if it's too large, choose Canvas Size from the Image pulldown menu and increase the dimensions by 50 pixels. Use the Move tool to reposition the marble to the middle of the window.

    NOTE: I created the blue1.pict marble texture from scratch using a great little piece of software called Specular TextureScape, but you can use any background or texture you find on the Web. Just remember your "netiquette" and ask permission before you take it.

11. Now to add the shadow. Create a new layer by choosing New, New Layer from the Layer pulldown menu and call it shadow. Move the shadow layer between the background and sphere layers by click-and-dragging it. Hide the sphere layer by clicking the eye icon.

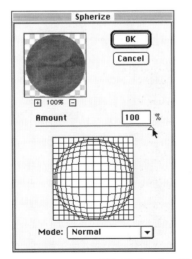

FIGURE 6.13. The Spherize dialog box

12. Select a shadow color from the browser-safe palette using the Eyedropper tool. This time, we used a dark olive green to bring out the beige-green ribbons in blue1 (browser-safe color #999966).

13. Draw a circle using the elliptical Marquee tool and choose Fill from the Edit pulldown menu. The Fill dialog box will appear. (See Figure 6.14.)

    Play with the Opacity slider here to soften this circle, and click OK when you're finished (otherwise the 100%, default setting is fine). The circle becomes solid green.

    Amy: Does the Opacity slider change the intensity of the color, or how does it work?

    Rebecca: Yes, but it changes the RGB value of the color as well, so you don't want to choose a dark browser-safe color from the palette and use the Opacity slider to lighten it up. (Good question— you just saved some readers a whole heap of color trouble later on.)

14. Now select Blur, Gaussian Blur from the Filters menu, and the Gaussian Blur dialog box will appear. (See Figure 6.15.)

    Move the Radius slider to 4.0 pixels. This will drastically feather and diffuse the colors along the edge of the sphere. Click OK.

15. Finally, use the Move tool to position the shadow where you'd like it. (See Figure 6.16.) Imagine this on a white or pale yellow background as a linked button.

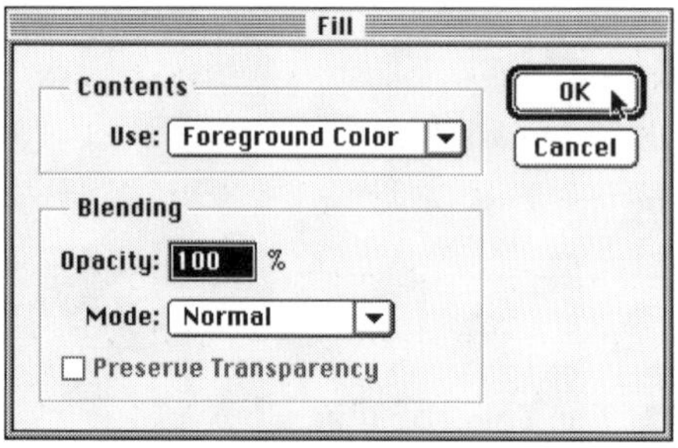

FIGURE 6.14. The Fill dialog box

Who's Afraid of Web Page Design?

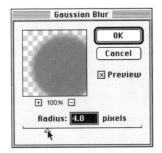

FIGURE 6.15. The Gaussian Blur dialog box

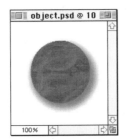

FIGURE 6.16. The finished product—a spherical object with a green shadow

Neon

1. Create a new file by pressing Control+N or choosing New from the File pulldown menu. The New dialog box will appear. Name this new Photoshop file neon.psd. Its height should be 75 pixels, its width should be 300 pixels, and its resolution should be 72 pixels/inch. Leave the rest of the settings as they are and click OK.

2. Make sure white is selected as the foreground color, and open the browser-safe color palette by choosing Show Swatches from the Window pulldown menu. Use the Eyedropper tool to select a bright color from the browser-safe palette—we chose a neon blue. Switch to the Marquee tool and draw a circle.

3. Choose Fill from the Edit pulldown menu, leave the settings as they are in the Fill dialog box, and click OK. Now choose Inverse from the Select menu, and then Feather from the Select menu. Set the radius in the Feather dialog box to 6 pixels and click OK.

Amy: What exactly does the Feather feature do?

Rebecca: The Feather feature is a heavy-handed blur that creates a more defined, circular, unfeathered area. This is what results in the distinctiveness of the halo at the end of the exercise.

4. Now change the foreground color to black by clicking on the Switch icon (right by the foreground/background color squares), and choose Fill from the Edit menu. Leave the settings as they are, click OK, and click again in the image to disable selection. You have a beautiful, simple, neon glow. (See Figure 6.17.)

FIGURE 6.17. The finished product—a spherical neon object

Halo

1. Create a new file by pressing Control+N or choosing New from the File pulldown menu. The New dialog box will appear. Name this new Photoshop file halo.psd. Its height and width should both be 100 pixels, and its resolution should be 72 pixels/inch. Leave the rest of the settings as they are and click OK.

2. Open the Layers dialog box by choosing Show Layers from the Window pulldown menu, and open the browser-safe color palette by choosing Show Swatches from the Window pulldown menu.

3. Switch the background color to black and choose Fill from the Edit menu. Fill with the background color (not the foreground color).

4. Choose New, New Layer from the Layer menu and call it Button. Now choose the elliptical Marquee tool and draw a circle.

5. Choose Feather from the Select pulldown menu and choose a radius of 10 pixels. Now use the Eyedropper tool to select a neon color from the browser-safe palette. We chose a vivid yellow. Choose Fill from the Edit pulldown menu.

6. Once more, choose Feather from the Select pulldown menu and choose a radius of 10 pixels. Now the neon color has diffused even further; with the yellow we can see hints of gold and mustard coming through against the black.

Choose Load Selection from the Select pulldown menu and click OK. Change the foreground color back to black and choose Fill from the Edit pulldown menu. Click OK, and you have a subtle halo glow. You could place a round object inside, or a bit of text for emphasis—whatever else you can imagine. (See Figure 6.18.)

FIGURE 6.18. The finished product—a spherical glowing halo

Contrast Glow

1. Create a new file by pressing Control+N or choosing New from the File pulldown menu. The New dialog box will appear. Name this new Photoshop file cglow.psd. Its height and width should both be 100 pixels, and its resolution should be 72 pixels/inch. Leave the rest of the settings as they are and click OK.

2. Open the Layers dialog box by choosing Show Layers from the Window pulldown menu, and open the browser-safe color palette by choosing Show Swatches from the Window pulldown menu.

3. If necessary, switch the background color to black and choose Fill from the Edit menu.

4. Choose New, New Layer from the Layer menu and name it Button. Now use the default rectangular Marquee tool to draw a square.

5. Choose Feather from the Select pulldown menu and choose a radius of 10 pixels. Now use the Eyedropper tool to select a neon color from the browser-safe palette. We chose an intense chartreuse green. Choose Fill from the Edit pulldown menu.

6. Once more, choose Feather from the Select pulldown menu and choose a radius of 3 pixels.

7. Choose Load Selection from the Select pulldown menu and click OK. Change the foreground color back to white and choose Fill from the Edit pulldown menu. Click OK, and you have an intense contrast glow between the white, the green, and the black. (See Figure 6.19.)

FIGURE 6.19. The finished product—a square object with a contrast glow

Plastics

Let's switch back to creating objects for this section on creating shiny effects.

For a hard, flat, plastic look:

1. Create a new file by pressing Control+N or choosing New from the File pulldown menu. The New dialog box will appear. Name this new Photoshop file plastic.psd. Its height and width should both be 100 pixels, and its resolution should be 72 pixels/inch. Leave the rest of the settings as they are and click OK.

2. Choose New, New Layer from the Layer pulldown menu, or click on the arrow in the upper right corner of the Layers dialog box

and choose New Layer from that menu. Name it Layer 1, leave the rest of the settings as they are, and click OK.

3. Next, select the elliptical Marquee tool and draw a circle. Use the Eyedropper tool to choose a browser-safe color from the palette—we chose a bright red. Choose Fill from the Edit pulldown menu, and click OK. You should have a bright red circle on a black background.

4. Choose Modify, Smooth from the Select pulldown menu, and the Smooth dialog box will appear. (See Figure 6.20.) Choose a setting of 3 pixels and click OK.

5. Now choose Blur, Gaussian Blur from the Filter pulldown menu. Make the setting 3.5 pixels and click OK.

6. Choose Load Selection from the Select pulldown menu, and the Load Selection dialog box will appear. Click OK, then choose Blur, Gaussian Blur again from the Filter pulldown menu. This time, choose a radius of 8 pixels and click OK.

7. Next, choose Render, Lighting Effects from the Filter pulldown menu. The Lighting Effects dialog box will appear.

Choose the settings shown in Figure 6.21: set the Style pulldown menu to Default, the Light type to Omni at an Intensity of 25, the Gloss Property scale to 100, the Material Property scale to −100, the Exposure Property scale to 0, and the Ambience Property scale to 6. The Texture Channel pulldown menu should be set to 1, with the Height scale set to 35. Feel free to play with these settings to see what each of these scales and settings does if you like. Click OK when you're done.

8. The final result, in Figure 6.22: a shiny, hard plastic sphere.

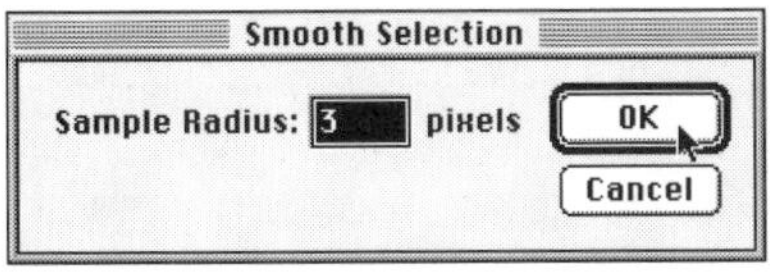

FIGURE 6.20. The Smooth dialog box

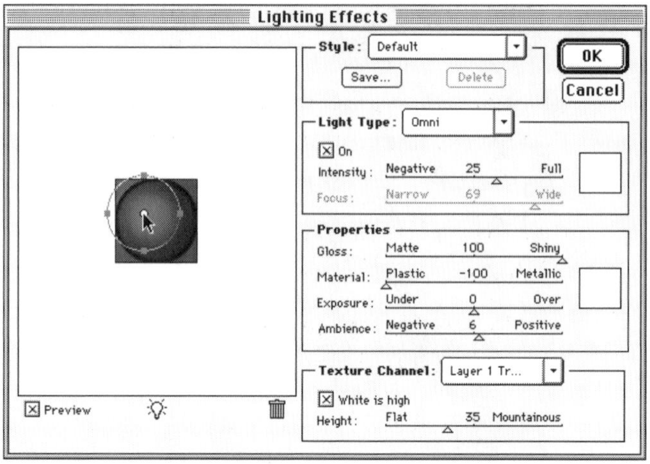

FIGURE 6.21. The Lighting Effects dialog box

FIGURE 6.22. The finished product—hard, shiny red plastic

For a softer-looking inflated plastic, first switch your background color to white, then:

1. Create a new file by pressing Control+N or choosing New from the File pulldown menu. The New dialog box will appear. Name this new Photoshop file plastic2.psd. Its height and width should both be 100 pixels, and its resolution should be 72 pixels/inch. Leave the rest of the settings as they are and click OK.

2. Choose New, New Layer from the Layer pulldown menu, or click on the arrow in the upper right corner of the Layers dialog box and choose New Layer from that menu. Name it Layer 1, leave the rest of the settings as they are, and click OK.

3. Next, select the Marquee tool and draw a square. Use the Eyedropper tool to choose a pale, browser-safe color from the palette—we chose a pastel pink. Choose Fill from the Edit

pulldown menu, and click OK. You should have a pale pink square on a white background.

4. Choose Modify, Smooth from the Select pulldown menu, and the Smooth dialog box will appear. Choose a setting of 3 pixels and click OK.

5. Next, select Stroke from the Edit pulldown menu, and the Stroke dialog box will appear.

   Choose the settings shown here in Figure 6.23: Stroke width 2 pixels, Outside location, Opacity 50%, mode Normal.

6. Choose Blur, Gaussian Blur from the Filter pulldown menu and choose a radius of 6 pixels. Then choose Adjust, Brightness/Contrast from the Image pulldown menu. The Brightness/Contrast dialog box will appear. (See Figure 6.24.)

   Leave the Brightness scale set to 0, but move the Contrast slider to the right till it reads +70. Click OK.

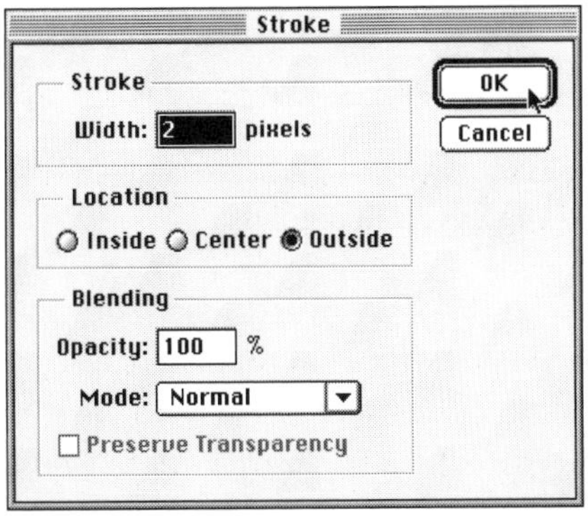

FIGURE 6.23. **The Stroke dialog box**

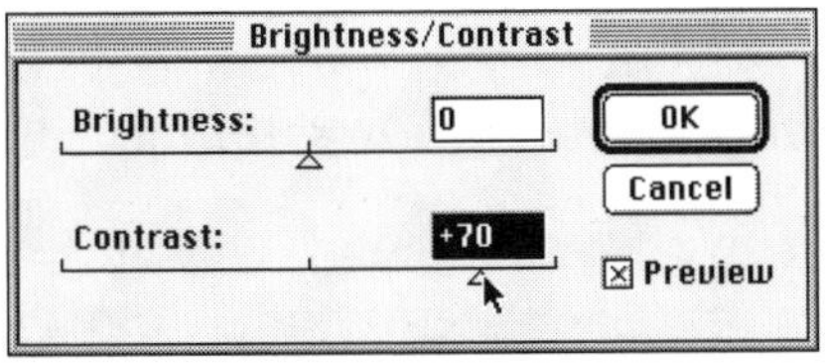

FIGURE 6.24. **The Brightness/Contrast dialog box**

7. Choose Stylize, Find Edges from the Filter pulldown menu. Next, choose Adjust, Levels from the Image pulldown menu. The Levels dialog box will appear.

   Choose the settings shown in Figure 6.25; input levels should be 0, 1.00, and 255, while the Output levels should be 0 and 245. Feel free to play with these settings as you like; the results and correct settings depend upon the size of the square.

8. Click OK when you're done, press Backspace to deselect the square, and there you have it—a softer, rounded plastic. (See Figure 6.26.)

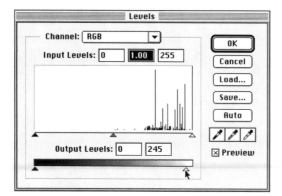

FIGURE 6.25. The Levels dialog box

FIGURE 6.26. The final product—a balloonlike plastic button

Creating Patterns and Textures from Filters

Here's a brief overview of how you can use some of Photoshop's filters to create original patterns and textures from a single color.

1. Create a new file by pressing Control+N or choosing New from the File pulldown menu. The New dialog box will appear. Name this new Photoshop file pttest.psd. Its height should be 300 pixels, its width should be 75 pixels, and its resolution should be 72 pixels/inch. Leave the rest of the settings as they are and click OK.

2. Use the Eyedropper tool to select a new background color, something not too dark and not too overwhelming—you are going to use this color as a baseline against which your eye will compare all the patterns and textures we'll create. We chose a medium blue (#99CCFF). Choose Fill from the Edit menu, leave all the settings as they are, and click OK.

3. Next, select the Marquee tool and draw a rectangle. Use the Eyedropper tool to choose another medium browser-safe color from the palette—this is the base color for all the textures and patterns we'll create with the filters. We selected a medium peach (#FFCC99). Choose Fill from the Edit pulldown menu, and click OK.

4. If you choose Artistic, Sponge from the Filters pulldown menu, you can create a simple, flat marbling effect with contrasting colors. (See Figure 6.27.)

5. If you choose Pointillize, Pixellate from the Filters pulldown menu, you can break down a single color into the various hues and tones ordinarily invisible to the naked eye. Adjust the slider to increase or decrease the size of the individual color circles. (See Figure 6.28.)

6. If you choose Sketch, Reticulation from the Filters pulldown menu, you can create a subtle, wrinkled or dehydrated effect. Our peach rectangle looks like a strip of orange peel. (See Figure 6.29.)

7. If you choose Texture, Grain from the Filters pulldown menu, you can create many texture effects on the Grain Type pulldown menu. (See Figure 6.30.)

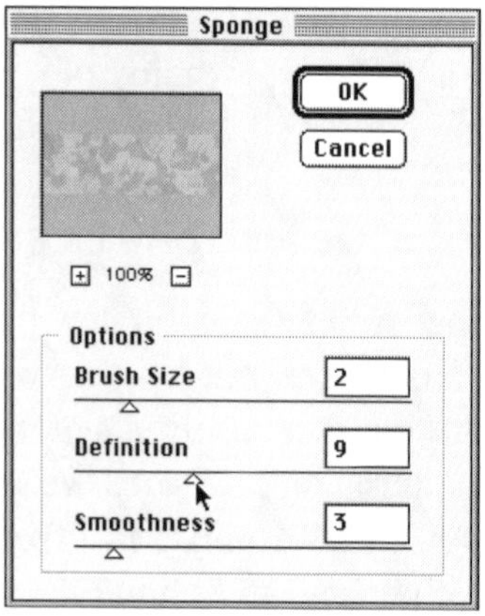

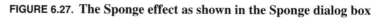

FIGURE 6.27. The Sponge effect as shown in the Sponge dialog box

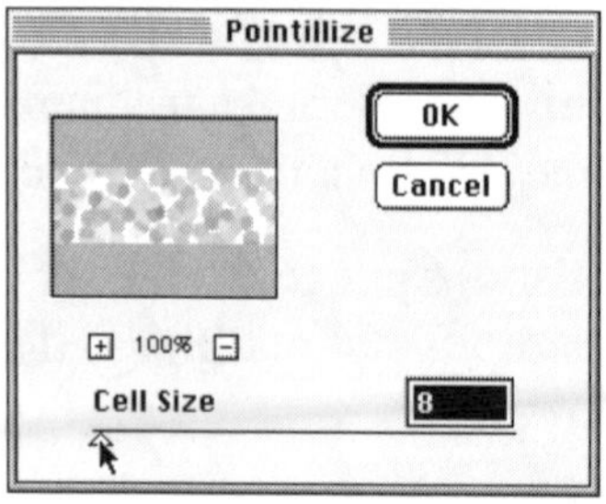

FIGURE 6.28. The Pointillize effect as shown in the Pointillize dialog box

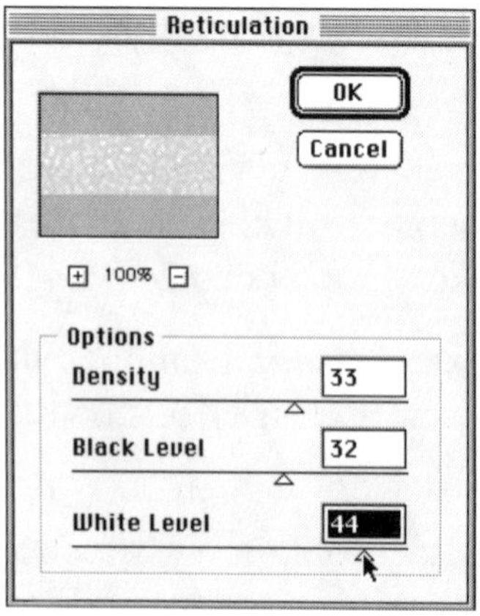

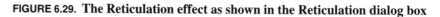

FIGURE 6.29. The Reticulation effect as shown in the Reticulation dialog box

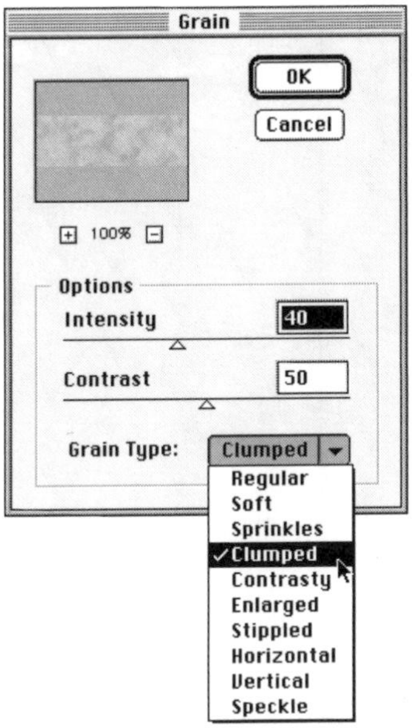

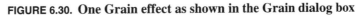

FIGURE 6.30. One Grain effect as shown in the Grain dialog box

Altering Patterns and Textures with Filters

1. Open blue1.pic from the CD-ROM. We're going to use this texture to demonstrate other Photoshop filters that are best used with existing multicolor samples, so choose All from the Select menu (or press Control+A).

2. If you choose Artistic, Rough Pastels from the Filters pulldown menu, you can create several streaky, smudged effects. Experiment with the Texture pulldown menu, too. (See Figure 6.31.)

3. If you choose Brush Strokes, Ink Effects from the Filters pulldown menu, you can create something that looks like chiseled, melted ice. Notice how the black ripples lend a shiny effect to the lighter colors. (See Figure 6.32.)

4. If you choose Distort, Twirl from the Filters pulldown menu, you can create a whirlwind or paint mixer effect by directing the twirl's direction, tightness, and so on. (See Figure 6.33.)

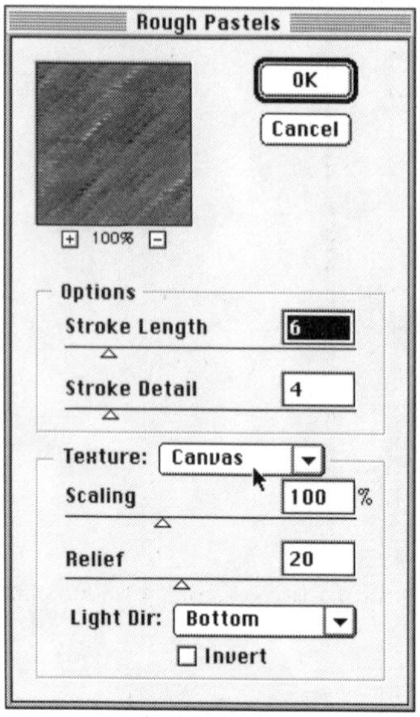

FIGURE 6.31. The Rough Pastels, Canvas effect as shown in the Rough Pastels dialog box

5. If you choose Texture, Stained Glass from the Filters pulldown menu, Photoshop separates the individual colors in the pattern into random pieces of "glass," complete with lighting and shading effects. (See Figure 6.34.)

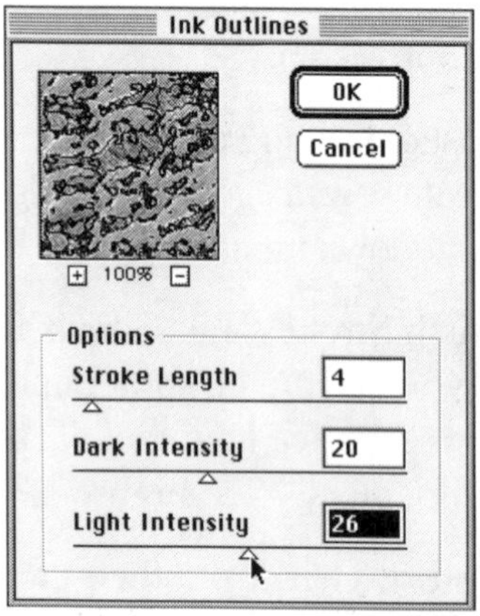

FIGURE 6.32. The Ink Effects effect as shown in the Ink Effects dialog box

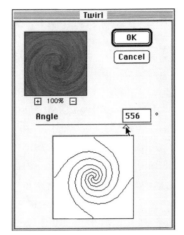

FIGURE 6.33. The Twirl effect as shown in the Twirl dialog box

NOTE: You should feel comfortable enough with the Filters menu by now that you can start experimenting on your own. Apply more than one filter, or select different areas of a color or texture with the Marquee tool and apply different filters to different spots. Feel free to make something ugly or make a mistake; to Undo the last thing you did, press Control+Z and it's gone.

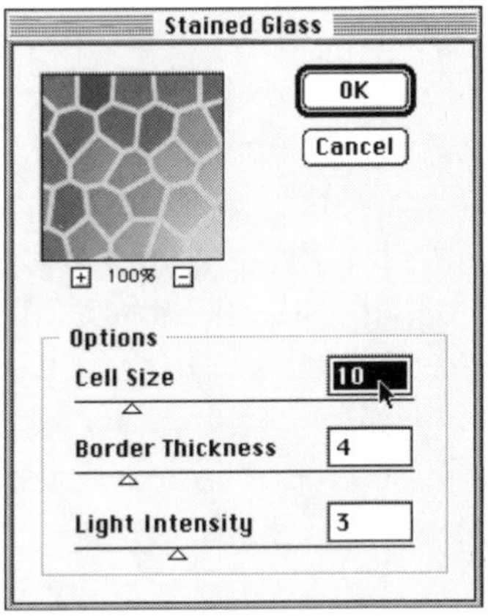

FIGURE 6.34. The Stained Glass effect as shown in the Stained Glass dialog box

Meta-Exercises: Preparing Artwork for the Web

In this section, we're going to use Photoshop to prepare scanned artwork for various uses on the Web—as backgrounds, assembly pieces, objects for linking, and so on. We will use some artwork I transformed for my own personal web site, so we'll talk a little more about scanning and file formats, as well as color and design strategy, as we work through these exercises with Photoshop.

Photoshop was not one of the required software packages we asked you to have handy in Chapter 2, so you may only be able to read along in this part, and that's fine. This is the section of this chapter Amy asked me (Rebecca) to write alone as an intermediate-to-advanced graphics lesson deliberately beyond the scope of the reader. We both feel that it will give you, the reader, something to reach for if you want to move beyond what you learned to do in Paint Shop Pro in the last chapter.

These are not really exercises, and you will not fall behind in this book or be unable to finish the sample sites if you don't do them.

The Prelude: Scanning Artwork

Two years ago, I was meandering through an exhibit of ancient Egyptian and Nubian art in the Indianapolis Museum of Art. It was time for a complete overhaul of my web site, but I had no idea where to start. Then a rack of note cards in the museum shop caught my eye, and inspiration struck. (See Figures 6.35 and 6.36.)

These two cards were the perfect springboard for a web site design. Most important, the designs are hand-painted onto strips of rough papyrus-like paper, so the color depth and texture look authentic to the eye. Also, they would scan well—ordinary note cards are usually printed with a glossy finish, which means that the moving, luminescent arm of the scanner can leave a glare in the finished file. Finally, they are detailed. I was already sketching out the look of the main, home page in my mind with the main figures as object links to secondary pages. But there are also plenty of smaller figures, such as the monkey on top of the scale, which would serve well as icons, Back and Forward buttons, or other subtle design motifs.

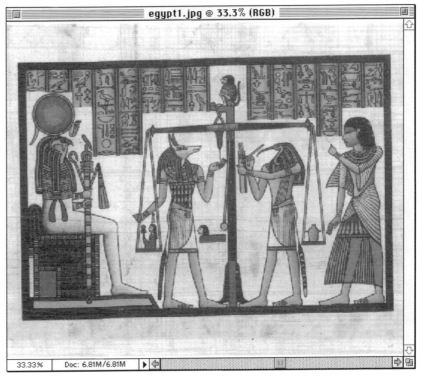

FIGURE 6.35. An entire web site strategy, Part One...

In fact, Figure 6.37 shows what my main, home page looked like when I was done.

To preserve as much detail as possible, I scanned these cards in as JPEGs. This goes against the simple credo for working with file format that we covered in the last chapter, but it's the exception that makes the rule. The unevenness of this papyrus surface creates millions of colors but also millions of tiny shadows, and none of the resolution options you have available for saving something as a GIF would preserve them. Remember: You can always reduce later, but you can never replace or add colors once you've removed them. So you should *always* judge with your eyes and not by the rules. (And you should always keep a little extra hard disk space available— check out the size of these scans to see why!)

I must add that I tried very hard to find the artist and the distributor of these cards. I asked the museum shop cashier, I

FIGURE 6.36. ...and Part Two

searched the Internet for the company name on the backs of the cards, I used white and yellow pages sites. No luck. So I put an extremely apologetic disclaimer on the Credits page and swallowed my guilt. I hope that the artist, wherever he or she is, considers imitation (optimization?) the sincerest form of flattery.

Using someone else's artwork without permission on a web page is still a less serious offense than putting it on a CD for all the world to own, so you will not find these two scans, or anything I create from them, on the CD. Still, take heart! I have a friend who created his whole web site from a sketch on a napkin using techniques and choices similar to mine. There are plenty of scanner-sized ideas out there just waiting to be discovered. Use these examples to help fire your imagination.

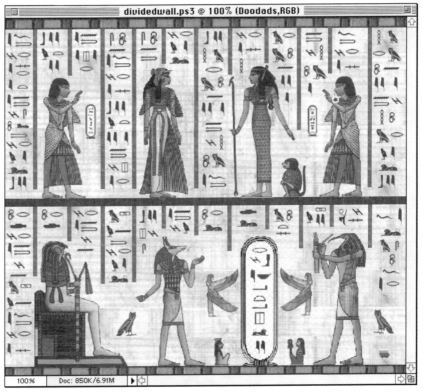

FIGURE 6.37. The final outcome: The Pyramid

Let's begin with the simplest, most basic kind of artwork you can use on a site: backgrounds.

Extracting Textures and Other Elements

The basic construction of my site, I knew, would revolve these eight figures against a "wall," like authentic ancient Egyptian art. I didn't have to worry about readability or "noise," because there would be no text. So what kind of background could I use?

I experimented with a sandstone texture, thinking I might create a tomb wall-painting effect, but the contrast of surfaces looked bad. Then I tried to settle on a single color, but there's no good beige or flesh tone in the browser-safe palette. So here's the solution I reached: a tiling papyrus background.

1. I opened the main scan or graphic and select the Marquee tool. Then I grabbed a generous, rectangular portion of the texture and pressed Control+C to copy it. (See Figure 6.38.)

2. Then I chose New, New File from the File pulldown menu (you can also press Control+N). The settings in the New dialog box are the dimensions of the papyrus slice I just copied, so I named it papyrus.psd and clicked OK. A blank window just the right size appeared. (See Figure 6.39.)

3. I pressed Control+V to paste, and Image Rotate, Rotate 90° clockwise from the Image pulldown menu. Next I resized the window accordingly and voilà: the background texture.

FIGURE 6.38. A nice slice of papyrus: good colors, good texture, no bruises or flaws

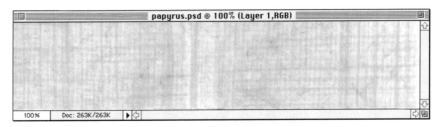

FIGURE 6.39. Papyrus.psd

4. To create a tileable, web-ready file, you have to convert this slice to Indexed color. So I chose Mode, Indexed Color from the Image pulldown menu. The Indexed Color dialog box appeared. (See Figure 6.40.)

Photoshop will automatically select Web from the Palette pulldown menu, and obviously it isn't going to work, so what do you do? Select Adaptive and begin deliberating over the different bit settings. I eventually settled on 6 bits, or 64 colors, and left the Dithering setting as None. (Dithering would smudge out the lovely papyrus fibers.)

Amy: Could you explain why the Web selection from the Palette pulldown menu doesn't work?

Rebecca: It has to do with my own personal judgment and the limited number of colors available in the browser-safe palette. When I applied the Web selection from the Palette pulldown menu, the effect was awful—all the detail and the contrast of the papyrus were gone, replaced with pink and yellow blotches. Photoshop had

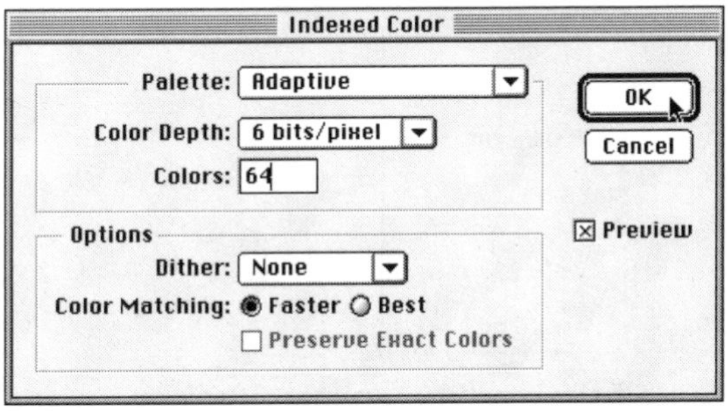

FIGURE 6.40. Optimizing the papyrus slice

dutifully replaced all the nonbrowser colors in the papyrus graphic with web-safe colors, which not only eliminated the texture and character but also obliterated the actual image. This is the most extreme example of why the browser-safe color palette is insufficient, and it shows when the Adaptive option should be chosen instead.

5. Finally, I chose Save As from the File pulldown menu and the Save As dialog box appeared. (See Figure 6.41.)

I chose GIF from the pulldown menu and clicked OK. In the Row Options dialog box, I chose Normal and clicked OK again. The basic papyrus background is finished.

This search-and-grab technique can work with anything. The friend I mentioned earlier with the lunch napkin grabbed just the rippled, crumpled edge of his napkin scan and used it to make the edge of a slice GIF. But he was using an entire unadulterated section

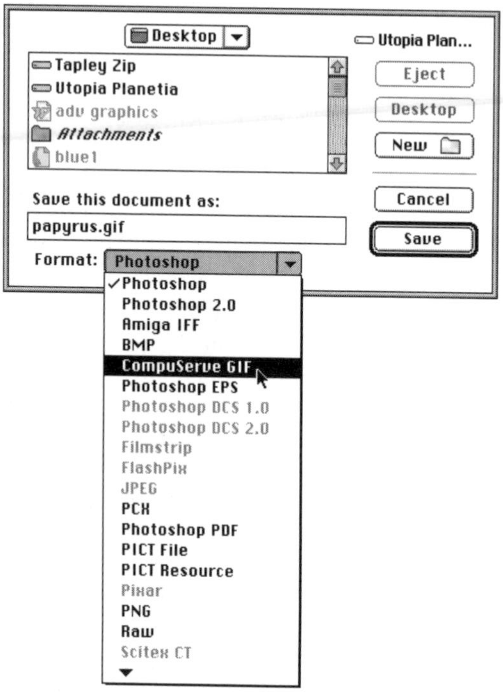

FIGURE 6.41. The Save As dialog box

of the napkin—what if he just wanted to grab the restaurant logo, for example? Then there would be a little more technique involved.

Let's extract a small object from a larger piece of artwork (in this case, the first Egyptian card scan).

1. I already mentioned how much I like that monkey perched on top of the scale in the first scan. So I grabbed him with the Marquee tool. (See Figure 6.42.)

You want to be generous with the Marquee tool when you select something small in this kind of situation. Don't try to get the edge of

FIGURE 6.42. This little monkey ornament will look good on a slice GIF

the Marquee right on the edge of the drawing—there are millions of colors making up that "solid" line, and you want them all.

2. I created a new file by pressing Control+N, named the new file monkey.psd (you could use something else equally logical), and then pressed Control+V to paste in the selection. This is the main graphic I'll work from to create this little ornament.

3. I made sure white was selected as the background color—it's easier to see the lighter colored pixels against it, rather than the black. Now you can shave a little off the top, so to speak. I selected the Crop tool from the Marquee tool options (it's the last one on the right end) and click-and-dragged it over the ornament. Let go once the moving dotted line appears; you can better manipulate this line by clicking-and-dragging the tiny boxes. When I was satisfied, I pressed Enter. Everything outside the dotted line at this point will be discarded.

4. I zoomed in to about 400% by pressing Control++ (that's Control plus the plus sign, +). Now you can clearly see all the pixels making up that "solid" line, but you can also discard a little more edge. You can see here with the monkey that I left lots of smudge along its black outline—saving the purples, blues, and grays that are invisible to the naked eye at 100%—but that I left lots of black beneath its feet. Why? He's sitting on something, so I need to create an artificial outline. I pressed Enter when I was satisfied. (See Figure 6.43.)

FIGURE 6.43. Shaving off a little more with the Crop tool

5. Now comes the subjective part. I don't want a crisp, clean line around this figure, but I don't want to leave too much papyrus, either. So I used the Eyedropper tool first to select a sample color from the papyrus area, and then I chose Show Options from the Window pulldown menu. The Tolerance measurement lets you widen or tighten the Wand's grabbing ability; I'm choosing a generous option of 10 pixels, and I'm unclicking the Use All Layers option.

6. Have a good close look at your graphic. Now you have to choose a background color that's not used anywhere on the part you want to keep—this is for the last step when you save this file as a transparent GIF. Zoom in even further if you have to; this is a critical step. I finally decided to use plain white, so I switched the foreground and background colors around, putting white on top.

7. Now comes the tedious part, at least for me. Use the Magic Wand tool to select all the areas around the image you want to discard. In this example situation, it took me lots of time because there were so many colors used in the papyrus. (You can see just how time-consuming this was in Figure 6.45.) I held down the Shift key to grab more than one selected area at a time, but I didn't grab too close to the part of the image I wanted to keep.

8. When I'd grabbed a large chunk of space, I pressed Backspace, and Photoshop filled the area with the background color I selected: white. I zoomed in a little more by pressing Control++ again, and continued to use the Magic Wand tool for one more pass.

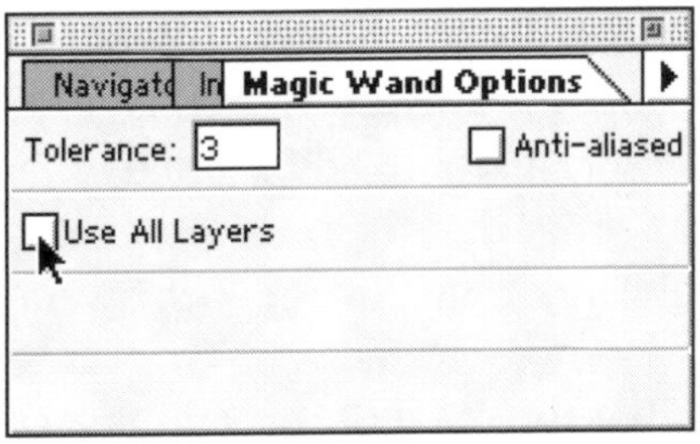

FIGURE 6.44. The Tool Options palette

FIGURE 6.45. Using the Magic Wand tool judiciously—takes time!

9. Eventually, however, I switched to the Pencil tool to clean up the very close edges. Go to the open Swatch dialog box, click on the Brushes tab, and choose a very small Pencil tip size—no more than 2 pixels. (See Figure 6.46.)

Why didn't I start with the Pencil tool from the beginning, and gradually work my way down to this tip size? Because the Pencil tool *adds* color; it would add a smudge of white if I were using a tip size any larger than 2 pixels. And this would leave residue colors in the area of the image that I want to be one hundred percent plain white. Remember, you're going to make the background of this kind of image transparent, but if there are any colors other than white present in the background, those pixels

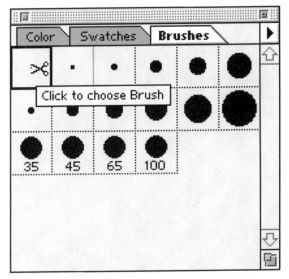

FIGURE 6.46. Choosing a small Pencil tip

will not be transformed. The result, then, would be a grainy or messy background—or, along the edge of your image, a white scratchy border. The Magic Wand tool is more time-consuming but it cleans up more effectively. Always use it first for one or two passes before switching to the Pencil tool.

10. In Figure 6.47, we're really close-up at 700%, but this is the only way to approach perfection. Zoom out by pressing Control+- (that is, Control plus the dash, -) from time to time to check your work, and use Control+Z to undo your last move.

11. When you're finished discarding everything except the ornament itself, it's time to save it as a transparent GIF. First, use the Crop tool once more, but this time do crop right to your lines to save file size, and press Backspace. Then choose Export, GIF89 Export from the File pulldown. The GIF89 Export dialog box will appear. (See Figure 6.48.)

12. Use the eyedropper to select your background color on the small preview image of your ornament, and press Enter. The background will go gray, signaling that it's transparent. Click OK when you're done.

FIGURE 6.47. Using the Pencil close-up to make final eliminations

13. Now choose Save As from the File pulldown menu, and choose CompuServe GIF from the File Type pulldown menu in the Save As dialog box. Change the name of your ornament to make it a GIF— my little monkey is now monkey.gif—and click OK. Click OK again when the Row Options dialog box appears, and you're done.

Assembling Extracted Elements

I also used this papyrus texture for a slice GIF on my secondary pages, the eight pages linked to the eight figures on the main, home page "wall." But I also did a little assembly work, selecting patterns and smaller design ornaments from the scans to create continuity. So let me demonstrate a little assemblage with the papyrus, the monkey, and some other designs to make a slice GIF.

Amy: Could you describe slice GIFs?

FIGURE 6.48. The GIF89 Export dialog box

Rebecca: Sure. A slice GIF is the long, thin graphic divided into vertical sections that tiles horizontally behind a VF web page as a background pattern. However, the vertical sections line up as stripes, creating left- or right-edge menu bars, text fields, and/or a beveled middle section between two strips of the same color. (During our tour of the web in Chapter 4, "More Basics of Site Creation," we called these page designs the left, the right, the double, and the triple VF.)

1. First, I created a new Photoshop file 1200 pixels wide and 90 pixels tall, and established its resolution at 300 pixels/inch. I called it eslice.psd.

Amy: Why 300 pixels/inch instead of the 72 that we've been using? Is that to show the complexity and detail of this particular image?

Rebecca: Yes. I chose to work at this high setting for two reasons. First, as you said, I wanted to keep the complexity by keeping the colors. This is another way of stating the axiom I mentioned earlier: You can always subtract color, but you can never put it back. Second, I could get away with this strategy because the monkey was going to be barely one inch tall. I also worked with the standing figures for the "wall" page at 300 dpi, thinking I could preserve detail there equally well. But those figures ended up about three and a half inches tall—I ended up having to choose between severely reducing the number of colors or physically reducing them in height. I went with the latter decision because I couldn't bear to look at the figures in 216 colors.

2. First, the papyrus background. I opened papyrus.gif and used the rectangular Marquee to select a decently sized chunk. Then I clicked on eslice.psd and press Control+V to paste.

3. Next I used the slider to move to the left end of eslice. Then I positioned the papyrus against the left side with the Move tool, leaving the rest of eslice untouched for now.

4. At this point, it was time to put in some Egyptian elements. I opened monkey.gif, but chose Rotate Canvas, Flip Horizontal to make him face the right way. I also reduced his size by selecting Image Size from the Image pulldown menu. Figure 6.49 shows what the Image Size dialog box looks like.

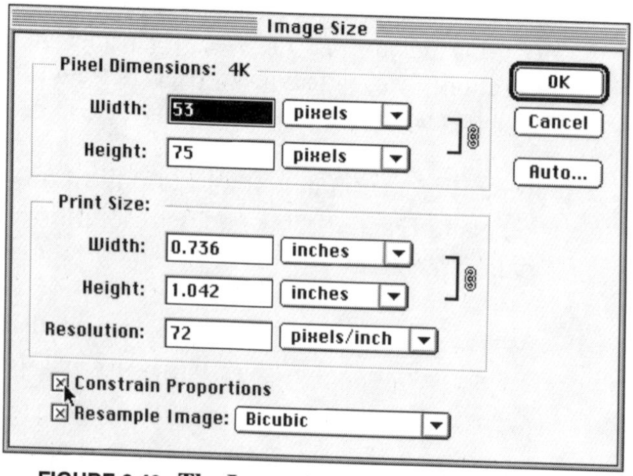

FIGURE 6.49. The Image Size dialog box

Who's Afraid of Web Page Design?

Before you reduce the size of an image like this, make sure Constrain Proportions is checked. Otherwise, the Height and Width measurements will change independent of one another, making your image look stretched. I played with the Width measurement, reducing the monkey gradually in 5-pixel increments, until I was satisfied. Then I clicked OK.

5. Now, to add this ornament to eslice, I pressed Control+A, clicked on the eslice window, and pressed Control+V. There's the monkey—I used the Move tool to position him on the very left edge of eslice. This is also the point at which I saved eslice.psd by pressing Control+S. I also clicked OK when the Save dialog box appeared to back up my work.

6. I wanted to separate this little ornament from the rest of the slice, as the text, graphics, and other page contents will appear to the left of him. So I went to the first scan with the four figures and the scale and hunted for a border. I found one I liked on the striped staff in the hands of the seated figure, so I zoomed in by pressing Control++ to make a clean grab.

NOTE: Notice that there are about ten border and texture possibilities just in this corner—look at the trailing ends of the seated figure's headdress, the variegated rows in his collar necklace, and the different designs on his chair. You can train your eyes to see such color, shape, and texture possibilities if you learn to look past the literal shapes.

7. Here's something important to remember if you're using a thin, vertical piece like this on a slice GIF: Imagine stacking two of these striped pieces end to end—if you want the seam between them to be invisible, you need to grab it like this. (See Figure 6.50.)

The first section at the top of the piece is golden orange, while the last section at the bottom of the piece is a black-and-red-stripe. So when a browser tiles this slice GIF, the striping will look continuous. I pressed Control+C to copy.

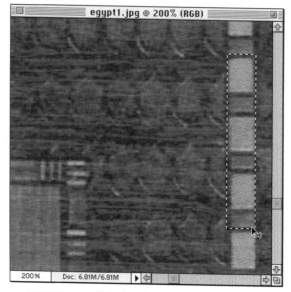

FIGURE 6.50. The border design as originally drawn, selected with the Marquee tool

8. Then I clicked on eslice and pressed Control+V. I used the Move tool to position the vertical border, leaving a nice amount of elbow room between it and the monkey.

9. Next, I chose Mode, RGB Color from the Image pulldown menu. Then I used the Eyedropper tool to select a single background color from the browser-safe palette. This color would fill the rest of eslice to provide a smooth reading surface—I chose a pale creamy yellow (#FFFFCC). Then I used the rectangular Marquee tool to select everything to the left of the vertical stripe border, and chose Fill from the Edit pulldown menu. I clicked OK to finish the Fill.

10. Last, I chose Save As from the Edit pulldown menu and CompuServe GIF from the File Type pulldown menu. I changed the file name to eslice.gif, pressed OK, and clicked OK in the Row Options dialog box.

    Figure 6.51 shows what the final product looks like by itself. Figure 6.52 shows what it looks like behind one of my old secondary pages, with more hieroglyphic ornaments added with the monkey.

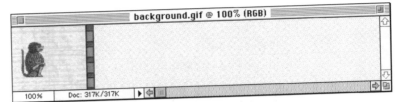

FIGURE 6.51. **The eslice.gif on its own...**

These are the basic Photoshop techniques I used to construct the entire "wall" page we showed you at the beginning of the chapter. The figures, the borders and dividers, even the individual hieroglyphic letters were all grabbed from scans, cleaned up with the Magic Wand and Pencil tools, and made into transparent GIFs.

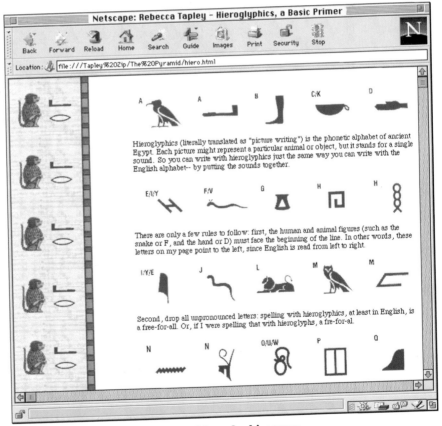

FIGURE 6.52. **...and behind my hieroglyphics page**

Amy: Wow! I thought this section was just great. When I sketch or find some art on which I want to base my page, I will return to this section to puzzle out the specifics of what to do with the scanned image. I think that much of this precise work can be duplicated in Paint Shop Pro, as well. For instance, I know that you can zoom in and use a paint brush tool to color in a pixel at a time.

Rebecca: Yes, Paint Shop Pro can be used to do this kind of work, albeit perhaps not as precisely. (I don't remember if PSP has a Magic Wand-type of tool or not, off the top of my head.) I don't believe PSP can do many of the effects in the first Exercises, though, which is the other half of the reason why I wrote this chapter.

Amy: Paint Shop Pro does have a Magic Wand tool for color selection. But you are right that many of the effects in the first half of this chapter would be very difficult to create in Paint Shop Pro. I didn't believe you at first, so I tried to duplicate the neon glow button in PSP. Though I used basically the same commands, the result was not the same. However, I read in the Help menu that Paint Shop Pro does accept Adobe-compatible plug-in filters, so maybe there's hope. And PSP does have its share of filters, feathering, deformations and special effects.

The arrangement of these elements on the page, however, was achieved by using a very complicated set of tables. You'll learn how to use table HTML in Chapter 8, "Positioning Elements with HTML," and you'll revisit tables again near the end of the book, where we bring together everything we've learned to put the finishing touches on our sample sites.

Review

- Photoshop relies heavily on layers when you're creating original artwork and filters when you're transforming existing colors or files.

- Begin by creating a .psd or Photoshop Document as a file to play with, then save it as a particular file format later on after you've reached the first key step in your design process.

- Feel free—feel obliged, even—to noodle around with Photoshop's settings and filters. It's an extremely sophisticated program with lots more to offer than we've shown you here, and the best way to get to know it is to use it.

"Answers" to the Exercises

Once again, there are no real answers to the exercises—or, rather, the demonstrations we show you. In this chapter, particularly, if you have successfully completed the exercises this means that your curiosity has been piqued, whether or not you can make a neon button or a plastic bit of text.

On with the Show

Now that we've learned to optimize graphics and perhaps to create a few graphics of our own from scratch or by assembly, let's move on to a more detailed discussion of color. Go on to the next chapter, where we'll finish examining browser-safe color and we'll choose background, font, and other colors for our sample sites.

CHAPTER 7

Preparing Web Colors

In the last chapter we talked about optimizing graphics for the Web and briefly introduced the idea of browser-safe colors. Now that you've used the browser-safe palette to reduce some sample graphics, it's time to look at this group of colors more closely within the context of actual web page design.

> **Rebecca:** If the intricacies of color and color theory pertaining to the Web are a serious interest, you might read *The Web Designer's Guide to Graphics: PNG, GIF & JPEG* by Timothy Webster, and/ or *Coloring Web Graphics* by Lynda Weinman. These books are for intermediate to advanced web page designers who want a more involved discussion.

> **Amy:** You have also directed me to Lynda Weinman's web site at www.lynda.com. There is a lot to be learned there as well.

Definitions

First, general color definitions. A **palette** is just a group or selection of colors—in the general sense of the word. Within web page design, however, when you speak of palettes you're talking about groups of colors used by designers and supported by browsers. A **browser palette** is the group of colors supported or displayed by browser software, but, to repeat, different browsers support an almost entirely different array of colors. The **browser-safe palette**, then, is the short list of 216 colors that all browsers have in common. We already introduced this idea to you in the last two chapters.

For the purposes of this chapter, we will discuss individual colors three different ways: in terms of the **RGB** system; as hexadecimal colors or **hex values**, and as **color names**. RGB, quite logically, stands for Red, Green, and Blue. Computers, and therefore the Web, use the RGB system to express and display colors because monitors use different amounts of red, green, and blue light to interpret what appears on the screen—up to a maximum of 255 "points" per color. So when you see a particular color selected in Paint Shop Pro or Photoshop, you will always see it broken down into three values: R=255, G=102, and B=102, for example. That's a browser-safe brick red.

A **hexadecimal** color is another way of expressing colors numerically. We could go into the complicated math if you need a nap (!) but let's just say for our purposes, a "hex" browser-safe color is written as a combination of 00, 33, 66, 99, CC, and/or FF. (You can describe any color as a hex color, but if it's got other numbers and letters it in, it's not browser-safe.) We will explore how to use hex numbers properly within HTML in later chapters of the book, though we will also briefly refer to hex numbers later in this chapter.

Finally, in the Web environment, colors can be safely expressed as **color names**. This is a long way of saying that if you want a link or a block of text to be green and you're not picky about the exact shade, you can type in the word "green" instead of a hex number. However, only a handful of color names display properly—that is, in exactly the same way—on PCs and Macintoshes. We will find out which color names are web-safe later on in this chapter.

NOTE: The majority of what we're describing here can be visually absorbed and understood just by looking at the color chip chart on the CD-ROM. A quick, overall look at the 216 browser-safe colors listed by their RGB and hex values, and a similar look to the colors you can use by name, is also on the CD-ROM.

Now here's some color theory and technical terminology. Colors are created by combining different percentages of hue, value, and saturation. **Hue** involves the location of all the colors on the visible spectrum, which everybody can visualize as a rainbow. **Value** describes the varying degrees of lightness or darkness in a color. Finally, **saturation** is the degree of a color's intensity—the difference between a pastel and a darker shade of the same green, for example. Apply anywhere from zero to 100 percent of each of these, and you get a single color. (We'll go into the hows and whys later on in this chapter.)

Brightness adds either white to tint or black to tone a color image. If you play with the brightness settings on your computer monitor or TV, you can make the display look like high noon or the dead of midnight. **Contrast**, similarly, is the difference between the dark and light colors that already exist in a color image. If you mess with this setting on your computer or TV, you blur the distinctions between the individual objects you see on the screen. Again, we'll go into more detail later on.

Texture and noise are the last two color tech terms you need to think about in this chapter. They do not comprise or define actual colors, but they do affect the way the human eye perceives color. **Texture** is any sort of definable, recognizable pattern, either on its own or in relationship to another element, for us, on a web page. **Noise** is a sort of visual value judgment that measures the amount of activity on a web page—if there are too many elements, colors, and/ or textures and the eye cannot focus, then there's too much noise. We will definitely address these concepts in this chapter as we compare colors and patterns, but they will also apply to the rest of the chapters when our sample sites really start coming together.

Amy: So if a page has too much noise, you might also say its too busy, right? I ask because Photoshop has a Noise filter that adds speckles to an image. It seems that your definition is about having too many design elements on one page.

Rebecca: Noise is both a criticism and a design tool—in a word, it's about *context*. It's true that if a web page has too many elements competing for someone's attention, then you can say it's too "noisy." But careful use of Noise, as with Photoshop's Noise filter, can create an interesting texture or background.

Now for related HTML and other web page definitions. Most of these are common sense, but let's review them anyway.

The **background color** of your web page is the solid color behind all text and elements displayed by your browser. The **font color** is the color of all plain nonlinked text displayed on your web page. Also, there are three **link colors** you can customize: the color of the unvisited link (a link that's never been clicked); the color of the active link (the color a link turns when the visitor holds the mouse key down on it); and the color of the visited link (the color of a link that's already been clicked). Sounds simple, right? It's not. We will discuss how these color settings can be overwritten, underestimated, and altogether messed up by HTML, by default browser settings, and by color choices themselves later on in the exercises.

Objectives

The objectives of this chapter are just as simple and as difficult as those in the last chapter. Learning to use color, particularly in the limited and limiting sense of the 216-color web-friendly palette, is extremely difficult. It is a skill not even experienced desktop publishers, painters, or other kinds of nonweb designers can master easily. So again, this chapter is merely meant to serve as a springboard to get you thinking about and looking at web-friendly color in ways that will help you build better web pages.

We will discuss RGB values, hex colors, and color names in detail before we incorporate them using HTML. And we will also discuss why hue, saturation, value, texture, and noise can mess up or otherwise mess with your good web design intentions. Finally, we are also going to apply color in practical ways now that we've prepared all our graphics. It's time to assign background, font, and link colors, so we will be preparing what graphic designers call **individual palettes**, or groups of colors to be used in a single project. We will create three individual palettes, one for each of our sample sites, and we'll discuss the reasons for our choices.

Color My World (Wide Web)

Since we already went over how to apply the 216-color palette to graphics in the last two chapters, we should focus on how individual colors are used on the Web.

We speak of the RGB colors because, if you remember, monitors display colors by using red, green, and blue dots, but web technology only accepts and interprets colors by hex numbers and/or color names. There is no place to input the three different RGB values per se, except in Paint Shop Pro or other graphics software you use to generate web graphics.

So let's move on to discussing colors as hex values and as color names, and then we'll expand on some of the other terms introduced in the definitions.

Hexadecimal Values

Hexadecimal (hex) values are used in web page design to represent any color to be displayed on a web page—backgrounds, text, links, borders, cells, tables, and so on. They also serve as a quick visual reference, as you can always tell if a color is browser-safe by looking at it in hex form. That is, if a color's hex value contains any number other than 0 (zero), 3, 6, or 9, or any letter other than C and F, it is not browser-safe, and you should not use it.

A hex value is actually comprised of an R, a G, and a B value represented by these letters and numbers. In the example #0033FF, the 00 is the R value, the 33 is the G value, and the FF is the B value. This color is a medium violet, and if you use hex values often enough, you will begin to recognize colors by the position of their individual letter and number representations.

When you use a hex value in a web page, it is always preceded by a number sign (#), which is why you will always see a number sign before a hex value in this book. (It's not actually part of the number itself.)

As a quick example, this medium apple green:

```
<BODY BACKGROUND="#CCFF99">
```

You should always surround colors in quotes to allow for early browsers, and there shouldn't be any spaces between the R, G, and B representations. You do not, however, have to use capital letters. That constitutes the proper syntax for using hex values; we'll cover the HTML more thoroughly in the exercises.

Color Names

Color names are colors you can use in HTML just as you use hex values, but without having to remember the six-digit letter-and-number combination. That's the benefit. The drawback of using color names is that you cannot be choosy about the exact color you get. If you type "red" you'll get a cherry red, period. If it's too bright or doesn't exactly meet your expectations, too bad.

The color names are included in the color chip chart on the CD-ROM, but here they are again for good measure.

Color Name	Hex Value
Aqua/Cyan	#00FFFF
Black	#000000
Blue	#0000FF
Fuchsia/Magenta	#FF00FF
Lime	#00FF00
Red	#FF0000
White	#FFFFFF
Yellow	#FFFF00

In the case of aqua and cyan, and fuchsia and magenta, you can use either color name and get the same color. But that's all, folks. The list is definitely not long.

When you use a color name in a web page, you don't need to use a number sign (#). As a quick example:

```
<FONT COLOR="blue">
```

"Blue" in this sense will always and only mean a bright royal blue, #0000FF. It doesn't stand for anything more, and it's not a nickname for a different shade you can specify elsewhere in your HTML document. That's the good and the bad of using color names.

You should always surround color names in quotes to allow for early browsers, but you still don't have to use capital letters. That constitutes the proper syntax for color names; we'll cover the HTML more thoroughly in the exercises.

Hue, Value, and Saturation

Hue, value, and saturation are important in all the ways to apply color, but they are particularly important in terms of web color. Why? Because our options are so limited, which makes every individual color choice so crucial.

Hue, remember, is just another word for a color on the rainbow. Most people (well, perhaps those of us about thirty and older) also remember their elementary school art teacher's color wheel. This simple wheel contains **primary** colors (red, blue, and yellow) and **secondary** colors (orange, green, and purple). For those of you who don't remember elementary school—or those of you who may not have had art classes at all—here's how it works: Secondary colors are made by combining two primary colors; red and yellow make orange, blue and yellow make green, and red and blue make purple. If you were to mix all these colors together so every color was present, you'd make black. If you removed all color completely, you'd make white. You can make millions of colors by adding and/or subtracting varying amounts of blue, yellow, red, white, and black. This way of combining color forms the basis for all color theory in every kind of artistic expression.

However, we're not in the real world—we're on the Web. With this limitation and the six basic hues in mind, go to the CD-ROM and have a look at the 216 browser-safe colors. Can you see how few colors are actually present? In the last chapter we casually mentioned the absence of a true beige or flesh tone on the browser-safe color palette, when we were selecting a solid background color for the slice GIF. That's a good example of what we're trying to show you here; among the 216 browser-safe colors, there are very few, if any, "between" colors because there are few basic hues to be mixed, and they can only be combined in fixed amounts.

Here's how that plays out with regard to value and saturation. If the value of your colors is too extreme—remember, value has to do with the lightness and/or the darkness of a color—then your pages will fall prey to the value difference between PCs and Macintoshes. That is, darker colors that look fine on a Macintosh may be too dark for a PC, and lighter colors that look fine on a PC may be too light for a Macintosh. So you want to choose mostly medium values, colors without too much lightness or darkness, to make sure your pages are readable in both environments.

Similarly, too much saturation can make your web pages unreadable. In the RGB world of the computer, the most highly saturated colors are pure red, pure blue, and pure green. So you might think you could grab the most attention by using lots of these pure colors in your backgrounds, your fonts, and yours links. The effect, however, would be blinding—all three colors would be so intense and visually competitive that visitors to your page would not know where to look first. What would happen then? They'd move on. Contrasting saturation, then, is the answer: utilize more tint (white) or tone (black) by choosing a few less-saturated colors to complement one highly saturated color.

We'll demonstrate how to choose and combine colors into readable yet compelling individual palettes in the exercises.

> **Amy:** Please remind readers again about the color difference between PCs and Macs, and give the URL for that Furbo Filter thingy again.

> **Rebecca:** Okay. To put it briefly, colors appear darker on a PC than they do on a Macintosh because of the way the hardware is constructed. So web page designers should account for this appearance in their design strategy—you can easily compare a graphic in PC and Macintosh "colors" by using the Browser Preview filter from Furbo Filters available at http://www.furbo-filters.com.

> There's another color utility called ColorMix that readers might find useful. It's a little program that enables you to "mix" two browser-safe colors to come up with a new color that's not on the

browser-safe palette, but is still browser-safe. It works by alternating colors pixel by pixel—so if you wanted to create a turquoise color by using a safe green and a safe blue, ColorMix would color all the even pixels green and all the odd pixels blue. The URL for this utility is http://www.colormix.com.

Brightness and Contrast

Brightness and contrast, as we said at the beginning of the chapter, have to do with the presence and/or absence of light in color. In the world of the Web, though, Brightness and Contrast are also control knobs on the visitor's monitor. So you as a web site designer should assume that visitors are looking at your web site through all kinds of contrast and brightness settings. How can you design for this scenario? Here are a few pointers.

Choose background and font colors with high contrast, such as black text against a yellow background, or pastel-pink text against a medium-green background. If you were to switch these color combinations—black against green, and pastel pink against yellow—you'd get into trouble on a PC and a Macintosh, respectively. Also, don't underestimate the number of people out there who surf the Web in grayscale and/or 1-bit color mode to reduce download time. How does your web page look in black and white? If you can't read the text or see details in your graphics, it's time to rethink your colors.

> **Amy:** How do I view pages in grayscale? I couldn't find an option to toggle in Internet Explorer 4.

> **Rebecca:** Don't mess with your software; use the Brightness and Contrast settings to turn down the color on your monitor. (How's that for a low-tech, everybody-can-do-it solution?)

> **Amy:** That is a decent solution. I also did a little more poking around and found that you can change colors in IE4 by selecting Internet Options from the View pulldown menu. In NN4 you choose Preferences from the Edit menu.

If you use large-sized text, or if you incorporate your text into a GIF or JPEG graphic, you can effectively beat most brightness and contrast problems. If you insist on using a background pattern or texture (don't say we didn't warn you), do the opposite of what we suggested above; combine colors of similar contrast such as black and green, or pink and yellow. It will make your text more readable, and it will wash out evenly if a visitor is looking at it through customized brightness and/or contrast settings.

Texture and Noise

The human brain has a very definite threshold for noise and texture, which we developed over the past three thousand years to help us conserve our energy. Behavioral scientists might even say this threshold has narrowed considerably with the emergence of the Web (or even remote control TV) as we make instant, or nearly instant, decisions purely on the basis of visual appeal.

We've already discussed texture and noise in a concrete way by looking at the sites that use backgrounds effectively in Chapter 4, "More Basics of Site Creation." Careful use of texture and noise adds both color and visual interest to a page, and contrast and emphasis to the text and graphics. Visitors can tell at a glance if a page contains something interesting, just by the combination of colors. Too much texture and noise, though, distracts and confuses visitors to your page, because their eye is drawn in too many different directions at once. If there are too many colors, too much pattern, and/or too complicated a texture, the brain interprets this confusion as unworthy of our time and attention. Our hand clicks the mouse, and we move on to the next possibility.

You can test this threshold a little by creating textures made of similar or analogous colors—a combination of different blues, greens, and dark yellows, for example. Or you can choose darker and lighter hues of the same color, such as a medium and dark purple. Be certain your text color is completely different, though, ideally from the other side of the color wheel—such as purple text against the blues/greens/ yellows, or orange text against the purples. Also, if your pattern or texture is particularly rough, you should increase the size and width of your text so it is less likely to be lost.

To put all this discussion into practice, let's jump into the HTML we use to apply color to web pages. It's time to do some exercises.

Exercises

When we look at the temporary or UC pages for our three sample web sites, we see many color challenges to be addressed. (See Figures 7.1, 7.2, and 7.3.)

The HTML used to add color is relatively simple. Choosing colors, and/or patterns or textures, is the tough part. It is also, naturally, a matter of subjective judgment. So if you don't like our color choices, or you have a moral objection to patterns and textures, feel free to design your own individual palette.

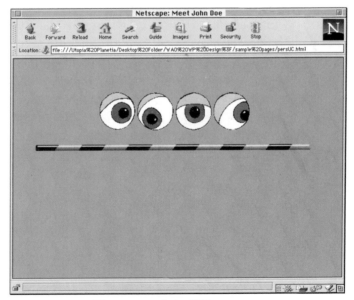

FIGURE 7.1. The personal site UC page

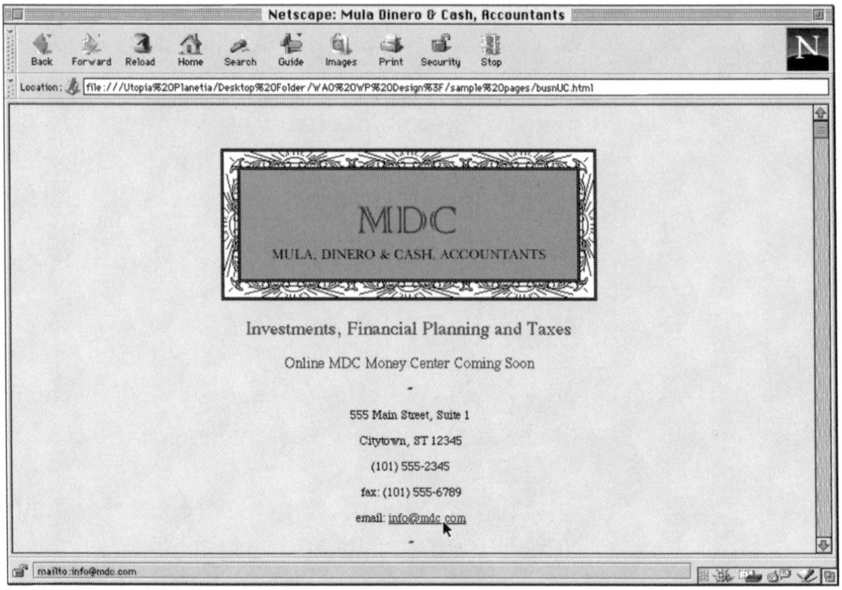

FIGURE 7.2. The business site UC page

With that disclaimer out of the way, here's our strategy: We're going to add a solid, nontiling background pattern behind the eyeballs on the personal UC page to demonstrate pattern effects. We're also going to choose a set of background and text colors to contrast nicely against the greens we already established in the business page palette. Then, finally, we'll address the challenge of choosing an appropriate palette of background and text colors to complement all the different graphics on the informational page. So let's get started.

Background Patterns

Part of the way we see and evaluate color is relational, in comparison to other nearby colors and how they are arranged. In this exercise, you should open your HTML editor and your browser, and put in the CD-ROM. You're going to compare various swirl patterns behind the eyeballs on the personal page and choose one to be the background.

Here's the HTML you need to add to the <BODY> tag:

```
BACKGROUND="pswirl.gif"
```

FIGURE 7.3. The informational site UC page

so that the HTML we'll begin with in this exercise looks like this:

```
<HTML>
<HEAD>
<TITLE>Meet John Doe</TITLE>
</HEAD>
<BODY BACKGROUND="pswirl.gif">
<BR>
<P><IMG SRC="eye1.gif">
<IMG SRC="eye2.gif">
<IMG SRC="eye3.gif">
<IMG SRC="eye4.gif"></P>
</BODY>
</HTML>
```

Save it as phome.html now, to create a new document, and also when you're finished with this exercise, to save your final changes.

Eventually, these four eyeballs will be grouped in the middle of the swirl, and they might even blink or roll around when the cursor touches them—but that's covered in Chapters 8 and 12, respectively. Right now we're strictly making color comparisons: some things that work, and some things that don't.

This purple swirl is a demonstration of a don't. The two purples within the background pattern might work well together, but they don't work against the purples in the eyeballs. We want a different kind of contrast, so next try bswirl.gif instead. Change the p to a b in the <BODY> tag HTML, save your HTML document, and reload it in your browser.

The blues swirl is another don't. It doesn't look as bad as the purple swirl, but it doesn't jump out and grab you, either. This is because these purples and blues do not have enough contrast against each other as color groups. Remember, you can create every shade of purple by combining blue with red, so the hues you select when contrasting blues, purples, and reds are very important. You can make something look dull just as easily as you can make something look spectacular.

Now experiment with cswirl1.gif and cswirl2.gif. These swirl backgrounds have contrasting colors built in, but do they blend harmoniously with the purples of the eyeballs? In our opinion, no. There's not a lot of pattern or texture to contend with on this page, but your brain can, and might, still interpret these color combinations as too noisy. The design purpose of this swirl, after all, is to draw attention to the eyeballs. The competition between the pairs of colors in these swirls prevents this from happening.

Finally, experiment with gswirl.gif and oswirl.gif. Here, at last, are two do's. The oranges and greens by themselves do not contrast significantly, so there's no distraction from the eyeballs. And as color groups compared with the purples in the eyeballs, there's just the right amount of relative contrast. Which one do you prefer? We'll keep oswirl.gif as the background for the personal page, just because there are many greens in the business site palette. But if green is one of your favorite colors (it's the second most popular favorite color in the world, by the way, with blue being the first) feel free to keep it.

> **Amy:** I notice that cswirl1.gif and gswirl.gif are similar in that they use what appears to be the same main color. But cswirl1.gif is no good, because the contrast between the green and yellow swirl, and the contrast between the purple eyeball and the background, is just too noisy or busy for the visitor's eye, correct?

> **Rebecca:** Yes, that was the visual point I was trying to make. Although now that I look at them again, I think the cswirl1.gif background rates higher than bswirl.gif and pswirl.gif. With cswirl1.gif at least there's some contrast—green and yellow individually complement purple pretty well.

> **Amy:** On the other hand, gswirl.gif uses the same green background with a lighter green swirl—less contrast in the background. Is this your point?

> **Rebecca:** Yes, the green background is less contrasty, which can be a good thing or a bad thing, depending upon the other design elements in your page. In this situation, I just exercised my authorial prerogative and went with the oswirl.gif because I liked it better.

> **Amy:** For me, the red tones in the background orange of oswirl.gif clash with the red tones in the purple center of the eyeball. If I were designing this page, I would definitely use the green swirl instead.

> **Rebecca:** Vive la différence!

Selecting Background and Text Colors

Now let's turn our attention to the business site. Open busnuc.html in your browser, and look at the greens used in the logo for a moment— it's the only part of the temporary page we'll use in the final product, so it will determine which other colors we use for backgrounds and fonts.

When you're designing a personal site, you can be as wacky and wild as you like. But for business sites you're not only constrained by good taste; you're limited to whatever message the business in question wants to send. Think back to the Homewrecker site, and the NetGrocer site. Think about Snapple's temporary page, and revisit them on the Web if you have to. All these sites are well designed, and they also use color very effectively, but the individual color palettes are all quite different. This is because a fashion designer can, and probably should, make bolder color statements than a grocery store, while a beverage company aims to appeal to both markets. Color is a language all its own, with as many dialects as it has applications.

So what kind of color language should you use to describe a CPA firm? Something conservative, something sophisticated. The MDC logo is designed to look like money, so why not take it from there? Pull an American one- or a twenty-dollar-bill from your wallet and have a look.

> **Amy:** Looking at American dollars is a good idea! I mention it because this is the kind of thing you have to do to get ideas—look at things in the world around you. I tend to forget that sometimes, as I'm sure others do.

You can see at a glance that you have a five-color palette at your disposal: black, gray, off-white or white, dark green, and light green. Now hold the bill under the light and take a close look. Unless your money is counterfeit, there should be tiny red and blue fibers in the paper—reds and blues that register on a subconscious scale. A highly saturated true red and true blue would do well against the rest of the more subtle colors we've chosen. So we've expanded our palette to seven colors. How should we apply them?

At this point, open the CD-ROM file called bpalette.gif in your browser. We created this palette in a graphics program in order to compare and contrast the seven colors we've chosen, to place them alongside the MDC logo, and to demonstrate some color combinations with regard to background and font selection.

As this palette demonstrates, the lighter green will be the background color throughout the business site. The font/color area at the bottom juxtaposes all the other colors against this green, so you can choose font and link colors.

The white and the gray are too bright for plain text, but perhaps not for highlights elsewhere. The black, similarly, is too contrasty compared with the dark green. Our decision, then, was to select the dark green for the plain text color, the blue for the link color, and the red for the visited link color. For the active link color—the color a linked word will turn when the visitor clicks it—we will use the same light green as the background. This makes the linked word disappear, and gives the visual illusion that it's being activated.

It's important, however, to choose link and visited link colors of similar or equal saturation. They will usually be located in proximity to one another on the page, such as in a navigational list, and you don't really want one to be more or less noticeable than the other. Some designers deliberately choose a visited link color that's much lighter or less saturated to make unvisited links stand out more clearly. If you think about it, this is questionable logic.

On a bank's web page, for example, you may have two text links right next to each other: one for online banking, the other for business hours. The visitor to this web page is probably going to use the online banking link all the time to pay bills, to transfer funds, and so on. If you make the visited link color less visible compared to the color of the unvisited business hours page, which link is going to jump out at a glance? The link to the business-hours page—the page that person will rarely, if ever, actually use.

Therefore, let's apply our text, background and link colors to the business page HTML as follows, using TEXT, BGCOLOR, and LINK/ALINK/VLINK.

Under </HEAD> insert:

```
<BODY TEXT="#006600" BGCOLOR="#66CC66"
LINK="#0000FF" ALINK="#66CC66" VLINK="#0000FF">
```

Check the answers for the complete HTML, which is how the business page should look, and save the new business page as bhome.html.

Choosing a Graphics-Intensive Palette

Some sites make use of lots of graphics, as does the informational page. That vertical row of historic houses down the left side of the page would be a nice visual reference, but if only they were all the same color! What does one do in such a situation?

Take a good, close look at these four houses. The orange and the yellow ones are in the same general color family, so they are easily complemented. Also, notice that the mansard roof on the gray house is similar in hue to the shingling on the blue house, so they complement each other fairly well. These are the reasons that we chose the four colors in the slice GIF on the informational UC page: a darker goldenrod yellow, a pale pastel yellow, as well as small amounts of the darker and lighter grays. We will be using these four colors again in the final design because they work well, and for continuity between the temporary and permanent pages.

But we need more options! We've got secondary pages, links, plain text, and much more to consider other than these houses. Also, the four UC colors are nice, but there's no pizzazz. Time for some contrasting, stronger choices.

Notice we said stronger, not highly saturated. When was the last time you saw someone paint a house cherry red, or choose royal-blue siding? Most of the colors in the houses we'll come across on this site (remember, it's a gallery, so there will be many) will be soft, muted colors. Our four other colors are medium, yet they hold up well against the pale yellow, which we chose as our sample background color.

Clearly, the text color choices are the olive green, the dark gray, the purple, or a default black. We like the way the olive green warms up against the yellow, so that's our body text color choice. Similarly, the purple makes the yellow look more subtle and the green more brown, so that's our choice for the link color. We'll use the same disappearing trick for the active link color, but what choice for the visited link color? In the end we decided on the orange, because it stands on its own against the purple and the yellow. Here's how that translates in HTML:

```
<BODY TEXT="#999966" BGCOLOR="#FFFFCC"
LINK="#666699" ALINK="#FFFFCC" VLINK="#FF9900">
```

Using your browser, open infoUC.html to see this in color.

More Exercises

If you want more practice with these techniques, you can create a color palette for the personal page, using the greens or oranges in the swirl background and the purple eyeballs as a reference point. You can also experiment with the business palette against a white background versus the light green. Last but not least—and here's a challenge indeed—see if you can come up with a background pattern for the slice GIF behind the houses on the informational site. Can you find both colors *and* textures to complement all these graphics together? You know how we feel about background patterns. Prove us wrong!

Amy: Yes, I love a challenge! I did play with the Historic House Style Gallery's background, and I learned a lot. Obviously mine was just one approach of many, but for those who are interested, here's what I did.

After creating a Photoshop document that was 900 pixels wide by 20 high, I pulled up the salem1s.jpg and used my eyedropper tool to get a good sample of the gray-blue roof color. I switched that to the background square on the toolbar, then used the eyedropper on the browser-safe palette to select different colors that might match. I couldn't find an exact match, but I did find a color with the same grayish hue that's just a touch greener. I drew a line in that color about 1 inch from the left margin (I guessed at that distance), and filled that section with the gray-blue color.

Then I pulled up salem4s.jpg, the picture of the goldenrod-yellow house, and used the eyedropper tool to get a sample of its color. I used the same procedure and found a great match in the browser-safe palette. I created a new layer, drew a yellow line right next to the edge of the blue fill, and filled the remainder of the canvas with the yellow. Then I added some subtle noise and despeckled it, so I have a very subtle, rich texture underneath the text. It looks like wallpaper that you might find in an old home—fitting, I think. The houses stand out against the blue, but my eye is drawn to the similarities between the colors of the background and the blues in the top and bottom houses. The olive-green text against the yellow texture works a balance of low contrast and good readability, and I find it very warm and pleasing to the eye. And I know that you can create just about the same thing in Paint Shop Pro, since I did something similar with my own UC page.

One problem: I do have to adjust the blue left margin a bit to make sure the blue fill stays underneath the houses and not the text. Is there a more precise way to do that than just guessing?

Rebecca: Yes—there are two possible solutions.

You can import one of the houses into your graphics program and use it as a reference point. This is easier in Photoshop than in Paint Shop Pro, because you can put the house on its own layer and make that layer visible or invisible by clicking the eye in the Layers dialog box.

However, you can also move the text and graphics around one pixel at a time just by changing a number in your HTML document—this is your second and, in my humble opinion, your better option. In a graphics program, you can't see the whole page put together; also, it's laborious to add and subtract. But in your HTML editor you can change a <TABLE> value, switch to your browser window and press Reload/Refresh, and instantly view your changes.

If you want to see Amy's VF background pattern in color, it's on the CD-ROM (homeslice.gif). Just change the <BODY> tag information, save your changes, and open the Gallery page in your browser.

"Answers" to the Exercises

Here's what the final HTML for the three sample sites should look like:
The personal page:

```
<HTML>
<HEAD>
```

```
<TITLE>Meet John Doe<TITLE>
</HEAD>
<BODY BACKGROUND="oswirl.gif">
<BR>
<P><IMG SRC="eye1.gif>
<IMG SRC="eye2.gif>
<IMG SRC="eye3.gif>
<IMG SRC="eye4.gif>
</BODY>
</HTML>
```

The business page:

```
<HTML>
<HEAD>
<TITLE>Mula Dinero & Cash, Accountants</TITLE>
<META NAME="keywords" CONTENT="mula, dinero,
cash, accountants, accounting, taxes, IRAs,
retirement, financial planning, estate planning,
wills, bequests, inheritance, stocks, bonds,
futures, investments, investors, investing">
</HEAD>
<BODY TEXT="#006600" BGCOLOR="#66CC66"
LINK="#0000FF" ALINK="#66CC66" VLINK="#0000FF">
<CENTER>
<IMG SRC="blogo1.gif" ALT="Mula, Dinero & Cash"
ALIGN=center>
<BR>
<P>Investments, Financial Planning and Taxes
<BR>
<P><BLINK>Online MDC Money Center Coming Soon</
BLINK>
<BR>
<P>555 Main Street, Suite 1
<P>Citytown, ST  12345
<P>(101) 555-2345
<P>fax: (101) 555-6789
<P>email: <A
HREF="mailto:info@mdc.com">info@mdc.com</A>
<BR>
```

```
</CENTER>
</BODY>
</HTML>
```

The informational page:

```
<HTML>
<HEAD>
<TITLE>The Historic House Style Gallery</TITLE>
<META NAME="description" CONTENT="A gallery of
American residential architectural styles popular
between 1750 and 1950.">
</HEAD>
<BODY TEXT="#999966" BACKGROUND="infoslice.gif"
BGCOLOR="#FFFFCC" LINK="#666699" ALINK="#FFFFCC"
VLINK="#FF9900">
<P>
<TABLE BORDER=0 CELLSPACING=0 CELLPADDING=0
WIDTH=600>
<TR>
<TD WIDTH=95 ALIGN=left VALIGN=top>
<P><IMG SRC="salem1s.jpg"><BR>
<P><IMG SRC="salem4s.jpg"><BR>
<P><IMG SRC="salem5s.jpg"><BR>
<P><IMG SRC="salem2s.jpg"><BR>
</TD>
<TD WIDTH=35>
</TD>
<TD WIDTH=470 ALIGN=left VALIGN=top>
<P><B><FONT FACE=Arial SIZE="+3" COLOR="blue">The
Historic House Style Gallery</B></FONT>
<P>
<IMG SRC="pixel.gif" HEIGHT=25 WIDTH=1>
<CENTER><B><FONT FACE=Arial SIZE="+2"
COLOR="brown">Coming Soon. . .</CENTER></B></FONT>
<FONT FACE=Arial SIZE="+1">
<B><UL>
<LI TYPE=square>A gallery of historical residential
styles built in America between 1750 and 1950<BR>
<LI TYPE=square>Background information on trends
```

```
and architects behind each style<BR>
<LI TYPE=square>Examples from across the country,
including regional adaptations<BR>
<LI TYPE=square>Notable architectural details and
features of each style<BR>
</UL></B>
<P><FONT FACE=Arial>Questions? Submissions? Email
<A HREF="mailto:curator@hhsg.com">curator@hhsg
.com</A>.
</TD>
</TABLE>
</BODY>
</HTML>
```

You might also take a look at the individual palette we created for the personal site, based on using the orange swirl background. You might want to make different choices, though, so if your palette contains different colors, it's okay.

Review

- A palette is just a group of colors. The browser-safe palette contains only the 216 colors that all the browsers have in common, and an individual palette is the group of colors you select to use in a single web site.

- For our purposes, colors are described as RGB values, hexadecimal values, or as color names. You can choose a browser-safe color in a graphics program by typing in its RGB values, but you use a hex value or a color name in the HTML of a web page.

- Hue, value, and saturation are all color theory terms used to describe how colors relate to one another on the spectrum. Brightness and contrast illustrates the difference between colors existing in an image and/or on the screen.

- Texture and noise involve how the human eyes and brain perceive grouped colors. If you combine too many colors and patterns to create texture on a page, visitors will not know where to focus—the page will have too much noise—and they will move on.

- It's good to combine like colors in a background pattern—for example, lighter and darker shades of red. It's not good to choose a text or link color that's similar to a background, such as light blue on white.

- Similarly, it's not good to combine dissimilar colors, such as light yellow and dark purple, in a background pattern, or visitors will have difficulty reading your text. But it *is* good to choose a dark text color for a light background color, or a light text color for a dark background color.

- Try to use a blend of hues and saturations in your web site palette. Combine light, medium, bright, and dark colors imaginatively and in balance, so visitors will know where you want them to look and what's most important.

On with the Show

Are you intrigued by the use of the <TABLE> tag in the informational site UC page? Does it bug you that the eyeballs on the personal UC page aren't centered over the swirled background? Let's fix those problems in the next chapter by learning how to position elements on a web page. Turn the page to get started.

CHAPTER 8 ——— *Positioning Elements with HTML*

Now that we've taken some time to cruise the Web and establish the form, the function, and the content of our fledgling web site(s), it's time to attack the HTML.

Definitions

There's only one definition you should keep in mind throughout the course of this chapter, and that's the definition of **HTML**. HTML is more than just a string of code. It serves the same task as the frame of a painting—it provides structural support, it displays the contents, and it sets off or in some way accentuates everything within it, hopefully without drawing attention to itself.

Our definition of what is and is not essential within an HTML document does not fall in line with what the W3, or World Wide Web Consortium, requires. (The W3 is the recognized authority on HTML and provides the HTML standard for the entire Web community.) We have admittedly, but deliberately, left out certain tags that some of you may believe are necessary to the proper syntax. So if you feel that this chapter shortchanges you, or you get to the end of the chapter and wonder what else should be in your framework, visit the W3 web site at http://www.w3.com and check out the official HTML 4 specifications. Remember that this book is merely a guideline, and not the definitive recipe for what a web page "should" be, and adjust your HTML accordingly.

Another word we will begin using is **syntax**, which is more or less a synonym for HTML grammar. When people discuss how to properly use a language such as English, they talk about how verbs are conjugated (I see, you see, he or she or it sees, and so on). Similarly, when people discuss how to properly write HTML, they talk about syntax—where a particular HTML tag should be located, how to use its attributes and values, what it can and cannot contain (plain text, other HTML tags), and so on.

The most important thing to keep in mind here is that there's very little, if any, HTML slang. You can use "ain't" and "him and me" in regular everyday English, but you can't fudge HTML, not even by as much as one tiny extra space. HTML is too much like other programming languages; writing HTML code requires precision and memorization of many rock-solid rules.

Objectives

In this chapter, we will begin coding the main and secondary pages of our web sites by building on the crude under-construction pages we created in Chapter 4, "More Basics of Site Creation." We will cover the essential <HEAD> and <BODY> elements you'll need to use as the foundation for your HTML pages, and we will begin exploring basic page construction using the <P>, <BR>, <IMG>, and <A> tags as a springboard. Then we will proceed to intermediate and advanced placement and alignment using tables and frames.

> **NOTE:** Even if you are familiar with how these basic tags are used, read this chapter as a refresher so you will be up to speed on the other topics we touch upon here, such as platform differences and discrepancies. You should at least skip to the end of the chapter and do the exercises so the three sample sites will be up to speed (don't forget that the exercises in this book are cumulative). The three

Who's Afraid of Web Page Design?

under-construction pages we'll be using here are provided for you on the CD-ROM as busnUC.html (the business site under-construction page), infoUC.html (the informational site under-construction page), and persUC.html (the personal site under-construction page). You can open these HTML documents in whichever HTML editor you chose to download and install in Chapter 2. Open your editor now and look at these pages to see where we're starting.

The "Basic" Web Page

Here is what we consider a "basic" web page within the confines of this book; you, the reader, should have a simple understanding of what all these tags are and how they work before you proceed.

```
<HTML>
<HEAD>
<TITLE>Here is the title of this web page.</
TITLE>
</HEAD>
<BODY>
<P>This, right here, is some plain text.<BR>
<P>Here is an image: <IMG SRC="eye1.gif"><BR>
<P>Here is a <A HREF="nextpage.html">link</A>.<BR>
<P>Here is a list:<BR>
<DIR><LI>First thing
<LI>Second thing
<LI>Third thing
</DIR>
<P>Here is a table:<BR>
<TABLE>
<TR>
<TD>Cell No. 1</TD><TD>Cell No. 2</TD>
</TR>
<TR>
<TD>Cell No. 3</TD><TD>Cell No. 4</TD>
</TR>
</TABLE>
</BODY>
</HTML>
```

Now again, for the record, you need not fully understand the details of how all these tags work. Part of the purpose of this book, after all, is to extend and deepen your knowledge of HTML. Think of this code instead as a sort of benchmark; if you recognize most of it and you understand how tags, attributes, and values work together (even if you've never used some of these particular ones before) you're ready to use the rest of this book.

It is also worth mentioning at this point that this HTML has been written out this way so you can clearly see the opening and closing tags—<BODY> and </BODY>, just as an example. You can certainly arrange your HTML any way you choose, and there are many web page designers who write HTML code in one continuous straight line. The vertical layout you see here, however, makes the various individual tags much easier to see, so it is the standard format we will use throughout the rest of the book.

It may also help you to arrange your outer tags—<HTML>, <BODY>, <FONT>, and <TABLE>, for example—in corresponding, ascending and descending order:

```
<HTML>
<BODY>
<FONT>
<TABLE>
  (The rest of the HTML goes here)
</TABLE>
</FONT>
</BODY>
</HTML>
```

This makes it much easier to tell if you've left out a closing tag, which is a very common beginner-to-intermediate mistake. You need only run your finger down the first and last few lines of your HTML document to make certain all your tags are in place.

We will also do everything possible to show you HTML as it appears on both the PC and Macintosh platforms and in both the Netscape and Microsoft browsers. If you take a close look at Figures 8.1 through 8.6, representing our benchmark HTML, you can see why.

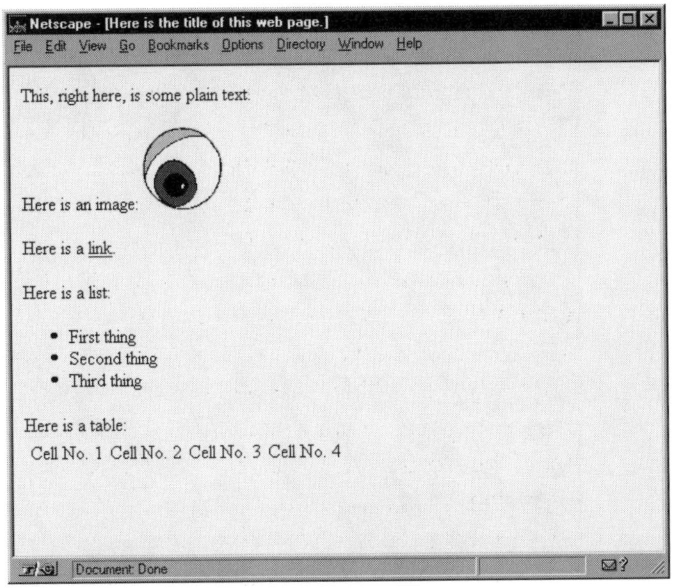

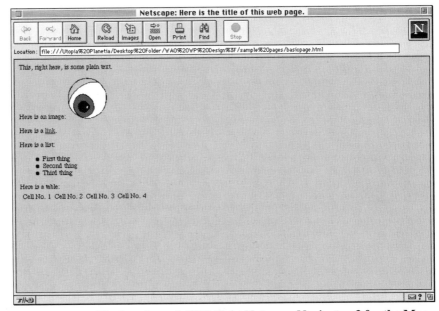

FIGURE 8.1. The benchmark HTML in Netscape Navigator 3 for the PC

FIGURE 8.2. The benchmark HTML in Netscape Navigator 3 for the Mac

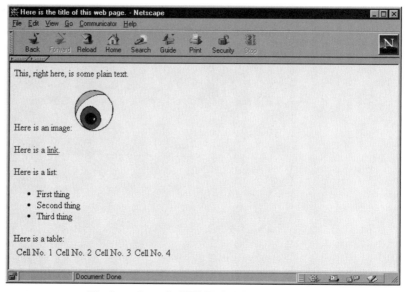

FIGURE 8.3. The benchmark HTML in Netscape Communicator for the PC

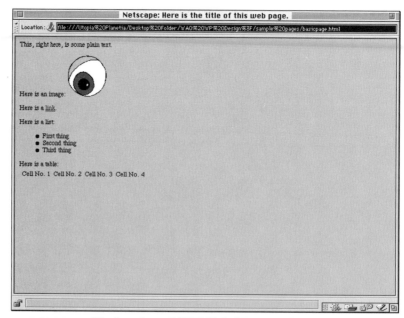

FIGURE 8.4. The benchmark HTML in Netscape Communicator for the Mac

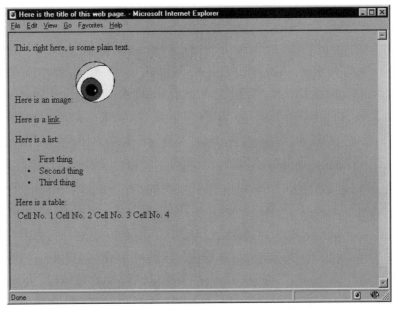

FIGURE 8.5. The benchmark HTML in Internet Explorer 4 for the PC

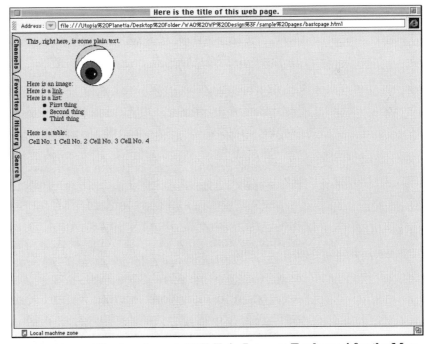

FIGURE 8.6. The benchmark HTML in Internet Explorer 4 for the Mac

The HTML used to create each of these figures is exactly the same, down to every letter, character, and space, but there are obvious and distinct differences. (We won't always show you all six at once like this, or this book will get very long very quickly.) As we begin our discussion of how to arrange elements on a page, keep these distinct differences in mind.

Amy: Could you point out some of the obvious and distinct differences in this page as displayed by Netscape Navigator and Internet Explorer? It would help me know what to look for in the future.

Rebecca: Just to name the most obvious (and the most frustrating), Navigator and Explorer use different default fonts and different default font sizes, so text in Navigator will be smaller and text in Explorer will be larger. Also, Explorer puts more of a "buffer zone" between paragraphs of text and between text and graphics, where Navigator puts less. You can imagine how these simple, but hardly minor, distinctions can wreak havoc with web page design. We'll talk about the cumulative effects of these differences, and some other disparities, later on.

Important <HEAD> Elements

A web page's structure is divided into two parts, the <HEAD> information and the <BODY> information, in that order. Both parts are enclosed by the <HTML> tag, as they always should be, with <HTML> always written first thing and </HTML> always written last. Everything else we write will occur between these two written elements, so let's proceed to the stand-out features of the <HEAD> tag.

<HEAD> tag elements—other HTML tags—serve a few important functions, although none of them work by themselves and nothing written within the <HEAD> tag appears on a web page. Some <HEAD> elements provide additional information about your page's exact location on your ISP server, and provide a very basic, rarely used form of keyword search. Other, more important <HEAD> elements, which we will address in later chapters, specify any scripting information used with JavaScripts and/or style sheets

instructions. The <HEAD> elements we will cover in this chapter, though, are the <TITLE> and <META> tags.

The <TITLE> Tag

The <TITLE> tag is one of those tags that does exactly what it says; whatever words are enclosed within it appear on the top edge of the browser window when your web page loads up. The title of the personal page we're creating might read like this:

```
<TITLE>Meet John Doe - John's Doe's Home Page</TITLE>
```

That's the correct syntax, meaning that the <TITLE> tag is in the right place, there are no extra spaces before or after the words themselves, and the closing </TITLE> is present. But the actual wording of this title is arguably wrong, for a couple of reasons.

First of all, when both Netscape Navigator and Microsoft Internet Explorer display a web page, they always, automatically throw in a little <TITLE>-like text of their own. Navigator 3 will always precede a title with "Netscape:" plus one space, while Navigator 4 and Explorer will always follow a title with a dash and "Netscape" or "Microsoft Internet Explorer." This leaves you with only a limited number of characters to work with—including spaces between individual words—if you want your entire web page title to display without running off the screen edge. (Hint: You do.)

So the watchwords here are *short* and *sweet*. For the business site we're working on, that's a simple task—we'll use the name of the company: Mula Dinero & Cash, Accountants. The other two sites—including John Doe's, of course—present a bit more of a challenge. How can we sum up the entire content of these two web sites in a handful of words?

For the personal site, we will use the first half of what's already written above: "Meet John Doe." We can afford to be informal and candid, and even a little wacky, because this site does not pretend to be high-level or corporate content. It's recreation, so the title can be relaxed. Also, "Meet John Doe" is nice and short—it will always load up in entirety.

Similarly, we will be straightforward with the title of the informational page: "The Historic House Style Gallery." This is about the maximum length you can reasonably use in a title—35 to 40 characters *including the spaces*—without fear of Netscape cutting it off. (Internet Explorer browsers give you almost the entire width of the browser window for your title but more people use Netscape, so you should be conservative and aim for the middle.)

The <META> Tag

If the brevity of the titles we just chose troubles you because you feel they're not descriptive or inclusive enough, here's a tag to ease your concerns: <META>. And here's how it works:

```
<META NAME="keywords" CONTENT="mula, dinero,
cash, accountants, accounting, taxes, IRAs,
retirement, financial planning, estate planning,
wills, bequests, inheritance, stocks, bonds,
futures, investments, investors, investing">
```

<META> is the tag search engines use to compare the text of a web page against the keywords a searcher uses. So if somebody is using Excite or HotBot to look for a new financial advisor and they type "investing" in the search field, Mula Dinero & Cash's web site will be among the list of sites that match their search. If we did not use the <META> tag to assign keywords to this site, the would-be client would be less likely to find it using a keyword search in a search engine.

The best feature of the keywords value is that there's no limit to the number of keywords you can assign. So get out your thesaurus, brainstorm, and come up with as many good keywords as you can think of, and use this tag and attribute combination for all it's worth. It might make the difference in whether or not your site is seen by the audience you're seeking.

Another effective way to use the <META> tag to help visitors find your page is to use the NAME and CONTENT attributes like this:

```
<META NAME="description" CONTENT="A gallery of
American residential architectural styles popular
between 1750 and 1950.">
```

When you specify the description value with the NAME attribute, the phrase or paragraph of text you write following CONTENT will appear on a search engine's results page, rather than the first bit of plain text on the web page itself. This way, you can zero in on the essence of your web page, and give potential visitors a quick summary of what they can expect to find.

A few side notes worth mentioning: To use both NAME keywords and NAME description in the same document, you must use the META tag twice. (This is one of the few times in HTML you can do this.) Also, make sure you understand the specifics of using the CONTENT attribute correctly in both circumstances. Too often a search for a web page will turn up a string of keywords listed as a site's description, which makes a poor impression of both the web site and its author's HTML skills.

Important <BODY> Elements

We know you're familiar with the basic <BODY> elements: <P> and <BR> for text, <IMG> for images, and <A> for links. But we haven't discussed how to manipulate and position page content using these tags and their attributes. So let's have a discussion about margins, spacing, and general page appearance using <BODY> tag attributes and values.

Simple Positioning with <BODY> Tags

The P in <P> stands for paragraph, and the BR in <BR> stands for line break, but understanding how to use these tags effectively is not so simple. Let's refer back to the basic benchmark/HTML page for an example. (See Figures 8.7 through 8.10.)

The figure captions list the three main comparisons you should make and remember between Netscape and Microsoft browsers, and between the PC and the Macintosh: type size, the presence or absence of automatic line breaks, and the width of the buffer zone (if any) between graphics and any text nearby. These disparities are, for now, written in stone and cannot be changed. But we can still get around them and/or learn to live with them through wise design choices.

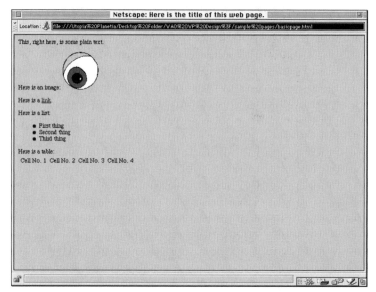

FIGURE 8.7. The benchmark in NN4 for the Mac revisited: smaller type, automatic line breaks after the <P> tag, and a smaller buffer zone between the eyeball GIF and surrounding text

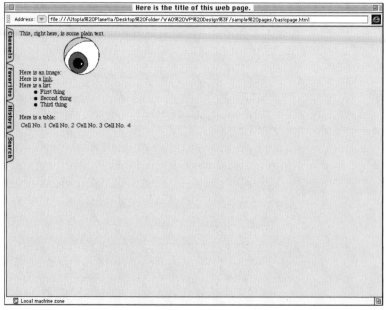

FIGURE 8.8. The benchmark in IE4 for the Mac revisited: smaller type, no automatic line break after the <P> tag nor a buffer zone between the eyeball GIF and surrounding text

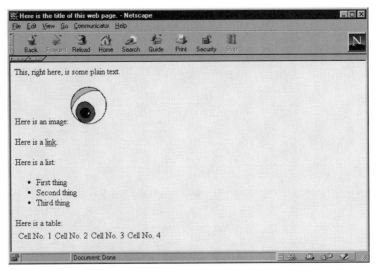

FIGURE 8.9. The benchmark in NN4 for the PC revisited: larger type, lots of space between lines of text, a larger buffer zone between the eyeball GIF and surrounding text—and a default white background, not gray like the others

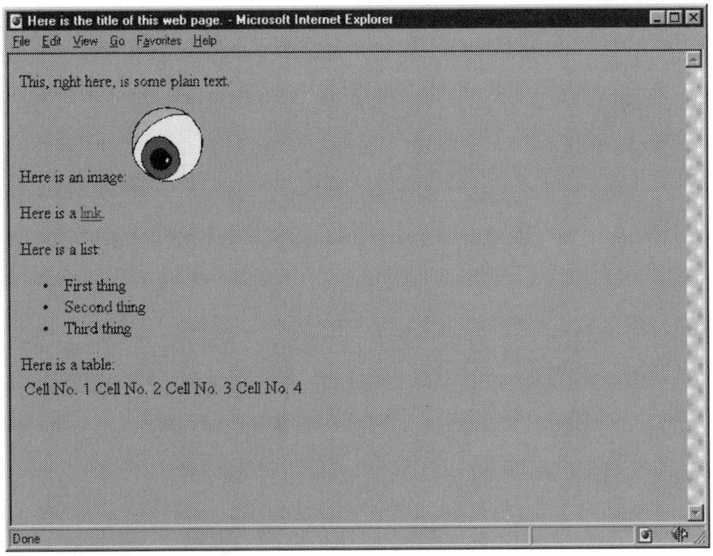

FIGURE 8.10. The benchmark in IE4 for the PC revisited: larger type, lots of space between lines of text, a larger buffer zone between the eyeball GIF and surrounding text

Let's bring up the personal under-construction page to get started. (See Figures 8.11 and 8.12.)

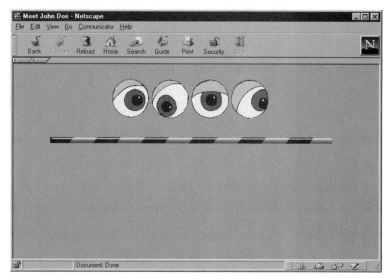

FIGURE 8.11. persUC.html in NN4 for the PC

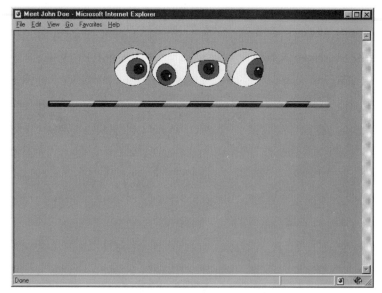

FIGURE 8.12. persUC.html in IE4 for the PC

Who's Afraid of Web Page Design?

This UC page will become the entryway to the final personal web site, with each of the four eyeballs linking the visitor to four secondary pages: one each for John Doe, Jane Doe, Jack Doe, and Jill Doe. So let's get rid of the under-construction bar and arrange these other four GIFs more effectively on the page.

We can arrange the four GIFs in a square using the ALIGN attribute of the <P> tag and judicious use of the <BR> tag. First, open persUC.html in your browser and save a copy of it as doe.html so you won't overwrite your changes onto the original file. The HTML for persUC.html looks like this:

```
<HTML>
<HEAD>
<TITLE>Meet John Doe</TITLE>
</HEAD>
<BODY BGCOLOR="#ff9900">
<BR>
<P><CENTER><IMG SRC="eye1.gif">
<IMG SRC="eye2.gif">
<IMG SRC="eye3.gif">
<IMG SRC="eye4.gif"></CENTER></P7>
<BR>
<P><CENTER><IMG SRC="UCbar2.gif></CENTER></P>
</BODY>
</HTML>
```

First, remove the UC bar and everything else on that line. For kicks, remove the <CENTER> and </CENTER> tag around the eye GIFs to see what it looks like. (We'll talk about align tags next.) Now add a second <P> tag before the <IMG> tag containing eye3.gif, so that the HTML looks like this:

```
<HTML>
<HEAD>
<TITLE>Meet John Doe<TITLE>
</HEAD>
<BODY BGCOLOR="#ff9900">
<BR>
<P><IMG SRC="eye1.gif">
<IMG SRC="eye2.gif">
```

```
<P><IMG SRC="eye3.gif">
<IMG SRC="eye4.gif">
<BR>
</BODY>
</HTML>
```

Now the eyeballs are separated onto two lines, albeit packed together in the upper left corner of the screen. (See Figures 8.13 and 8.14.)

Let's move the whole group of eyeballs toward the middle of the page. We'll use the ALIGN attribute for the <P> tag like so:

```
<P ALIGN=center><IMG SRC="eye1.gif">
<P ALIGN=center><IMG SRC="eye3.gif">
```

The ALIGN attribute for the <P> tag has three values—right, left, and center—with left being the **default**, or where the text/graphics will automatically be placed by the browser if nothing different is specified. This is an all-or-nothing, imprecise way of moving elements around a web page, but it's also the simplest.

You can also use the ALIGN attribute with the <IMG> tag, with varying results and unreliable support between browsers. Here are all the possible ALIGN values, with an explanation of what they do:

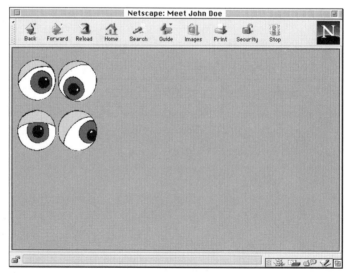

FIGURE 8.13. doe.html in NN4 for the Mac

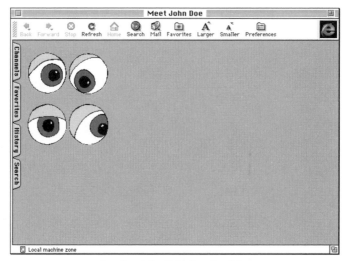

FIGURE 8.14. doe.html in IE4 for the Mac

bottom The bottom edge of the graphic is aligned with the bottom line of the next graphic or corresponding text.

left The graphic "floats" on the page with its left side flush against the edge of the browser window while the corresponding graphic or text flows around it.

middle The exact middle line of the graphic is aligned with the baseline of the next graphic or corresponding text.

right The graphic "floats" on the page with its right side flush against the edge of the browser window, while the corresponding graphic or text flows around it.

top Any corresponding text or graphic is aligned with the top edge of the graphic. (This is the ALIGN attribute's default setting in both Netscape Navigator and Microsoft Internet Explorer.)

Take a few minutes now to incorporate these values of <IMG> ALIGN to see what they do to the four eyeballs. View the results in both Navigator and Explorer to see how each browser interprets this HTML.

Amy: So the HTML with these values looks like:
`<IMG SRC="eye1.gif" ALIGN=bottom>` Correct?

Rebecca: Pretty much—there are good arguments for always placing the value (in this case, bottom) in quotes just to be safe. But for version 4, and usually version 3, browsers it's not necessary.

Amy: I can really see the difference between the browsers when I use the "middle" value on eye1.gif. NN4 set the two top eyeballs farther apart and at a greater angle than IE4. I can see how this can be a problem if you're trying to place a lot of graphics using the ALIGN attribute.

Rebecca: Yes, ALIGN is only good in simple situations such as this one. Read on, though, for more sophisticated solutions to positioning—and we'll revisit the <A> tag a little more thoroughly in Chapter 10, "Adding Multimedia and More."

It is extremely important that you learn to feel comfortable experimenting with HTML. Unless you try different attributes and values, and unless you try different attributes and values in different situations, you will never acquire a thorough understanding of how HTML works. This is the best and the worst of the HTML language all at once—it's flexible, so that the same tag, attribute, and value you might use successfully on one page might be a bad choice on another. Yet it's also very rigid, so you cannot rely exclusively on proper syntax to determine whether or not your coding is "correct." So let's repeat something we said in the preface to this book: You are not just learning a new pastime or hobby you can do in a couple of hours; you are learning a state of mind you can only develop with practice.

Now that we've learned simple HTML positioning just using tags, attributes, and values alone, let's move on to a more intermediate method: the "pixel.gif" trick.

Positioning with the "pixel.gif" Trick

This handy little gimmick for positioning elements on a web page makes use of the <IMG> tag and its HEIGHT, WIDTH and ALIGN attributes. We will take a tiny transparent GIF image that's merely one pixel high and one pixel wide and use it to "push" all the other elements on our web page into position.

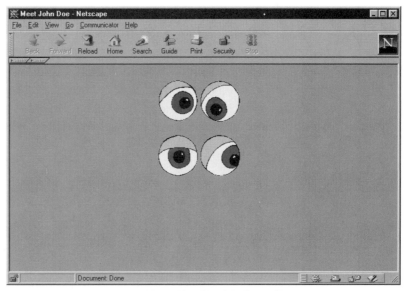

FIGURE 8.15. doe.html in NN4 PC, with final alignment

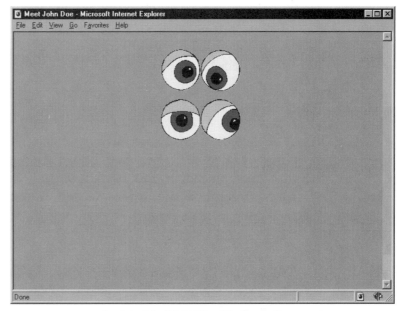

FIGURE 8.16. doe.html in IE4 PC, with final alignment

First, go to the book's CD-ROM and copy pixel.gif into the folder on your desktop or hard drive with all the other practice files you're using to complete the exercises in this book. Now open your HTML editor if you haven't already done so, and let's start coding.

The idea behind this trick is simple: we begin with the transparent one-pixel by one-pixel GIF to establish a fairly uniform size (images are not affected by the size disparities between the PC and the Macintosh and/or Netscape Navigator and/or Microsoft Internet Explorer).

Then we trick browsers into thinking this GIF is taller and wider than it actually is by giving it absolute size instructions in the form of HEIGHT and WIDTH values. So the browser creates an area for the GIF on your web page that's much larger than it really needs, scooting over everything else around it. (This is part of the HTML I used on the Pyramid main page to position those eight Egyptian figures on the wall of hieroglyphics.)

In the last section, we succeeded in creating an evenly distributed cube shape for the four eyeballs on the personal home page just by manipulating the <P> tag. But we did not try to use the <P> and <BR> tags to position the eyeballs vertically—that is, to push them further down the browser window into a more centralized position. This is because <P>, <BR>, <PRE>, and other plain HTML tags designed to give you blank space on a web page do not work reliably when the blank space must be large. Internet Explorer, for example, will not recognize more than one <BR> tag if you place a string of them in your HTML to create many blank lines. And the <PRE> tag is chancy in either Navigator or Explorer because it's intended for use with preformatted text, not blank space.

First, create a simple <IMG> tag string and place it within the HTML for doe.html:

```
<HTML>
<HEAD>
<TITLE>Meet John Doe</TITLE>
</HEAD>
<BODY BGCOLOR="#ff9900">
<BR>
<IMG SRC="pixel.gif" ALIGN= HEIGHT= WIDTH=>
```

```
<P ALIGN=center><IMG SRC="eye1.gif" HSPACE=6
VSPACE=1>
<IMG SRC="eye2.gif" HSPACE=6 VSPACE=1>
<P ALIGN=center><IMG SRC="eye3.gif" HSPACE=6
VSPACE=1>
<IMG SRC="eye4.gif" HSPACE=6 VSPACE=1>
<BR>
</BODY>
</HTML>
```

You should place these instructions before that first <P> tag so pixel.gif will not be positioned next to the first eyeball. Choose bottom as the value for ALIGN, and 1 (one) as the value for WIDTH—we are mucking about with vertical space, remember, so the HEIGHT attribute measurement is most important. Now you can begin positioning the eyeball cube farther down the page by assigning an arbitrary HEIGHT value—try 30 for starters—and then increasing or decreasing it as you please. (We are satisfied with a value of 55, so that's what will appear in this page's HTML for the rest of the book.)

Amy: The numbers (such as 55) represent a quantity of pixels, correct?

Rebecca: Yes, you can always assume that a number such as 55 in this case refers to a pixel measurement, unless you are told otherwise or unless there's a sign of some sort—such as a percentage (%) sign, which you can use in forms.

Figures 8.17 and 8.18 demonstrate a comparison of the eyeball cube after the last section, and after the <IMG> tag is added with pixel.gif in this section.

Now let's combine both the last two sections with the <TABLE> tag to demonstrate the most precise positioning of all.

Positioning with the <TABLE> Tag

<TABLE> Tag HTML

The <TABLE> tag had a relatively humble beginning as the friend of scientists looking for neat little charts in which to put their numbers

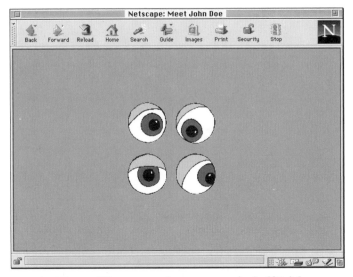

FIGURE 8.17. The personal page sans pixel.gif trick...

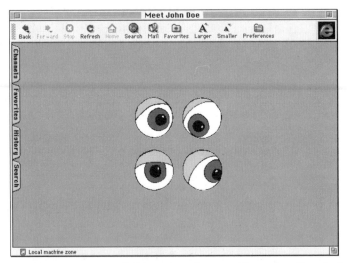

FIGURE 8.18. ...and the personal page after using the pixel.gif trick

and other calculations. Today it has been recruited (to use a nice word) for other purposes, most popularly as a way of enhancing the other primitive positioning HTML tags we've already visited. A word of warning, then: We are getting into one of those areas where HTML purists sometimes scowl and complain about improper usage. But the <TABLE> tag does work for positioning, and it works relatively well.

Here is all the HTML that goes into creating a table, for those of you who haven't used the <TABLE> tag in this manner before.

```
<TABLE>
<TR>
<TD>Cell No. 1</TD><TD>Cell No. 2</TD>
</TR>
<TR>
<TD>Cell No. 3</TD><TD>Cell No. 4</TD>
</TR>
</TABLE>
```

The <TABLE> tag itself works like the <BODY> and the <HEAD> tags; it specifies everything between <TABLE> and </TABLE> as belonging, as you may have guessed, in table format. <TR> specifies any information pertaining to one row in a table (such as Cell #1 and Cell #2, above), while <TD> specifies any information pertaining to one cell in a table (such as Cell #3). You can also control columns of cells within a table (such as Cell #2 and Cell #4) though columns are not specified by means of a particular HTML tag as cells and rows are here with <TD> and <TR>.

The <TABLE>, <TR>, and <TD> tags possess many attributes that control appearance, alignment, internal and external spacing, and more. Here is a quick reference for the most useful and reliable crossplatform attributes for the <TABLE> tag, their values, and what function they serve.

<TABLE>

BGCOLOR   Specifies a background color for all cells in the table, either by hexadecimal value or by color name.

BORDER   Specifies the presence and width of the border around each cell, row, and column in a table in pixels (a value of zero makes this border invisible).

CELLPADDING   Specifies the amount of blank space between a cell border and its contents in pixels.

CELLSPACING   Specifies the amount of blank space between two cells.

COLS   Specifies the number of columns in a table so browsers can load up a table more quickly.

HEIGHT   Specifies the exact table height in pixels; must be used in conjunction with a WIDTH setting.

WIDTH   Specifies the exact table width in pixels; must be used in conjunction with a WIDTH setting.

`<TR>`

ALIGN   Specifies the horizontal alignment of text within all the cells in a single row (values are center, justify, left, and right); works in conjunction with VALIGN.

VALIGN   Specifies the vertical alignment of text within all the cells in a single row (values are baseline, bottom, middle, and top); works in conjunction with ALIGN.

`<TD>`

ALIGN   Specifies the horizontal alignment of an individual cell's contents (values are center, justify, left, and right); works in conjunction with VALIGN.

COLSPAN   Specifies an individual cell as being more than one column wide.

ROWSPAN   Specifies an individual cell as being more than one row wide.

VALIGN   Controls the vertical alignment of a cell's contents (values are baseline, bottom, middle, and top); works in conjunction with ALIGN.

These are the attributes and values you will use to control how individual areas of a table appear on your web page. We will not be using all of them in this book, but you might find them useful later on as you create other web pages on your own.

There are also several Internet Explorer-only attributes for these three tags that may or may not be reliably supported by Navigator in the future. There is supposedly an ALIGN attribute for the `<TABLE>` tag, and a BGCOLOR attribute for both the `<TR>` and `<TD>` tags, for example. And all three tags supposedly have BACKGROUND, BORDERCOLOR, BORDERCOLORDARK, and BORDERCOLOR-LIGHT attributes, which specify individual background patterns, solid background colors, and/or contrasting dark and light borders around cells for a 3-D effect. However, at this writing you should only use them in page designs where their impact is optional.

Applying the <TABLE> Tag

Now let's put all of this HTML to use. Open your HTML editor and bring up the Historic House Gallery site UC page—infoUC1.htm.

Here's what the HTML should look like before we begin.

```
<HTML>
<HEAD>
<TITLE>The Historic House Style Gallery</TITLE>
<META NAME="description" CONTENT="A gallery of
American residential architectural styles popular
between 1750 and 1950.">
</HEAD>
<BODY BACKGROUND="infoslice.gif">
<P>
<TABLE BORDER=0 CELLSPACING=0 CELLPADDING=0
WIDTH=600>
<TR>
<TD WIDTH=95 ALIGN=left VALIGN=top>
<P><IMG SRC="salem1s.jpg"><BR>
<P><IMG SRC="salem4s.jpg"><BR>
<P><IMG SRC="salem5s.jpg"><BR>
<P><IMG SRC="salem2s.jpg"><BR>
</TD>
<TD WIDTH=35>
</TD>
<TD WIDTH=470 ALIGN=left VALIGN=top>
<P><B><FONT FACE=Arial SIZE="+3" COLOR="blue">The
Historic House Style Gallery</B></FONT>
<P>
<IMG SRC="pixel.gif" HEIGHT=25 WIDTH=1>
<CENTER><B><FONT FACE="ARIAL" SIZE=+2
```

```
COLOR="#996633">Coming Soon :</FONT></CENTER></B>
<UL>
<LI TYPE=square>A gallery of historical residen-
tial styles built in America between 1750 and
1950<LI TYPE=square>Background information on
trends and architects behind each style
<LI TYPE=square>Background information on trends
and architects behind each style
<LI TYPE=square>Examples from across the country,
including regional adaptations
<LI TYPE=square>Notable architectural details and
features of each style
</UL>
<P>Questions? Submissions? Email <A
HREF="mailto:curator@hhsg.com">curator@hhsg.com</
A>.
</TD>
</TABLE>
</BODY>
</HTML>
```

Amy: I should have asked this question in an earlier chapter, but I just noticed this bit of HTML: <LI TYPE=square>. The LI is for "list item," I know, which usually comes with a round bullet. I hadn't seen the attribute TYPE before: is that for the type of bullet, the value of which is square?

Rebecca: Yes, there are a couple different kinds of bullets you can apply to a <UL> list, but that's getting a little bit ahead of ourselves. (I don't mean to stick in HTML we'll cover in the near future, but it makes for nice teasers.)

Figures 8.19 and 8.20 show what this code looks like on the Web. Notice first of all that quite a bit of the important positioning on this page was accomplished using the simple techniques we've already covered. The <P> tag inserted by itself between the <BODY> and <TABLE> tags is the reason that there's a little blank space at the top of the web page. Without it, the page loads up with the top edge of

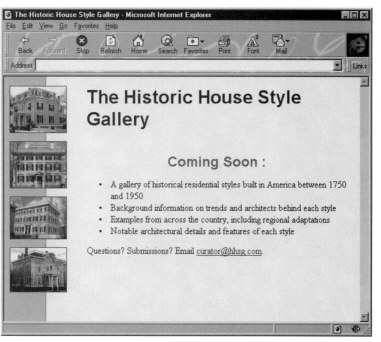

FIGURE 8.19. The Historic House Gallery UC page in Internet Explorer 4 for the PC

FIGURE 8.20. The Historic House Gallery UC page in Internet Explorer 4 for the Mac

the first house photograph right up against the top of the browser window. Also note that the pixel.gif trick was used to separate the blue and brown headers, lending a little breathing and reading room to the top half of the page design.

Now, however, let's turn our attention to this use of the <TABLE> tag. We'll chop out the pertinent HTML here below one cell at a time to make it easier. Here's the first cell in the table, along with the <TABLE> tag:

```
<TABLE BORDER=0 CELLSPACING=0 CELLPADDING=0
WIDTH=600>
<TR>
<TD WIDTH=95 ALIGN=left VALIGN=top>
<P><IMG SRC="salem1s.jpg"><BR>
<P><IMG SRC="salem4s.jpg"><BR>
<P><IMG SRC="salem5s.jpg"><BR>
<P><IMG SRC="salem2s.jpg"><BR>
</TD>
```

Let's take the <TABLE> attributes and their values first. The <TABLE> tag on this web page encloses all the text and graphics, so that everything can be properly positioned with the slice background in mind. The BORDER attribute has been established at zero so that the borders that usually surround the edges of each cell are invisible, or zero pixels wide. CELLSPACING and CELLPADDING have also been established at zero so that the edges of the table cell will coincide precisely with the edges of the house photos. Most of the time this is the value you'll want to set, because it provides the most precision. Finally, the WIDTH of the table has been established at 600 pixels, the standard "default" setting you should fix in your mind as the ideal browser window width. This is based on the fact that the most popular screen size is still 640 by 480.

Now skip down a few lines to the first <TD> tag, specifying the first table cell, which contains the four house photographs. The ALIGN and VALIGN attributes have been established as left and top respectively so that the upper left corner of the first photo is flush with the edge of the table (again, for precision, as in the CELLSPACING and CELLPADDING example in the previous paragraph). The

WIDTH value, however, is the key to positioning these photos. Take a little time now to increase and decrease this pixel setting and see how it affects the entire layout of this web page. Cell width is unlike overall table width in that each increment one pixel up or one pixel down can have a profound effect on your entire web page design. (With this in mind, you should always jot down your original setting so you don't forget it.)

> **Amy:** Design question: So your slice GIF background is designed so that the right one-third of each JPEG will hang out over the light-yellow main area of the page, correct? I hadn't thought of doing that; I was designing my slice GIF in the last chapter to have the blue left margin end evenly between the column of pictures and the left edge of the text. I didn't get the dimensions of the blue area right, though. Not yet, anyway.

> **Rebecca:** Both design strategies have merit if you take the visitor's assumptions into account. You can use a vertical edge to make a clean separation between different areas on a web page, or you can offset it a little as a means of emphasis. I thought the offset gold stripe on this page would help tie together all the different colored houses on the main page, especially because they're not links. If the gold part of the slice GIF lay wholly behind the houses, visitors to the page might misinterpret the house graphics as buttons on some sort of unlabeled navigation bar. Then my design strategy would have looked like an HTML mistake.

Here's the HTML for the other two cells in this table, though the closing </TD> tag is missing for the second one.

```
<TD WIDTH=35>
</TD>
<TD WIDTH=470 ALIGN=left VALIGN=top>
```

This second cell is used to establish the amount of vertical space between the right edges of the house photos and the left margin of the text, hence the WIDTH setting of 35 pixels. Finally, the third and last table cell affects the positioning of the text itself, so the closing </TD> tag is way down at the bottom of page just before the </TABLE> tag.

Its WIDTH value here is 470 pixels, but it, combined with all the WIDTH values of a table's cells, should always total whatever you establish as the <TABLE> WIDTH.

In other words, in this particular situation 95 + 35 + 470 = 600, the WIDTH value established at the top of the HTML document in the <TABLE> tag. Why does this need to happen? If you don't coordinate the combined widths of cells in your tables, your page will take more time to load up as browsers will need to spend more time "thinking" through the dimensions of your page. Your visitors won't get an error, and your page will eventually load up, but you will have caused needless waiting.

> **Amy:** So you're saying to always include the HTML <TABLE WIDTH=600> (as well as border, cell padding and cell spacing specifications) right when you introduce the table itself, so that the page will load more quickly? Or are you saying that the *width* needs to always be 600?

> **Rebecca:** Both. You must always declare a <TABLE> width at the beginning, *and* I also recommend a total measurement of 600 pixels to get your table contents centered properly on the average monitor screen.

One quick comment before we move along: Learning to use the <TABLE> tag efficiently was one of the most frustrating and time-consuming tasks I (Rebecca) ever undertook in learning HTML. It is very easy to add a few pixel-widths here without remembering to subtract a few pixel-widths there, or to spend a good five to ten minutes tweaking the position of one single graphic. So ... as you noodle around with the <TABLE> tag in conjunction with your own web pages, schedule yourself *lots* of time. Don't sit down "just for a minute" in the beginning to "fix just this one thing," or you'll likely be pulling your hair out ten minutes later. I tell you that from personal experience on behalf of my own poor scalp.

Now let's tackle the use of frames, the ultimate and most-maligned positioning HTML tool.

Positioning with Frames

The Truth about Frames

Let's make this clear right from the start, before we even touch frames HTML: There are *many* people on the Web who loathe frames. They hate them. They view them with a most profound abhorrence, as one of my favorite novelists would say.

This certainly doesn't make for a very encouraging introduction to this particular tag, but you should be forewarned. If you design your web page using frames, there are indeed people who will leave your site immediately upon first glimpse, unless you have designed a completely separate page without frames they can choose instead. That's the bad news, part one.

The bad news, part two, is that there are relatively decent reasons to, er, dislike frames. Most early browsers (versions 2 or earlier, plus non-Netscape and -Internet Explorer products) do not recognize frames-based HTML. Also, visitors looking at a frames page cannot bookmark it, and if the web page author hasn't coded his or her frames pages properly, visitors cannot use the Back button to get to their previous location and exit out. On top of these functional problems, frames are also considered by some design authorities to be somewhat ugly unless they are "seamless"—without borders.

On the other hand, there are design advantages from a functional standpoint. It's nice to have your site menu stay put in the same place, all the time, for example. Or to put banner ads in their own special frame so any GIF animations, JavaScripts, or other doodads can load and reload without affecting the usability of the rest of the page. So don't dismiss the benefits of frames out of hand because of the drawbacks, either. You must consider your entire site plan when you consider how frames works.

Frames HTML

When you look at a web page that uses frames, you are actually looking at the results of your browser loading up a set of several small web pages. Each individual frame displays one individual HTML document—three documents for three frames, and so forth. So in order to create the look of one web page with, say, four frames, you will have to create five separate web pages: four to tell the browser what information to load in each frame, and one to tell the browser how to arrange all the frames together.

The two primary HTML tags used to create frames pages are `<FRAMESET>` and `<FRAME>`. `<FRAMESET>` functions like the `<TABLE>` tag in that it tells the browser everything inside it should be displayed in frames; similarly, the `<FRAME>` tag specifies the contents of one particular frame just as the `<TD>` tag specifies all information inside a table cell.

The `<FRAMESET>` and `<FRAME>` tags possess many attributes that control functionality, alignment, internal and external spacing, and more. Here is a quick reference for the most useful and reliable crossplatform attributes for these tags, their values, and the purpose they serve.

`<FRAMESET>`

ALIGN   Specifies the alignment of an individual frame within a frameset with respect to any surrounding text (values are bottom, center, left, right, and top).

FRAMEBORDER   Specifies the presence (with a value of 1) or the absence (with a value of zero) of the default three-dimensional border around an individual frame. The border will appear by default unless this attribute is used with a corresponding value of zero.

MARGINHEIGHT   Specifies the amount of vertical space between the contents of a frame and its border in pixels. Used in conjunction with MARGINWIDTH.

MARGINWIDTH   Specifies the amount of horizontal space between the contents of a frame and its border in pixels. Used in conjunction with MARGINHEIGHT.

NORESIZE   Prevents the browser from resizing a specified frame if the visitor changes the width or height of the browser window.

SCROLLING   Specifies the presence (with a value of yes) or the absence (with a value of no) of a click-and-drag slider bar in the specified frame. The slider bar will appear by default if a frame's contents exceed its size and unless this attribute is used with a corresponding value of no.

SRC   Specifies the file name or URL of the HTML document to be displayed in the corresponding frame.

<FRAME>

COLS   Specifies the creation of a frame within a vertical column on the web page in pixels (with a numerical value), as a percentage of the overall browser window area (with a numerical value plus a percentage sign %), or as a relative size (with an asterisk *).

Amy: What do you mean by "as a relative size"? And does the asterisk stand alone as a value, as in <FRAME COLS=*>, or does it stand with a number, as in <FRAME COLS=300, *>?

Rebecca: <FRAME COLS=300, *> is correct, and I'll explain why in just a few pages.

FRAMEBORDER   Specifies the presence (with a value of 1) or the absence (with a value of zero) of the default three-dimensional border around an individual frame. The border will appear by default unless this attribute is used with a corresponding value of zero.

FRAMESPACING   Specifies the amount of space between individual frames in pixels.

ROWS   Specifies the size and number of horizontal rows within a frames document in pixels (with numerical values), as a percentage of the overall browser window area (with numerical value plus a percentage sign %), or as a relative size (with an asterisk * and a numerical value).

SCROLLING   Specifies the presence (with a value of yes) or the absence (with a value of no) of a click-and-drag slider bar in the specified frame. The slider bar will appear by default if a frame's contents exceed its size and unless this attribute is used with a corresponding value of no.

Again, as when we explored the <TABLE> tag in the previous section, we will not be using all these attributes. It is up to you to experiment on your own to learn how these tags and attributes work in different web pages. Now, though, let's apply what we've learned by creating a new main page for the business site.

Applying Frames HTML: The Main Page

Before we delve into writing frames pages, open your HTML editor and the browser of your choice, and put in the CD-ROM.

We will be creating a main home page for Mula, Dinero & Cash with two frames. One will run vertically along the left side containing the site menu and the MDC logo, and a second will constitute the rest of the browser window where the visitor can view the rest of the web site's contents. Start by opening bhome1.htm in your HTML editor. The HTML looks like this:

```
<HTML>
<HEAD>
<TITLE>Mula Dinero & Cash, Accountants</TITLE>
<META NAME="keywords" CONTENT="mula, dinero,
cash, accountants, accounting, taxes, IRAs,
retirement, financial planning, estate planning,
wills, bequests, inheritance, stocks, bonds,
futures, investments, investors, investing">
</HEAD>
<FRAMESET>
</FRAMESET>
</HTML>
```

Now here are a few general notes about frames HTML: If you noticed that the <BODY> tag is missing, it's deliberate. (And you're developing a good eye!) The first rule of frames HTML is that you

cannot use \<FRAME\> and \<BODY\> in the same document, or nothing will appear on the screen. You also cannot use \<FRAMESET\> by itself without specifying something with the \<FRAME\> tag within it. So don't test the HTML we wrote just yet.

The two attributes of \<FRAMESET\> that determine general layout are COLS (columns) and ROWS (uh, rows). Which do you use in your base frameset—the \<FRAMESET\> tag we've already written in? If you want a vertical frame area extending completely across the screen, either on the left or on the right—or if there are no frame areas extending all the way across the screen in either direction—you need to begin by establishing a COLS value. Otherwise, if there are only horizontal frame areas on your page, begin with ROWS.

We do want a horizontal frame area along the top edge of our page, so let's begin by inserting this HTML:

```
<HTML>
<HEAD>
<TITLE>Mula Dinero & Cash, Accountants</TITLE>
<META NAME="keywords" CONTENT="mula, dinero,
cash, accountants, accounting, taxes, IRAs,
retirement, financial planning, estate planning,
wills, bequests, inheritance, stocks, bonds,
futures, investments, investors, investing">
</HEAD>
<FRAMESET ROWS="18%, 82%"
<FRAME SRC="lhead.html">
<FRAME SRC="info.html">
</FRAMESET>
</HTML>
```

The pair of percentages tells the browser to divide the page into two horizontal frames, one at 18% of the window's width and the other at 82%. We do this first because of the way Netscape interprets each \<FRAMESET\> definition; it can divide a page horizontally or vertically, but not both, and ROWS is the attribute it prefers to work with first.

Amy: Does Internet Explorer interpret the \<FRAMESET\> definition differently than Netscape? Apparently we don't have to be as concerned with that. Why?

Rebecca: IE interprets <FRAMESET> differently only with regard to things we've already covered—text is larger, spacing is different, and so on. Establishing ROWS first is a Netscape-only precaution, nothing more.

Now, to divide the top horizontal frame and achieve the final look we outlined in our sketch, we're going to nest a second frameset within the first. Here's the HTML:

```
<FRAMESET COLS="23%, 77%">
<FRAME SRC="menu.html" NAME="left">
<FRAMESET ROWS="18%, 82%">
<FRAME SRC="lhead.html" NAME="rtop" SCROLLING=no>
<FRAME SRC="info.html" NAME="rbottom">
</FRAMESET>
```

Amy: Now I'm really confused. I thought we were going to specify the ROWS first because that's what Netscape likes to read first. And I still don't get the part about why we do the ROWS first because of the way Netscape can "divide a page horizontally or vertically, but not both."

Oh, wait; are we inserting the COLS first in the HTML to force the browser to split the page vertically first, and then to split the second column horizontally, so we have a menu frame running the height of the left margin? If that is so, why did you want us to write out the ROWS HTML first, before the COLS?

Rebecca: Frames are confusing, aren't they? You did touch on the answer in your second paragraph, though.

If you only want vertical *or* horizontal frames, then you use the <FRAMESET> tag once and just COLS or ROWS. However, if you want vertical *and* horizontal frames, as we do in our sample site, things get even more complicated. (That is, you write your frames HTML with one expectation, and your browser turns out something utterly and completely different.)

As you've already seen in the HTML above, when you want both vertical and horizontal frames, you **nest** (tuck) one <FRAMESET>

tag inside another. Now, when you specify ROWS in the outside frameset and COLS in the inside frameset, your browser will divide rows into columns. When you reverse the settings by specifying COLS in the outside frameset and ROWS in the inside frameset, the browser will divide columns into rows. Look here:

```
<HTML>
<FRAMESET ROWS="33%, 33%, 34%">
<FRAMESET COLS= "49%, 51%">
<FRAME SRC=one.html>
<FRAME SRC=two.html>
</FRAMESET>
<FRAME SRC=three.html>
<FRAME SRC=four.html>
</FRAMESET>
</HTML>
```

If we write our frames HTML like this, specifying three rows and two columns, the browser starts dividing up rows first and then columns like the ones in Figure 8.21.

Get it?

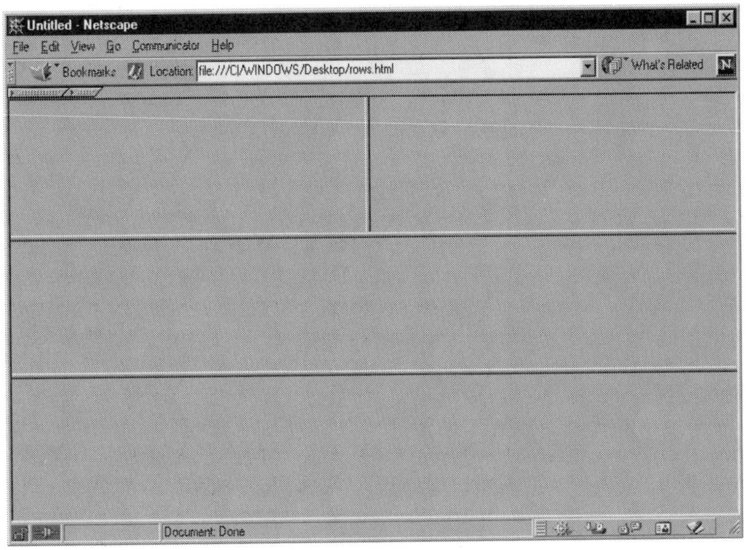

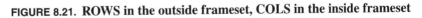

FIGURE 8.21. ROWS in the outside frameset, COLS in the inside frameset

Amy: Got it! You can write either ROWS or COLS first as you decide the layout dimensions of your page, but you must *place* them in the order you want the browser to read them.

You could specify ROWS and COLS as two specific measurements in pixels or as one specific measurement in percentages or pixels plus an asterisk. The asterisk means "and everything else"—it's a relative measurement in relation to whatever else you specify. But we prefer percentages. They're not fixed as pixel measurements would be, but they are precise, although a visitor to your web page can still resize the browser window and get good results.

Amy: So to use an asterisk, would you write <FRAMESET ROWS="200,*">? Then would the first row be 200 pixels wide while the second row took up the rest of the screen?

Rebecca: Yes, that's it exactly. But if we switch the attributes, specifying COLS in the outside frameset and ROWS in the inside frameset, the browser starts dividing up columns first and then rows, as in Figure 8.22.

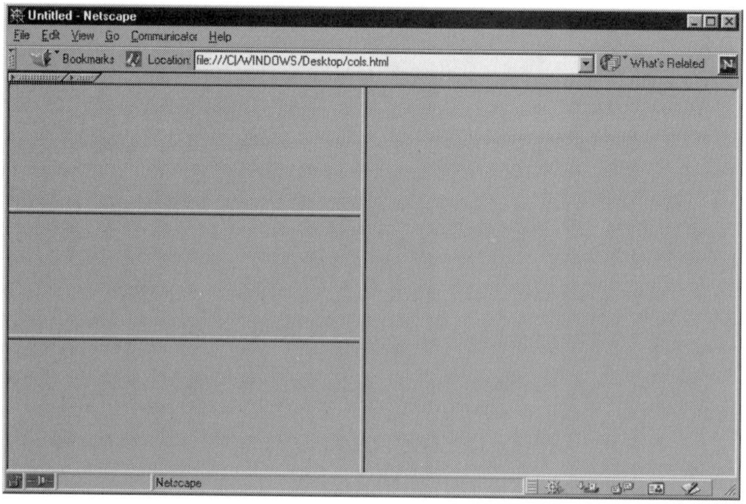

FIGURE 8.22.   COLS in the outside frameset, ROWS in the inside frameset

Amy: Do we prefer percentages because they adjust better to different screen and window sizes?

Rebecca: Yes, but the word *prefer* is the catch there. I prefer and recommend percentages for the very reason you mentioned. But there are good reasons to use a fixed measurement for a frame—you don't have to use the same combination of measurements throughout, either. You can use percentages in one frameset and a pixel measurement plus an asterisk in another, depending upon your design.

The only situation in which I would suggest using a firm, pixel-based measurement with an asterisk is if you had a graphic such as an imagemap or button bar. You would establish the width or height of the frame to the dimensions of the graphic, so then visitors would always see the logo no matter how much they mess with the browser window, even at the expense of other frames. But as I already said, this is what I prefer. Other designers will tell you something else.

Finally, let's use the <NOFRAMES> tag to insert a little message for visitors to this page who are using a very early browser:

```
<NOFRAMES>
<BODY BGCOLOR="#ccffcc" TEXT="#006600"
LINK="#0000FF" ALINK="#ccffcc" VLINK="FF0000">
<P>This web page requires frames, but your
browser can't read them. Call MDC instead at
(101) 555-2345 or email us at <A
HREF="mailto:info@mdc.com">info@mdc.com</A>.
</BODY>
</NOFRAMES>
```

Now save this file as bhome.html.

Notice that it requires the <BODY> tag, and that we can even established background and link colors. This is the message that would appear if a visitor to your web page were browsing with software that does not support frames. Most people on the Web do not fall into this category, but it's still good "netiquette" to provide this message anyway.

So here's the final HTML for the entire main page, bhome.html:

```
<HTML>
<HEAD>
<TITLE>Mula Dinero & Cash, Accountants</TITLE>
<META NAME="keywords" CONTENT="mula, dinero,
cash, accountants, accounting, taxes, IRAs,
retirement, financial planning, estate planning,
wills, bequests, inheritance, stocks, bonds,
futures, investments, investors, investing">
</HEAD>
<FRAMESET COLS="23%, 77%">
<FRAME SRC="menu.html">
<FRAMESET ROWS="18%, 82%">
<FRAME SRC="lhead.html" NAME="rtop" SCROLLING=no>
<FRAME SRC="info.html" NAME="rbottom">
</FRAMESET>
<NOFRAMES>
<BODY BGCOLOR="#ccffcc" TEXT="#006600"
LINK="#0000FF" ALINK="#ccffcc" VLINK="FF0000">
<P>This web page requires frames, but your
browser can't read them. Call MDC instead at
(101) 555-2345 or email us at <A
HREF="mailto:info@mdc.com">info@mdc.com</A>.
</BODY>
</NOFRAMES>
</FRAMESET>
</HTML>
```

Let's move on to create the three other pages needed to make this frames page work. However, don't close bhome.html in your editor. We'll be creating a link among these four pages—the one we just worked on and the three we'll construct in the next section.

Applying Frames HTML: The Individual Frame Pages

The first thing we will do here is create the individual three pages that will be displayed within the frames page. Here's the first and the simplest, containing the firm's address and so forth: lhead.html:

```
<HTML>
<HEAD>
```

```
<BODY BGCOLOR="#ccffcc">
<P><IMG SRC="lhead.gif">
</BODY>
</HTML>
```

Notice that we decided to go with a different background color, #CCFFCC, a light mint green. You need to establish <BODY> tag attributes here in your individual pages because, remember, you can't use <BODY> within <FRAMESET>.

Here's the second frame page containing the site menu: menu.html:

```
<HTML>
<BODY BGCOLOR="#ccffcc" TEXT="#006600"
LINK="#0000FF" ALINK="#ccffcc" VLINK="FF0000">
<IMG SRC="blogo2.gif">
<FONT FACE="arial, helvetica" SIZE="+1">
<P><A HREF="bhome.html">Home</A>
<P><A HREF="services.html">Services</A>
<P><A HREF="staff.html">Meet Our Staff</A>
<P><A HREF="survey.html">Are You Fiscally Fit?</A>
<P><A HREF="links.html">Links</A>
</FONT>
</BODY>
</HTML>
```

And, finally, here's the third frame page where visitors can see the results of what they choose from the menu: info.html:

```
<HTML>
<BODY BGCOLOR="#ccffcc" TEXT="#006600"
LINK="#0000FF" ALINK="#ccffcc" VLINK="FF0000">
<CENTER>
<FONT FACE=Arial SIZE="+2">
<P>Mula, Dinero & Cash, Accountants
</FONT>
</CENTER>
</BODY>
</HTML>
```

Figures 8.23 and 8.24 show what the final product looks like.

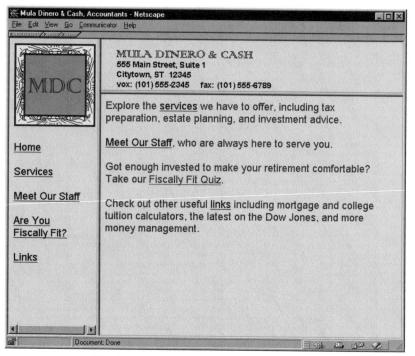

FIGURE 8.23. The MDC frames page in Netscape Navigator 4 for the PC

Amy: I do have one more question. You mentioned earlier that "visitors looking at a frames page cannot bookmark it, and if the web page author hasn't coded his or her frames pages properly, visitors cannot use the Back button to get to their previous location and exit out." I'm assuming that there's no way to get around the bookmarking problem; the visitor has to bookmark the main page and get to a secondary page through the frames menu. But about the browser Back button problem—if we continued to make pages for all the links on the menu.html page in the above site, is it coded so that the visitor can use his or her Back button to navigate this site and to exit it? If it's not in this code, how can we put it in?

Rebecca: Thanks for reminding me. These are actually two separate questions, so let's answer the bookmarking one first.

Bookmarking is asking your browser to remember not the contents of a page, but rather their location. Updates and dead links aside,

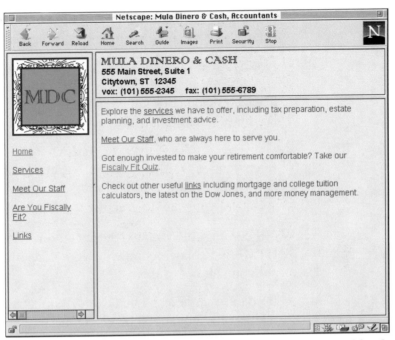

FIGURE 8.24. The MDC frames page in Netscape Navigator 4 for the Mac

this strategy is fine if you're looking at a nonframes page, because its display instructions and its contents are all in one place. The problem with a frames page is that the display instructions and the contents are separate. You can only access the content through a link in the display instructions—if that link changes or disappears, so does the content.

The Back button problem has to do with the NAME and TARGET attributes we'll be learning how to use in the next chapter, so I'll save that discussion until we have the right context.

Review

- Syntax is synonymous with grammar in HTML. It tells you how and where to locate a tag, how to write out its attributes and values, and what other tags can be placed within it. But unlike with real grammar, there are no shortcuts or slang in HTML—you cannot even add or forget one single space, or your code will not work.

- Arrange your opening and closing tags in corresponding ascending and descending order. This will help you read it more easily, and discover whether or not you've left something out. Also, arrange a tag's attributes alphabetically if you're using more than six for one tag for the same reasons.

- Keep your page titles short and sweet. Neither Netscape Navigator nor Microsoft Internet Explorer gives you much room to work with, and you want to grab the user's eye quickly.

- Get comfortable with experimentation. The best way to learn HTML is to play around with your code, make mistakes, and then get yourself out of them.

- If you use more than one table cell on a page, their combined widths must equal 600 pixels. Otherwise your page will take longer to load up because browsers will have to do the math them-selves, and they're slow.

- Consider both the pros and the cons of a frames-based web site. There are legitimate reasons for both opinions. If you do go ahead and decide to use frames, give your visitors a warning in your entryway, and/or provide a non-frames version of your web site as an alternative.

"Answers" to the Exercises

Here is what your HTML should look like after you've completed all the exercises in this chapter.

The HTML for the personal site's home page, doe.html, should look like this:

```
<HTML>
<HEAD>
<TITLE>Meet John Doe</TITLE>
```

```
</HEAD>
<BODY BGCOLOR="#ff9900">
<BR>
<IMG SRC="pixel.gif" ALIGN=bottom HEIGHT=55
WIDTH=1>
<P ALIGN=center>
<IMG SRC="eye1.gif" HSPACE=6 VSPACE=1>
<IMG SRC="eye2.gif" HSPACE=6 VSPACE=1>
<P ALIGN=center><IMG SRC="eye3.gif" HSPACE=6
VSPACE=1>
<IMG SRC="eye4.gif" HSPACE=6 VSPACE=1>
<BR>
</BODY>
</HTML>
```

The HTML for the informational site's main page, infoUC.html, should look like this:

```
<HTML>
<HEAD>
<TITLE>The Historic House Style Gallery</TITLE>
<META NAME="description" CONTENT="A gallery of
American residential architectural styles popular
between 1750 and 1950.">
</HEAD>
<BODY BACKGROUND="infoslice.gif">
<P>
<TABLE BORDER=0 CELLSPACING=0 CELLPADDING=0
WIDTH=600>
<TR>
<TD WIDTH=95 ALIGN=left VALIGN=top>
<P><IMG SRC="salem1s.jpg"><BR>
<P><IMG SRC="salem4s.jpg"><BR>
<P><IMG SRC="salem5s.jpg"><BR>
<P><IMG SRC="salem2s.jpg"><BR>
</TD>
<TD WIDTH=35>
</TD>
<TD WIDTH=470 ALIGN=left VALIGN=top>
<P><B><FONT FACE=Arial SIZE="+3" COLOR="blue">The
```

```
Historic House Style Gallery</B></FONT>
<P>
<IMG SRC="pixel.gif" HEIGHT=25 WIDTH=1>
<CENTER><B><FONT FACE=Arial SIZE="+2"
COLOR="brown">Coming Soon :</CENTER></B></FONT>
<FONT FACE=Arial SIZE="+1">
<B><UL>
<LI TYPE=square>A gallery of historical residen-
tial styles built in America between 1750 and
1950<BR>
<LI TYPE=square>Background information on trends
and architects behind each style<BR>
<LI TYPE=square>Examples from across the country,
including regional adaptations<BR>
<LI TYPE=square>Notable architectural details and
features of each style<BR>
</UL></B>
<P><FONT FACE=Arial>Questions? Submissions? Email
<A HREF="mailto:curator@hhsg.com">cura-
tor@hhsg.com</A>.
</TD>
</TABLE>
</BODY>
</HTML>
```

And finally, the HTML for the business site, bhome.html, should look like this:

```
<HTML>
<HEAD>
<TITLE>Mula Dinero & Cash, Accountants</TITLE>
<META NAME="keywords" CONTENT="mula, dinero,
cash, accountants, accounting, taxes, IRAs,
retirement, financial planning, estate planning,
wills, bequests, inheritance, stocks, bonds,
futures, investments, investors, investing">
</HEAD>
<FRAMESET COLS="23%, 77%">
<FRAME SRC="menu.html">
```

```
<FRAMESET ROWS="18%, 82%">
<FRAME SRC="lhead.html" SCROLLING="no">
<FRAME SRC="info.html" NAME="rbottom">
</FRAMESET>
<NOFRAMES>
<BODY BGCOLOR="#ccffcc" TEXT="#006600"
LINK="#0000FF" ALINK="#ccffcc" VLINK="FF0000">
<P>This web page requires frames, but your
browser can't read them. Call MDC instead at
(101) 555-2345 or email us at <A
HREF="mailto:info@mdc.com">info@mdc.com</A>.
</BODY>
</NOFRAMES>
</FRAMESET>
</HTML>
```

On with the Show

Now that we've covered basic alignment and positioning of text, let's proceed to basic alignment and positioning of graphics. We will be expanding on what we learned here, particularly about tables and frames, as we move through this last quarter of the book. So turn the page to keep going.

CHAPTER 9

Positioning Text with HTML

You've chosen your color palettes, prepared your graphics, and perhaps even created your own buttons or imagemaps. Now it's time to fill in the rest of the page with text: plain text, linked text, and lists of all sizes, fonts, and styles, as well as forms.

Definitions

Text in the sense that we will be using it here is plain, unlinked text that you type into your HTML document. It can be customized, however, by style sheets (see Appendix A, "Adding DHTML: JavaScript, Style Sheets, and More"). We will also sometimes refer to text as plain text, when we compare it with **linked text**, words or phrases that are hyperlinked to other pages in the site or to other URLs elsewhere on the Web.

We will also be looking at fonts, font sizes, and font styles. A **font** is a type style; in Chapter 7, when we created each site's individual palette, we used various fonts in different colors against our sample background to choose text and link colors. Choosing **font size** on the

Web, however, is not the same as choosing the font called Geneva, for example, in a standard size of 10 or 12. It has to do with how PCs and Macintoshes display text differently, the limited number of preset values associated with the SIZE attribute of the <FONT> tag, and the way these two things work together. **Font style** on the web, though, is just the same as in word processing; you have bold, you have italics, you have underlining and strikethrough. You can even use superscript and subscript if you have a scientific inclination. That aspect of text on the Web is relatively unchanged and easy.

When we speak of lists and forms in this chapter, we'll be referring to ways of organizing text with HTML. A **list** is a short catalog of items specified by the <LI> tag, which applies standardized spacing and bullets to and around each individual list item. Lists as a whole, and the individual items on them, are interpreted by browsers with standard margins and spacing, and at a preestablished size. This makes them a bit of a design challenge; we will address those issues later on in the chapter.

A **form**, on the other hand, organizes question-and-response–type text on a web page and sends it back to the web site author's server to be processed. So a form is actually a two-part structure; there's the HTML you code to create the interface for the visitor to your page, and the **gateway program,** which processes the information the visitor types in. (We will go into this in more detail later.) Forms appear on a web page in many ways. Common types include the **text box**, a one-line blank area you can click and type in, while the **text field** works the same way but is two or more lines wide and usually scrolls. A **radio button** is a round hollow button that fills in when the visitor clicks it, and a **checkbox** is a square hollow button that fills in with an X when the visitor clicks it. A **pulldown menu** is a menu of short items to be clicked and highlighted, though it scrolls rather than unfurling as a regular pulldown menu, such as the File menu on your browser on Windows or Mac software, does. Finally, the Reset and Submit buttons work just as they sound; the **Reset button** allows the visitor to clear all the forms on the page and begin again, while the **Submit button** sends all the form information to the web page author's server.

Objectives

Our objectives are to round out the pages we began creating in the last chapter by adding new text or reformatting existing text. We will also begin creating secondary pages so we can establish links, and therefore begin work on our sites as a whole. Both these tasks will involve all the ways to manipulate and add text, as we described in the definitions. So open your HTML editor and your browser, have the CD-ROM handy, and we'll begin.

Plain Text, <BASEFONT>, and <FONT>

Let's begin by comparing plain and default text, as well as plain text that has been bolded and italicized, in order to create a benchmark for our discussion of text appearance. (See Figures 9.1 through 9.6.)

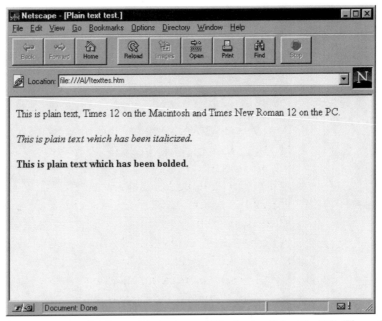

FIGURE 9.1. Plain text in Netscape Navigator 3 for the PC: Times New Roman 12 in black

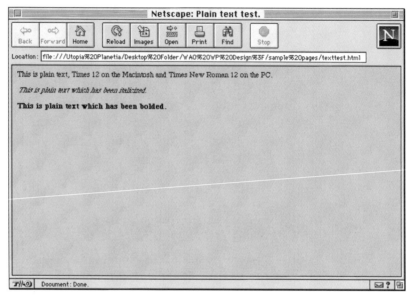

FIGURE 9.2. Plain text in Netscape Navigator 3 for the Mac: Times 12 in black

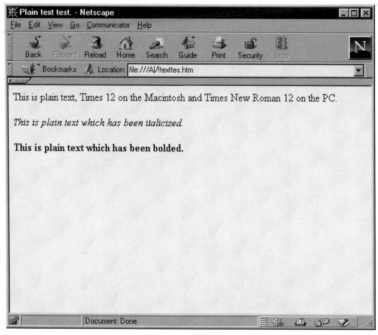

FIGURE 9.3. Plain text in Netscape Navigator 4 for the PC: Times New Roman 12 in black

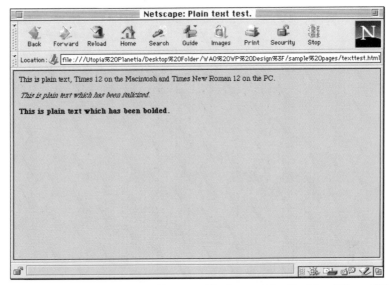

FIGURE 9.4. Plain text in Netscape Navigator 4 for the Mac: Times 12 in black

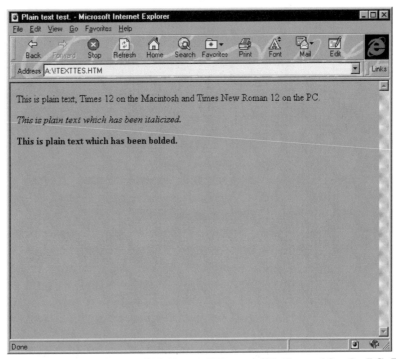

FIGURE 9.5. Plain text in Microsoft Internet Explorer 4 for the PC: Times New Roman 12 in black

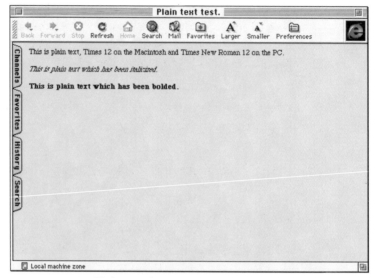

FIGURE 9.6. Plain text in Microsoft Internet Explorer 4 for the Mac: Times 12 in black

If this is where we all start from scratch, you can well imagine how quickly things can get complicated with customizations. If your imagination isn't that good, we'll show you.

The <BASEFONT> tag does allow you to change the size, color, and font of all your "default" plain text—all the plain text in your entire HTML document—but only to a limited degree. The HTML to do so looks like this:

```
<HEAD>
<BASEFONT SIZE="+2" COLOR="#999933" FACE="helvet-
ica, arial, chantilly">
</HEAD>
```

Sounds great, doesn't it? The problem is that <BASEFONT> is not yet well supported by any of the major browsers. This has not changed significantly with versions 5 and above of Navigator and Explorer, either. Fortunately, the <FONT> tag enables you to change the size, color, and font of a selected area of text in a web page, from a single word to an entire paragraph, *in relation to your* <BASEFONT> *settings, if any*. This is the important point: You can use <FONT> alone, and you definitely should. If you haven't used the

<BASEFONT> tag, or if you cannot get good crossplatform support for <BASEFONT>, <FONT> uses your browser's defaults instead of the <BASEFONT> settings. The HTML is very similar, but the <FONT> tag is placed within the <BODY> tag:

```
<BODY>
<FONT SIZE="+1" COLOR="#99CC33" FACE="courier,
geneva, chicago">
</BODY>
```

Let's take these attributes and their values one at a time.

The SIZE Attribute

The SIZE attribute can be used to increase the default font size in fourteen increments, from the smallest -7 to the largest +7. Here's what these increments look like in all our browsers and on both platforms, using the <FONT> tag to demonstrate so we can fit all fourteen examples in the same document. (See Figures 9.7 through 9.12.)

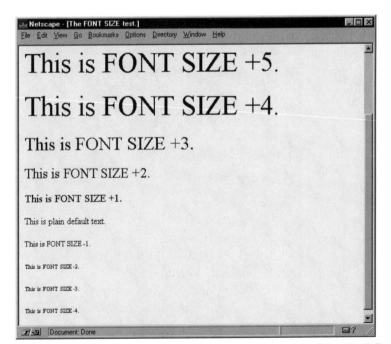

FIGURE 9.7. Font increments in Netscape Navigator 3 for the PC

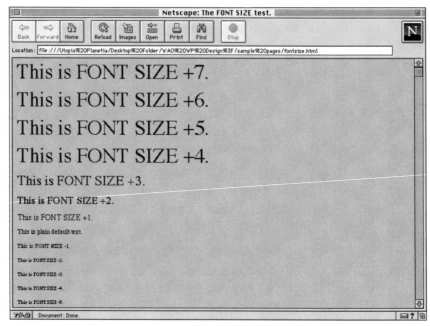

FIGURE 9.8. Font increments in Netscape Navigator 3 for the Mac

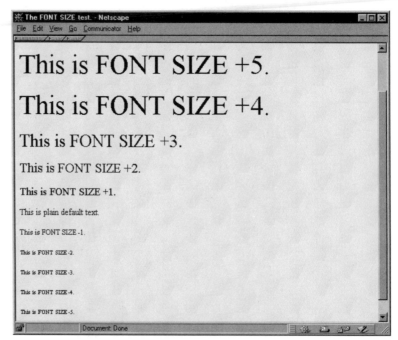

FIGURE 9.9. Font increments in Netscape Navigator 4 for the PC

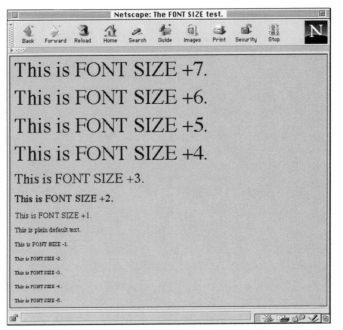

FIGURE 9.10. Font increments in Netscape Navigator 4 for the Mac

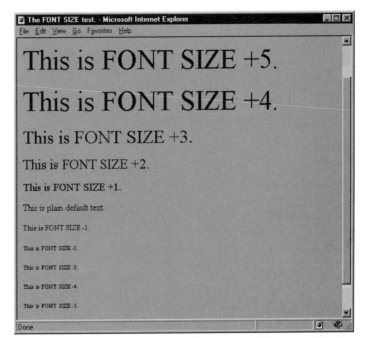

FIGURE 9.11. Font increments in Microsoft Internet Explorer 4 for the PC

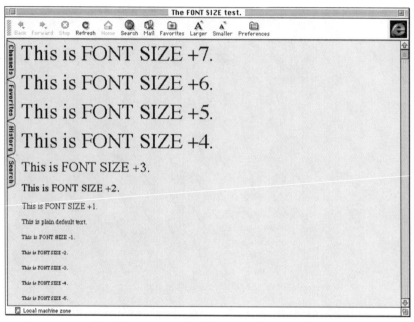

FIGURE 9.12. **Font increments in Microsoft Internet Explorer 4 for the Mac**

Here the disparity between the PC and the Macintosh is even more obvious; the larger increments on the PC are so large that they make it impossible to view all fourteen choices at a glance, as you can on the Mac. Fortunately (or unfortunately), once you get to either extreme there's no difference, so we could take these screen shots. It's pointless, then, to go any lower than -3 and/or higher than +4 on this SIZE scale when you use <FONT> without <BASEFONT>.

Why would you do that? Because <BASEFONT> is not supported at all by versions 3 or earlier of Netscape Navigator. You are almost forced to use <FONT> and its attributes to get reliable browser support, even though <FONT> produces such drastic size and spacing differences between the PC and the Mac. Also, remember that <FONT> is a relative tag—if you do use <BASEFONT> to specify, say, a SIZE of +2, <FONT> will use that +2 as its starting point. So a paragraph you specify in that same document with <FONT SIZE="+1"> will not be one increment larger than the default, but *three* increments larger.

The COLOR Attribute

Here, at least, is a little good news: You can reliably assign any of the 216 browser-safe colors to either an entire HTML document using the COLOR attribute, with <BASEFONT> or <FONT>, for reasons we've already explained. And you can definitely use <FONT COLOR> to make even one single word a different color from its sentence, paragraph, or entire web page. COLOR is reliably and uniformly supported by both of the browsers and both of the platforms we're talking about. Isn't that good to hear at this point?

Here's the HTML for the complex use of <FONT COLOR> we just described:

```
<HTML>
<HEAD>
<TITLE>The FONT COLOR test.</TITLE>
<BODY>
<P>Add one color to a <FONT
COLOR="#FFFFFF">word</FONT> while leaving the
rest of the sentence black. <FONT
COLOR="#666666">Add another color to a sentence.
</FONT>
<FONT COLOR="#FFFF00">
<P>And start over with the next paragraph.
</BODY>
</HEAD>
</HTML>
```

We had to use all shades of browser-safe gray as well as pure yellow, because this isn't a color book, but look at the results, in Figures 9.13 through 9.18.

There's one catch after all: the default background color. In both browsers on the Mac, and in IE4 on the PC, it's gray. In NN3 and NN4 on the PC, it's white. So don't hunt for the word *word* too closely; it's specified in white. Most of the time this will not be a problem, as you will very likely design a palette that includes a custom background color or pattern. But there's always a visitor out there who's turned off all his colors, or established her own default palette with white or gray, depending on her browser. Try to keep this all in mind when you consider the COLOR attribute.

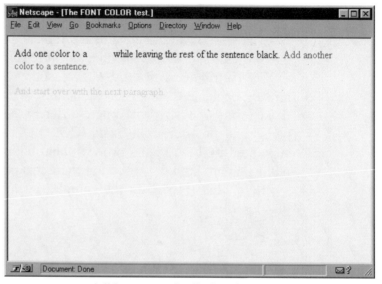

FIGURE 9.13. A "demonstration" of <FONT COLOR> in Netscape Navigator 3 for the PC

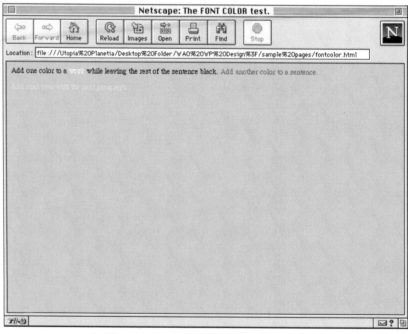

FIGURE 9.14. A "demonstration" of <FONT COLOR> in Netscape Navigator 3 for the Mac

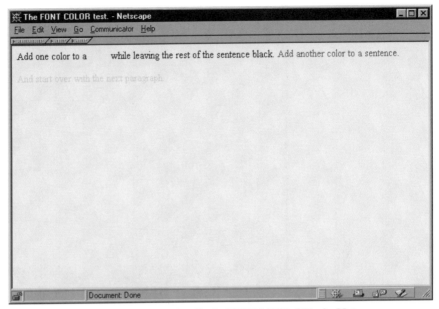

FIGURE 9.15. A "demonstration" of <FONT COLOR> in Netscape Navigator 4 for the PC

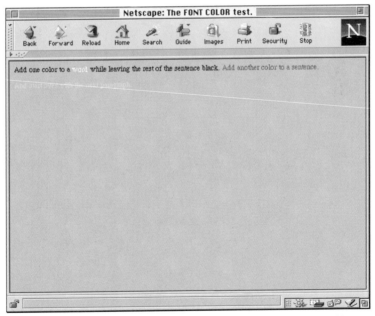

FIGURE 9.16. A "demonstration" of <FONT COLOR> in Netscape Navigator 4 for the Mac

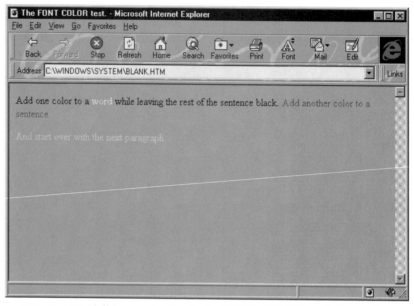

FIGURE 9.17. A "demonstration" of <FONT COLOR> in Microsoft Internet Explorer 4 for the PC

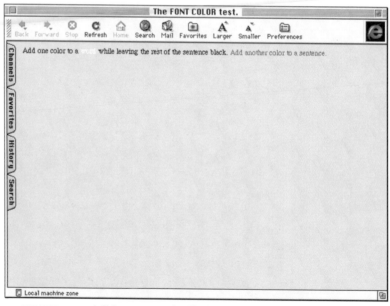

FIGURE 9.18. A "demonstration" of <FONT COLOR> in Microsoft Internet Explorer 4 for the Mac

The FACE Attribute

Now things get complicated again. The FACE attribute of the <BASEFONT> and <FONT> tags is supposed to permit you to choose a selection of alternate fonts; so you can specify not only something different from the default font, but also different fonts for different platforms. Sounds great, doesn't it? It is, and it isn't.

Here's the HTML:

```
<FONT FACE="times, arial, chantilly">
```

A browser will look at these three fonts in descending order of priority. It will look for Times on the visitor's computer first, then for Arial if Times isn't there, and then for Chantilly if neither of the first two options is available. If none of the font faces you specify is available, the browser will resort to Times for the Mac or Times New Roman for the PC.

You should always choose font faces that are 1) widely available, and 2) named correctly with regard to platform. In other words, don't be tempted by those curly copperplate fonts, or fonts that look like seventies poster script, because chances are, visitors looking at your page won't have them. You are better off using less common fonts in small doses on graphics.

> **Amy:** By that you mean typing or importing your fancy-font text into a graphics document and saving it as a GIF, correct?

> **Rebecca:** Yes. Any text you save as a GIF is unaffected by the <FONT> tag or other such HTML in your document (seems like a no-brainer, but it's good to state this clearly).

Second, the same font face can have two names, one for the PC, and one for the Macintosh. Also, the same font face name can result in two slightly different results; if you specify Times, for example, Times is what you get on the Mac, but Times New Roman is what you get on the PC. So your best strategy is to choose a font that's popular, that's present on both the PC and the Macintosh albeit with two possibly different names, and that will complement your overall design strategy. In other words, good luck!

So which fonts can you use all the time without any worries? Here's the master list: Arial, Helvetica, and Courier. It makes the browser-safe palette look generous by comparison, doesn't it? The good news is that you can specify as many font faces as your heart desires, so let's look at other options.

Fonts that ship with new Macintosh systems are: Chicago, Courier, Geneva, Helvetica, Monaco, New York, Palatino, Symbol, Times and Zapf Dingbats. Fonts that ship with Window 3.1x, Windows 95, and Windows NT are: Arial, Comic Sans, Courier New, Modern, MS Sans Serif, Symbol, Times New Roman and Wingdings. Windows 97 ships with the same fonts that come with Windows95, but there's a value pack many people choose to add on, including: Baskerville Old Face, Book Antiqua, Bookman Old Style, Century Schoolbook, Cooper Black, Copperplate Gothic, Eras, Eurostile, Franklin Gothic, Garamond, Gill Sans, Goudy Old Style, Impact, Lucida, Lucida Sans, and Stencil.

There are a handful of other fonts you can try—Bauhaus 93, Brittanic Bold, Brush Script, Colonna MT, Georgia, Kino MT and Verdana—because we've found them to be popular enough and as reliable as anything else listed above. Also, Microsoft has established a selection of popular fonts at its Typography site that are freely downloadable for Windows and for Macintosh: Arial, Arial Black, Comic Sans, Courier New, Georgia, Impact, Times New Roman, Trebuchet, and Verdana. The URL for this site is: http://www.microsoft .com/truetype.

Figures 9.19 through 9.24 show a <FONT FACE> test to demonstrate what these fonts look like, compared with each other and with the default Times and Times New Roman fonts. Almost all of them have been enlarged to show detail that would get lost at the standard setting of 12, particularly on the Mac.

You'll have the best luck conducting your own <BASEFONT FACE> and <FONT FACE> tests, and we strongly encourage you to do this kind of experimentation. Just have another glance at the individual palettes we created in Chapter 7, and you can see the influence the right (and the wrong) font face choices can make on your entire web site.

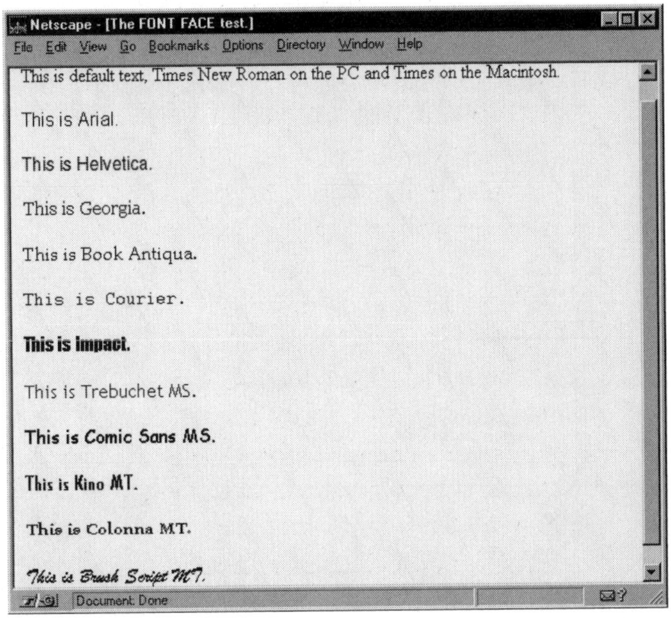

FIGURE 9.19. A comparison of common and popular fonts in Netscape Navigator 3 for the PC

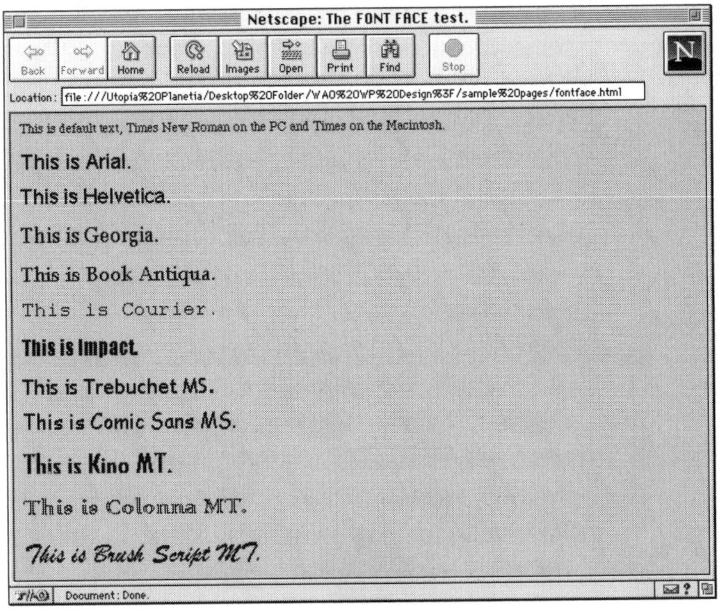

FIGURE 9.20. A comparison of common and popular fonts in Netscape Navigator 3 for the Mac

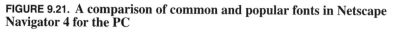

FIGURE 9.21. A comparison of common and popular fonts in Netscape
Navigator 4 for the PC

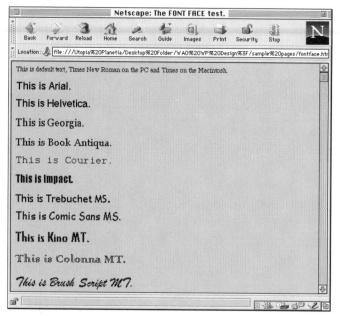

FIGURE 9.22. A comparison of common and popular fonts in Netscape
Navigator 4 for the Mac

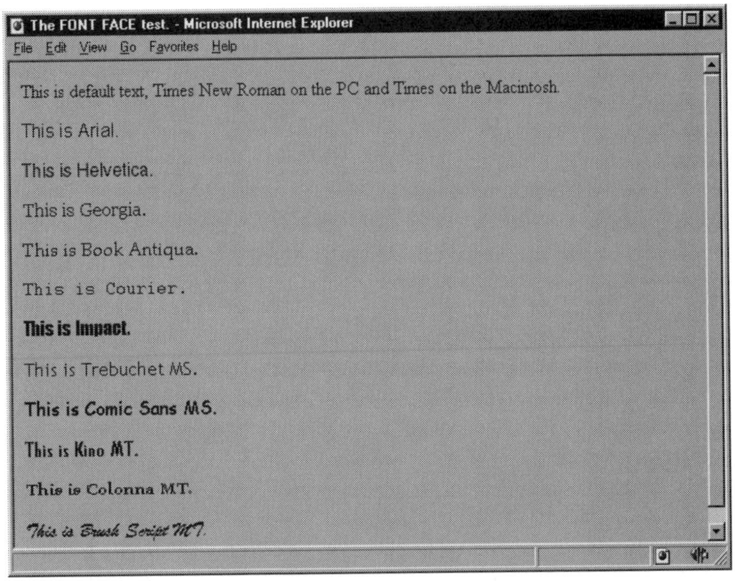

FIGURE 9.23. A comparison of common and popular fonts in Microsoft Internet Explorer 4 for the PC

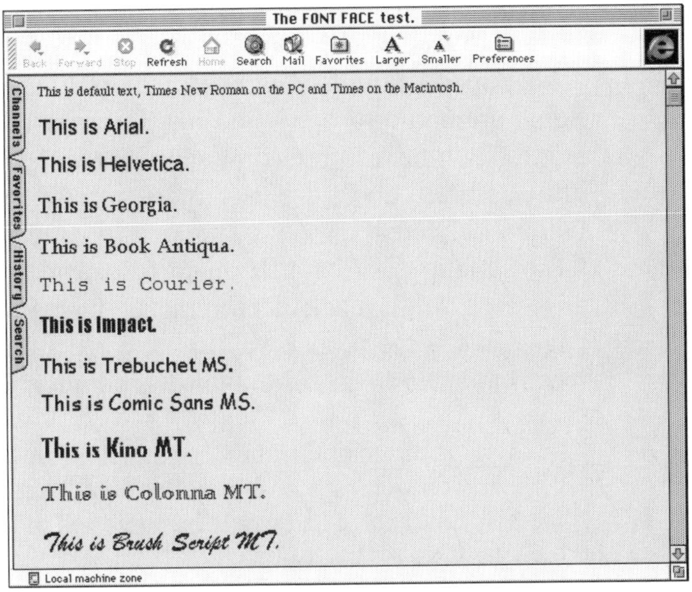

FIGURE 9.24. A comparison of common and popular fonts in Microsoft Internet Explorer 4 for the Mac

We'll incorporate all this information into our three sample sites later on in the exercises.

Lists

A list, as we defined it at the beginning of the chapter, is a short catalog of items. In a web page, they can be numbered by lowercase or uppercase Arabic letters (a, A), Arabic numbers (0, 1, and so on), or by lowercase or uppercase Roman numerals (i, I, ii, II, and so on). They can also be displayed with three different bullet types: a solid square, a hollow circle, or a solid circle.

While lists are a tidy way of displaying groups of links or other short bits of text, they are considered an outdated way of conveying online information. They've been around since the genesis of the Web when chemists and computer scientists were posting their doctoral theses in outline form. So for some designers, lists evoke the heyday of the typewriter and not the happening, here-and-now feeling of today's Web environment.

So why are we bothering to mention them here? Because they can serve a specific limited purpose in the right kind of page environment. Some online newspapers and magazines use lists of links to related stories right next to breaking news or regular columns. Sites such as eBay and NetGrocer use lists to categorize types of products, such as hot or cold cereal, or Elvis memorabilia and Beanie Babies. Lists, in these situations, are not the main focus of the reader's attention, nor are they given a place of prominence in the overall design of a web page. This is the proper way to use a list—unobtrusively, as a quick means to an end—in current third-generation web page design.

Amy: You might want to explain somewhere what a third-generation web page design is. I've read Siegel, so I know, but I bet others don't know and would be interested to learn.

Rebecca: Okay. Back in the dark ages of web pages, there were first-generation web sites. They were designed to look good on text-only, black-and-white, low-resolution screens. They looked as though someone had typed a paper report or proposal into the HTML document. Horizontal rules, edge-to-edge blocks of text, and other linear elements dominated. Most important, however, these pages went nowhere: perhaps there were links to other parts to the document, but there was no sense of relationship to other HTML documents somewhere else. You read, you scrolled, you got to the end.

Then Netscape created extensions to this basic HTML so more color and graphics could be added, and second-generation web sites were born. Instead of default gray, a background could be a color, or a tiled background pattern. Banners, colored borders, and three-dimensional linked buttons proliferated. But the overall concept and site structure did not change—second-generation sites have home pages and links to secondary pages, and perhaps more graphics. But there is no sense of passing through, no allowance for the way visitors use the Web right now.

Third-generation web sites recognize that visitors are just that: passersby. They seek to give visitors a rounded, psychologically three-dimensional experience so there is a beginning, a middle, and an end. Notice, however, that this concept of "best" design does not rely heavily on cutting-edge technology. A third-generation web site is *not* necessarily the site with all the latest doodads requiring visitors to have three or four trendy plug-ins. It is a site that presents the experience of surfing the Web with themes, metaphors, and other elements that tie the entire site together without words, guiding the visitor through with as few limitations as possible.

If you had the need to post an extremely formal document online, you would use the <OL> tag to enclose your list along with the <LI> tag to specify each list item, like so:

```
<OL TYPE=A>
<LI> Statement of Purpose
<LI> Statistics
<LI> Bar Charts
<LI> Conclusion
</OL>
```

To choose your numbering sequence, you would choose the TYPE attribute with a value of 1 for Arabic numbers, a for alphanumeric lowercase letters, A for alphanumeric uppercase letters, i for lowercase Roman numerals, or I for uppercase Roman numerals.

If you wanted to create a bulleted list, however, you'd use the <UL> tag with the TYPE attribute, like so:

```
<UL TYPE=square>
<LI> Men's Clothes
<LI> Children's Clothes
<LI> New Arrivals
<LI> Sale Rack
</UL>
```

The TYPE attribute has three possible values: circle, for a hollow spherical bullet; disc, for a solid spherical bullet that is also the default; and square, for a solid or hollow square bullet (see the bullet type test figures). Figures 9.25 through 9.30 show what they all look like in the browsers and on the platforms we're investigating.

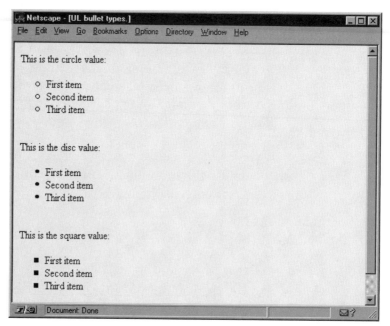

FIGURE 9.25. Bullet options in Netscape Navigator 3 for the PC

Who's Afraid of Web Page Design?

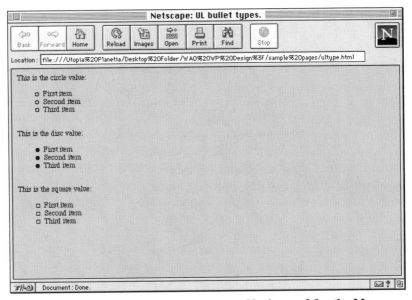

FIGURE 9.26. Bullet options in Netscape Navigator 3 for the Mac

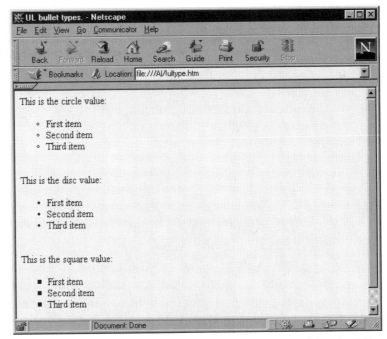

FIGURE 9.27. Bullet options in Netscape Navigator 4 for the PC

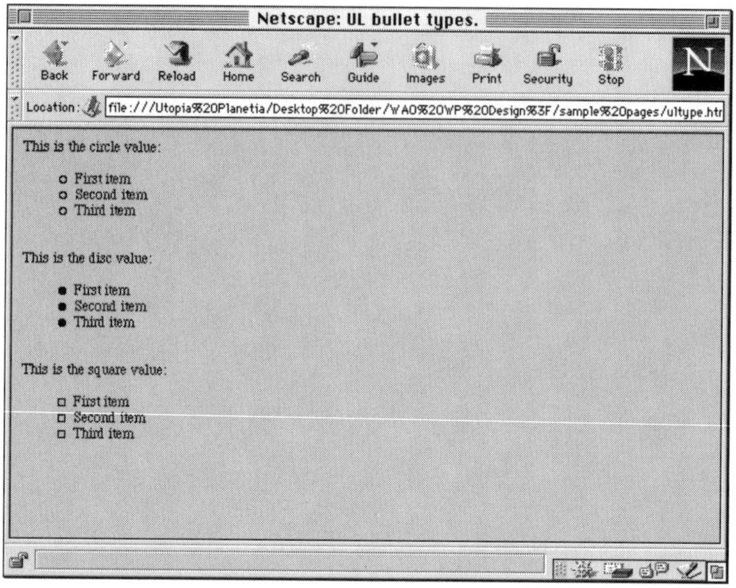

FIGURE 9.28. Bullet options in Netscape Navigator 4 for the Mac

As you can see, these bullets are actually of various sizes, and some of the bullet types aren't supported (IE4 for the PC only supports the disc value). There are also different amounts of spacing between list items, and between lists and other text on the page. This will draw more emphasis to a list than you might want, so consider all these things before you add a list to your page.

We will use lists sparingly in our sample sites later on in the exercises.

Forms

The word *form* tends to make most American people think of paying taxes, but on the Web it means something much different. A **form** on a web page is an interface between the visitor typing in text or numbers, or choosing options from sets of buttons, and the gateway program that processes the visitor's information. In plain English, you can use HTML to create a form on a web page, but you need to store a CGI script or some similar program on your server in order to make a form work.

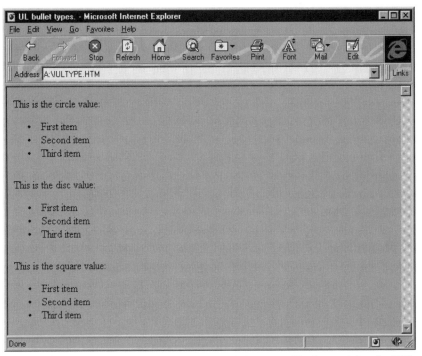

FIGURE 9.29. Bullet options in Microsoft Internet Explorer 4 for the PC

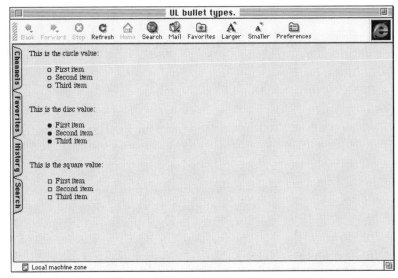

FIGURE 9.30. Bullet options in Microsoft Internet Explorer 4 for the Mac

CGI scripting is true programming and is not covered in this book. But we can discuss the incorporation of forms in a web page from a design point of view, and from a standpoint of strategy. First, the HTML.

The *<FORM>* Tag

The most basic, unvarnished form HTML looks like this:

```
<FORM ACTION=http://www.isp.com/cgiscript
METHOD=post>

The form's contents go here.

</FORM>
```

The ACTION attribute tells the browser where to send the visitor's information once he or she has finished filling out the form. The METHOD attribute has two values: post, for sending the form's contents one way to the server, and get, for sending form contents and retrieving a response. These two attributes are required, and a form will not work without them.

The <FORM> tag also has two other useful attributes, ENCTYPE and TARGET. ENCTYPE is not needed unless you are using a form to send feedback to an email address; in that case, you should add ENCTYPE="text/plain" to the <FORM> tag. Otherwise, the default setting (application/x-www-form-urlencoded) is implied, and you don't need to type it in.

Amy: So what does ENCTYPE actually do?

Rebecca: ENCTYPE is short for "enclosure type," and it tells the server what kind of information is headed its way when the visitor is done using the form. Since email is going directly to the site designer's mailbox, it doesn't get translated or processed by the gateway program the same way as other form information does, if at all. So ENCTYPE is like a fork in the road of form information: e-mail goes this way, everything else goes that way.

The TARGET attribute lets you instruct the gateway program to produce a response in a different window other than the one where the form is found.

Here are TARGET's four values:

blank   The response appears in a new, blank window.

parent   The response appears into the parent window.

self   The response appears in the same window where the form is found (the default).

top   The response appears in the full, existing window, excluding all other information.

As with ENCTYPE, you can usually omit a TARGET attribute and do perfectly well with the default. Now let's talk about the <INPUT> tag, which specifies the kind of form information you put on your web page, and requires more complicated attributes.

The <INPUT> Tag

<INPUT> has nine important attributes, not including CLASS and ID, which are used primarily for style sheets. They, and their established values and/or functions, are:

ALIGN   Wraps text around a form and aligns it on a web page.

bottom   Text aligns to the bottom edge of the form.

left   Text aligns to the left edge of the form.

middle   Text aligns to the center of the form.

right   Text aligns to the right edge of the form.

top   Text aligns to the top edge of the form.

MAXLENGTH   Establishes a maximum number of characters to be written in a text box.

NAME   Describes the text box to the gateway program.

SIZE   Specifies the height and width of a text box.

SRC   Lists the file name when an image is specified by the TYPE attribute.

TABINDEX   Forces the visitor to click on a text box to use it, rather than to use the Tab key as is the default.

TYPE   Specifies the kind of form to be displayed on the web page.

button   An oval gray button

checkbox   A square blank selectable box (used in groups)

file   An HTML file

hidden   Specifies the email address where the form results will be sent; nothing actually appears on the web page itself

image   An image

password   A blank password text box (will display asterisks or black dots instead of typed characters)

radio   A blank selectable radio button (used in groups for multiple choice)

reset   A Reset button

submit   A Submit button

text   A blank single-line text box

The CHECKED and NOTAB attributes do not have values; their presence or absence alone signals the browser to implement or not to implement the changes they specify. CHECKED works in tandem with the TYPE attribute when it has been used to specify radio or checkbox. It establishes a default selection among the whole group of checkboxes or buttons, in case the form's gateway program absolutely requires that an option be selected. Similarly, NOTAB removes a particular form from the tabbing order on a whole web page of forms. By default, a visitor to your forms page can use the

Tab key to move from one form to another, but you can use NOTAB either to emphasize or minimize the importance of a particular form, depending on what it is.

The <SELECT>, <OPTION>, and <TEXTAREA> Tags

The <SELECT> tag specifies a pulldown menu and how it appears as a text box on the actual web page. It has three attributes:

MULTIPLE Lets the visitor choose more than one item on the pulldown menu.

NAME Describes the pulldown menu's text box to the gateway program.

SIZE Specifies the number of items on the menu displayed on the web page and, accordingly, the presence or absence of a scrollbar.

The <OPTION> tag also pertains to pulldown menus, and it has two attributes. The SELECTED attribute works like <INPUT CHECKED>; if your gateway program requires that there be one selected item on the pulldown menu in order for it to work properly, SELECTED lets you establish a default selection. Similarly, the <OPTION> tag's VALUE attribute describes the pulldown menu to the gateway program the same way <INPUT NAME> works. It identifies each item on the menu as a separate answer, so the gateway program can distinguish them from one another.

Finally, <TEXTAREA> defines a large text box—anything more than one line—with four attributes:

COLS Specifies the number of vertical columns in characters.

NAME Describes the contents of the text box to the gateway program.

ROWS Specifies the number of horizontal rows in characters.

WRAP Forces the text box text to wrap once the end of the row is reached, so visitors can see what they have written. Without it, the text does not wrap, and visitors have to use a horizontal scrollbar to proof what they have typed, which is an annoyance and not good "netiquette."

Building Well-Designed Forms

Now let's put these tags, attributes, and values into practice. Here's what the HTML in our sample figures looks like:

```
<HTML>
<HEAD>
<TITLE>The FORM test.</TITLE>
</HEAD>
<BODY>
<FORM action="http://www.isp.com/cgiscript"
method="post">
<P>Your name:
<INPUT maxlength="25" name="namebox" type="text">
<BR>
<P>I like:
<INPUT name="check1" type="checkbox">
Paisleys
<INPUT name="check2" type="checkbox">
Stripes
<INPUT name="check3" type="checkbox">
Textures <BR>
<P>Choose a wallpaper you like:
<INPUT name="paper1" src="wallppr1.gif"
type="image">
<INPUT name="paper2" src="wallppr2.gif"
type="image">
<INPUT name="paper3" src="wallppr3.gif"
type="image">
<BR>
<P>I am wallpapering the:
<SELECT multiple name="wpprmenu" size="4">
<OPTION value="1">Living Room
<OPTION value="2">Dining Room
<OPTION value="3">Bedroom
```

```
<OPTION value="4">Bathroom
<OPTION value="5">Kitchen
</SELECT>
<BR>
<P>Bill me using my:
<INPUT checked name="ccard" type="radio"
value="visa">
Visa
<INPUT name="ccard" type="radio" value="mcard">
MasterCard
<INPUT name="ccard" type="radio" value="aex-
press">
American Express <BR>
<P>My credit card number is:
<INPUT maxlength="20" name="ccnumber" type="pass-
word" value="password">
<P>Additional specifications (i.e. room measure-
ments): <BR>
<TEXTAREA cols="40" rows="5" name="feedback"
wrap="virtual">
</TEXTAREA>
<BR>
<INPUT name="reset" type="reset" value="Reset">
<INPUT name="submit" type="submit" value="Sub-
mit">
</FORM>
</BODY>
</HTML>
```

Amy: Wow! Nothing like an example to help make sense of it all. With every NAME attribute, the value has to be one that the CGI script at the server will recognize, correct?

Rebecca: Yes, the NAME attribute is the way the gateway program distinguishes all the bits of information from one another.

Amy: So I'm assuming we'd have to contact our ISP to get a list of some sort?

Rebecca: No, the person who writes the gateway program decides on the NAME attribute values. Or you tell him or her what you want them to be, and they write them into the code. Your ISP can only tell you whether or not the server can host the kind of gateway program you have.

Figures 9.31 through 9.36 show what this HTML looks like on our browsers and platforms.

Notice all the little differences in the way the forms themselves are displayed, too—the ones that are working, that is. The wallpaper samples, for example, are sometimes outlined in blue and sometimes not; technically, they are links to the gateway program even though they're hypertext links. You should also notice how scattered and ugly these forms look on the page as they are—the unpredictable preset sizes, margins, and spacings around these forms individually and in relation to each other create a big headache you have to contend with.

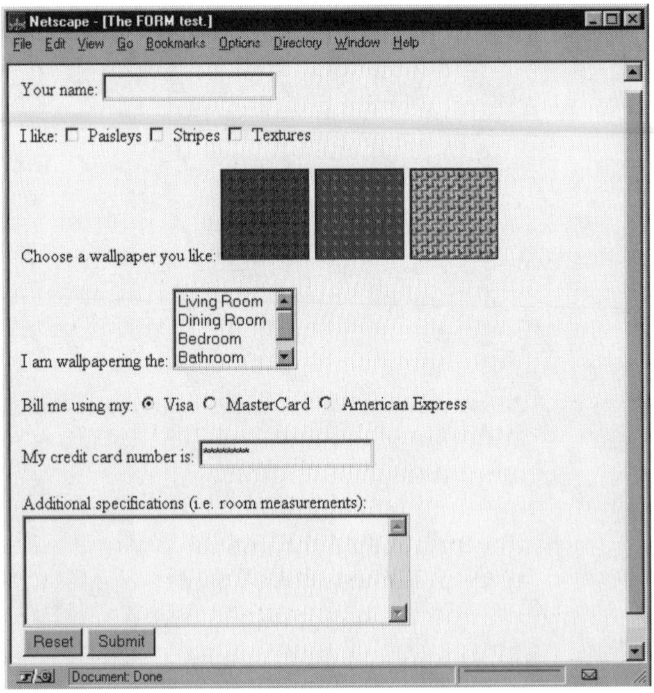

FIGURE 9.31. An assortment of forms in Netscape Navigator 3 for the PC

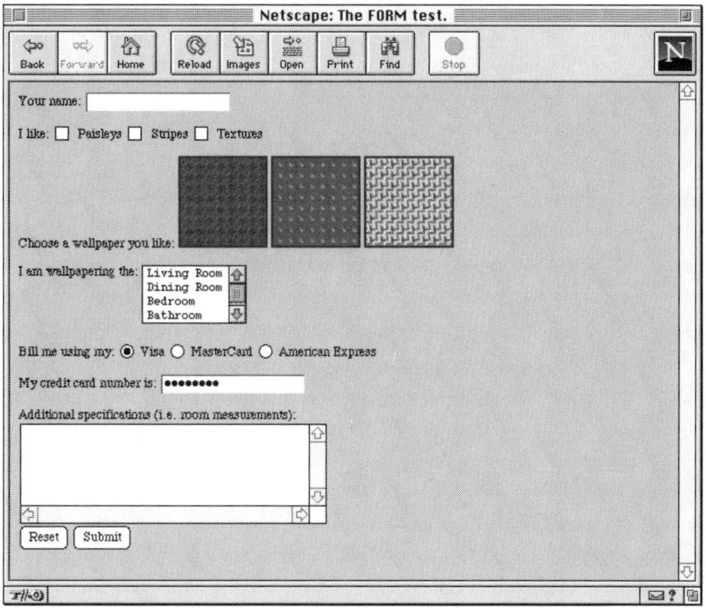

FIGURE 9.32. An assortment of forms in Netscape Navigator 3 for the Mac

Also, there are some minimum settings you need to remember when you use some of these forms. If you're using a pulldown menu, for example, with the <SELECT> tag, your minimum SIZE value should be 4. You can choose 3, 2, or 1, but the slider bar will not appear properly. The browser needs a width of four text lines at minimum, or the slider button will bleed off the top or the bottom of the menu, depending upon which way the visitor slides it. It's also not necessary to make a large <TEXTAREA> textbox if you use WRAP=virtual, which should make designing with text boxes a little easier. Visitors like to see about five lines of text visible at any given time, which are approximately half the width of the open window. Anything smaller gives the text box a cramped look, and anything larger is wasted space you could better design some other way.

We're going to do our best to incorporate forms in the business sample site in the exercises, so let's address the solutions to these problems here.

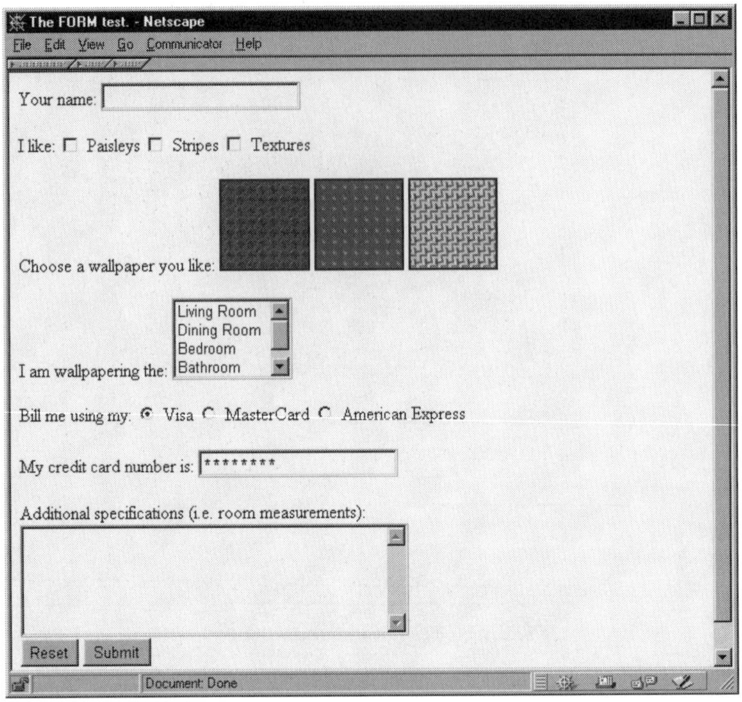

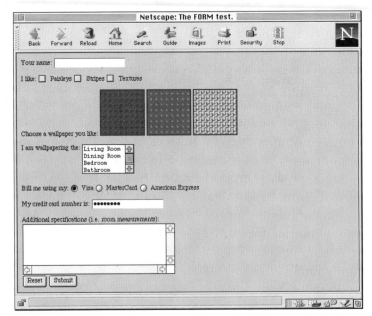

FIGURE 9.33. An assortment of forms in Netscape Navigator 4 for the PC

FIGURE 9.34. An assortment of forms in Netscape Navigator 4 for the Mac

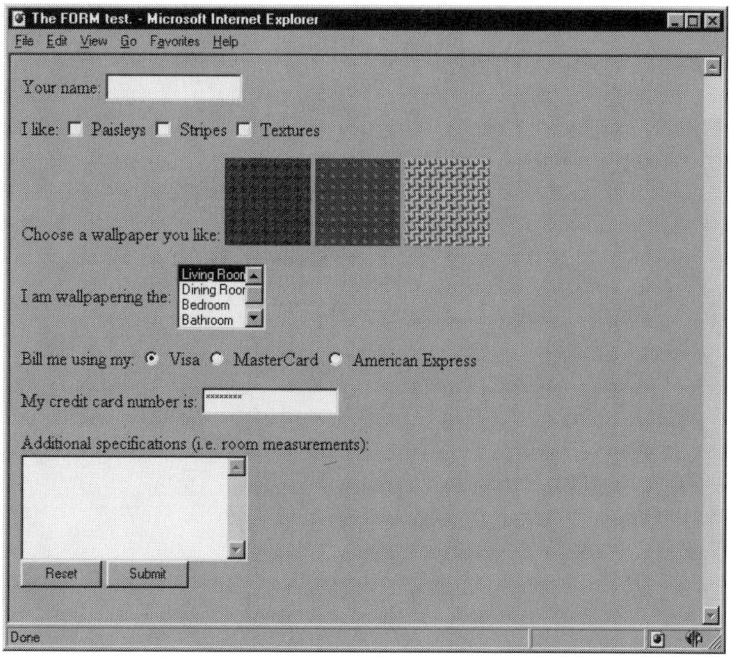

FIGURE 9.35. **An assortment of forms in Microsoft Internet Explorer 4 for the PC**

Exercises

In these exercises, we'll create a secondary page for the personal site, first by adding link HTML to the eyeballs page, and then by building John Doe's secondary page from scratch. We'll play with plain and linked text and all the <FONT> customizations to create something cool. Then we'll use the same techniques to link the main Historic Home Style Gallery page to a secondary house style page, and to mix links with plain text for smart, concise descriptions. Finally, we'll create the Fiscally Fit quiz on the business site with forms, and link it to the rest of the site.

Embellishing Plain Text

Open your HTML editor and your browser, and have the CD-ROM handy.

1. Open the main home page for the personal site in your HTML editor, doe2.html. It should look like Figure 9.37.

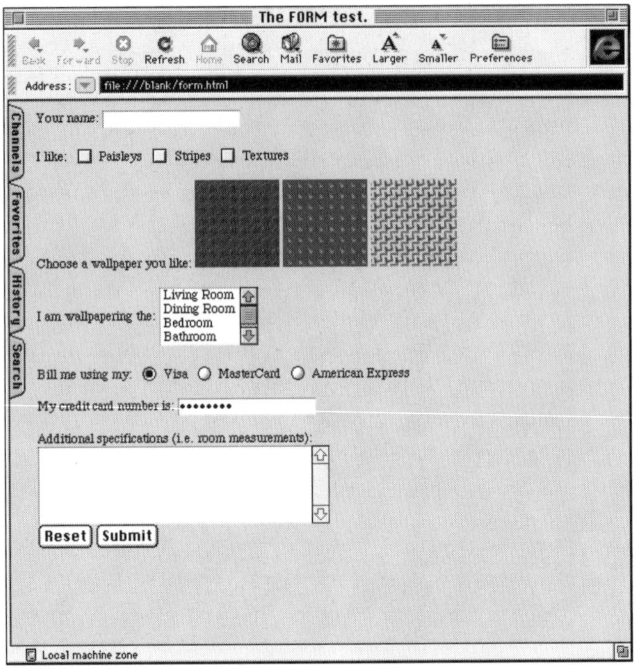

FIGURE 9.36. An assortment of forms in Microsoft Internet Explorer 4 for the Mac

The HTML should look like this:

```
<HTML>
<HEAD>
<TITLE>Meet John Doe</TITLE>
</HEAD>
<BODY BACKGROUND="oswirl.gif">
<BR>
<IMG SRC="pixel.gif" ALIGN=bottom HEIGHT=55
WIDTH=1>
<P ALIGN=center>
<IMG SRC="eye1.gif" HSPACE=6 VSPACE=1>
<IMG SRC="eye2.gif" HSPACE=6 VSPACE=1>
<P ALIGN=center><IMG SRC="eye3.gif" HSPACE=6
VSPACE=1>
<IMG SRC="eye4.gif" HSPACE=6 VSPACE=1>
<BR>
</BODY>
</HTML>
```

Who's Afraid of Web Page Design?

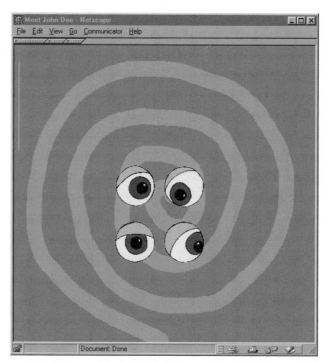

FIGURE 9.37. The main home page for the personal site, doe2.html

You'll notice doe2.html includes the background we decided on in Chapter 7 and the positioning we accomplished in Chapter 8.

Amy: Perhaps I missed it, but I don't remember talking about the attributes HSPACE and VSPACE. What do they do, exactly?

Rebecca: HSPACE and VSPACE add horizontal and vertical space, respectively, around a graphic like a picture frame. Only in this example, the horizontal portions of the frame are 6 pixels wide while the vertical portions are only one pixel wide. (I think I did neglect to mention these in the last chapter; good catch.)

2. First, let's link each of the eyeballs to the names of our would-be secondary pages, one for each member of the Doe family:

```
<A HREF="john.html"><IMG SRC="eye1.gif" BORDER=0
HSPACE=6 VSPACE=1></A>
```

```
<A HREF="jane.html"><IMG SRC="eye2.gif" BORDER=0
HSPACE=6 VSPACE=1></A>
<A HREF="jack.html"><P ALIGN=center><IMG
SRC="eye3.gif"  BORDER=0 HSPACE=6 VSPACE=1></A>
<A HREF="jill.html"><IMG SRC="eye4.gif"  BORDER=0
HSPACE=6 VSPACE=1></A>
```

Note that we also added the BORDER attribute to the <IMG> tag with a value of 0 (zero), which disables the telltale outline around a linked graphic. So the appearance of the four eyeballs hasn't changed, even though they are all now linked to what will become our secondary pages.

Now we can proceed to actually creating a secondary page, in this example, for John Doe.

3. Begin a new HTML document and name it john.html. Incorporate the individual palette choices you selected in Chapter 7 (this was listed under "More Exercises," remember). Give this page the title "Meet John Doe." Now we can add a little text before we begin tweaking its appearance.

Your HTML should look like this, with the exception of your own background and color choices:

```
<HTML>
<HEAD>
<TITLE>Meet John Doe</TITLE>
</HEAD>
<BODY BGCOLOR="#FFCC99" TEXT="#996666"
LINK="#663366" ALINK="#FF6699" VLINK="#FF6666">
<BR>
<P>John is a programmer at <A HREF="http://
www.acmetech.com">Acme Technology Inc.</A> where
he does plenty of technogeek stuff.
<P>His hobbies include racquetball, microbrewing,
and collecting Buddy Holly records.
<P>Email John at <A HREF="mailto:jdoe@acme-
tech.com">jdoe@acmetech.com</A>.
</BODY>
</HTML>
```

Have a look at this page in your browser, and make color changes accordingly. Notice that our initial color choice of bark brown as the text color looks purplish against the peach background color. This makes the deep purple we chose as the link color appear less distinct. Remember: Part of the way your eye measures color is in relationship to other colors around it. So you may want to use the color chip chart on the CD-ROM to modify your palette—the individual palettes we created and suggested in Chapter 7 are only a place to begin.

> **Amy:** Since I decided I would use the green swirl background instead of the orange swirl for the home page, I thought it would be best to continue with the contrasting green and purple colors for the secondary page. If you want to check it out, I used:

```
<BODY BGCOLOR="#66CC33" TEXT="#993399"
LINK="#006600" ALINK="#993399" VLINK="#660000">
```

4. Now let's add some visual interest with the `<FONT>` tag. First, bold John's name and increase its size +1. Do the same for the words "racquetball" and "Buddy Holly." Reload or Refresh john.html in your browser and have a look. Bolding and enlarging these few words has also had the effect of separating these three lines of text a little more, making the page contents easier to read.

> **Amy:** So the HTML will look like this: `<FONT SIZE="+1">` `<B>John</B></FONT>`. (This is for those readers who, like myself, had forgotten the HTML for bold text.)

> **Rebecca:** Sorry—I took you for granted there. Yes, the HTML you wrote just now is correct.

5. Next, change the text font to Verdana, with Georgia, and Helvetica being your second and third alternate choices, respectively. Save your changes and reload john.html in your browser accordingly. Test each font separately to make sure you like the effect; your second and third choices might not look perfect, but they should look acceptable though they're all different. (See Figures 9.39 through 9.41.)

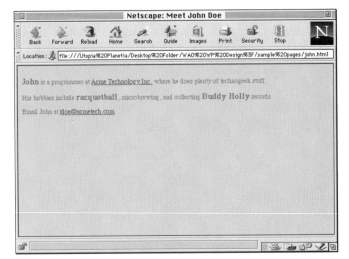

FIGURE 9.38. Initial <FONT> changes to john.html

For the record, we liked the font Kino MT best of all in the abstract, but when we tested it in the actual page with the actual text we would use, it didn't look as good. There's not necessarily a technical reason for this decision, although with some fonts, such as Colonna MT, the size of your text has to be a certain size before all

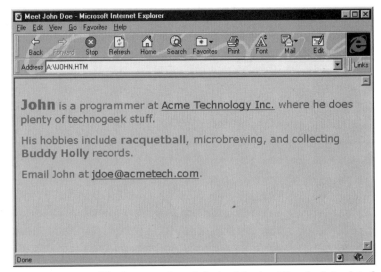

FIGURE 9.39. Verdana as the plain text font setting in john.html

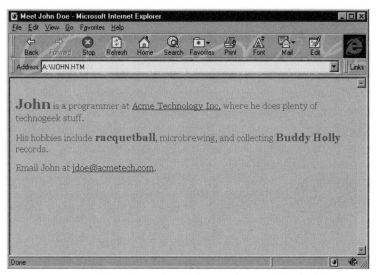

FIGURE 9.40. Georgia as the plain text font setting in john.html

the detail can be seen. The text and overall appearance of your page might not support larger-than-standard lettering, so do you change the design or choose a different face? This is why testing many <FONT FACE> choices at this stage is key, even if you tested the same choices while making a palette.

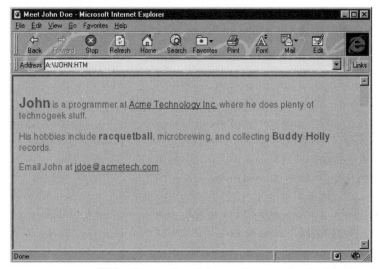

FIGURE 9.41. Helvetica as the plain text font setting in john.html

This is where we'll stop for now, even though this secondary page is still quite plain. We will be practicing the same HTML in the next exercise before we add lists.

Incorporating Effective List Text

If you don't have your HTML editor and browser open anymore, reopen them. Also be sure to have the CD-ROM handy, and let's get started with lists.

1. Open the temporary page for the informational site, infoUC1.html. Your HTML should look like this before we begin:

```
<HTML>
<HEAD>
<TITLE>The Historic House Style Gallery</TITLE>
<META NAME="description" CONTENT="A gallery of
American residential architectural styles popular
between 1750 and 1950.">
</HEAD>
<BODY BACKGROUND=infoslice.gif TEXT="#999966"
BGCOLOR="#FFFFCC" LINK="#666699" ALINK="#FFFFCC"
VLINK="#FF9900">
<P>
<TABLE BORDER=0 CELLSPACING=0 CELLPADDING=0
WIDTH=600>
<TR>
<TD WIDTH=95 ALIGN=left VALIGN=top>
<P><IMG SRC="salem1s.jpg"><BR>
<P><IMG SRC="salem4s.jpg"><BR>
<P><IMG SRC="salem5s.jpg"><BR>
<P><IMG SRC="salem2s.jpg"><BR>
</TD>
<TD WIDTH=35>
</TD>
<TD WIDTH=470 ALIGN=left VALIGN=top>
<P><B><FONT FACE=Arial SIZE="+3" COLOR="blue">The
Historic House Style Gallery</B></FONT>
<P>
<IMG SRC="pixel.gif" HEIGHT=25 WIDTH=1>
```

```
<CENTER><B><FONT FACE=Arial SIZE="+2"
COLOR="brown">Coming Soon. . .</CENTER></B></
FONT>
<FONT FACE=Arial SIZE="+1">
<UL>
<LI TYPE=square>A gallery of historical residen-
tial styles built in America between 1750 and
1950<BR>
<LI TYPE=square>Background information on trends
and architects behind each style<BR>
<LI TYPE=square>Examples from across the country,
including regional adaptations<BR>
<LI TYPE=square>Notable architectural details and
features of each style<BR>
</UL>
<P><FONT FACE=Arial>Questions? Submissions? Email
<A HREF="mailto:curator@hhsg.com">cura-
tor@hhsg.com</A>.
</TD>
</TABLE>
</BODY>
</HTML>
```

First, let's make some changes to this page text so we can easily save it as the final main, home page for the Historic House Style Gallery, which we'll call gallery.html.

The HTML of gallery.html should look like this:

```
<HTML>
<HEAD>
<TITLE>The Historic House Style Gallery</TITLE>
<META NAME="description" CONTENT="A gallery of
American residential architectural styles popular
between 1750 and 1950.">
</HEAD>
<BODY TEXT="#666699" BACKGROUND="infoslice.gif"
LINK="#666699" ALINK="#FFFFCC" VLINK="#FF9900">
<P>
<TABLE BORDER=0 CELLSPACING=0 CELLPADDING=0
WIDTH=600>
```

```
<TR>
<TD WIDTH=95 ALIGN=left VALIGN=top>
<P><IMG SRC="salem1s.jpg"><BR>
<P><IMG SRC="salem4s.jpg"><BR>
<P><IMG SRC="salem5s.jpg"><BR>
<P><IMG SRC="salem2s.jpg"><BR>
<P><IMG SRC="salem6s.jpg"><BR>
</TD>
<TD WIDTH=17>
</TD>
<TD WIDTH=470 ALIGN=left VALIGN=top>
<CENTER>
<P><FONT COLOR="#666699" SIZE="+3">The Historic
House Style Gallery</FONT>
<P><FONT COLOR="#999966" SIZE="+2">A gallery of
American historical residential styles<BR></FONT>
</CENTER>
<BR>
<FONT FACE="georgia" COLOR="#999966" SIZE="+2">
<P>More Styles Coming Soon
<IMG SRC="pixel.gif" HEIGHT=25 WIDTH=1>
<P>Questions? Submissions? Email <A HREF=
"mailto:curator@hhsg.com">curator@hhsg.com</A>.
</FONT>
</TD>
</TABLE>
</BODY>
</HTML>
```

Next, let's add more text to work with, along with links to what will be our first secondary page.

2. There will be five secondary pages on this site, four style pages (the Victorian, the Georgian, the Prairie/FourSquare and the Revivals) along with a Coming Soon page with brief introductions to forthcoming style pages. Add the following HTML after the two headlines to introduce this text:

```
<IMG SRC="pixel.gif" HEIGHT=25 WIDTH=1>
<FONT FACE="georgia" COLOR="#666666" SIZE="+2">
```

```
<P>Georgian Styles, 1700 - 1776
<P>Victorian Styles, 1850 - 1900
<P>Revival Styles, 1800 - 1870
<P>Prairie Styles, 1900 - 1920
</FONT>
<BR>
<FONT FACE="georgia" COLOR="#999966" SIZE="+2">
<P>More Styles Coming Soon
<IMG SRC="pixel.gif" HEIGHT=25 WIDTH=1>
<P>Questions? Submissions? Email <A
HREF="mailto:curator@hhsg.com">curator@hhsg.com</
A>.
</FONT>
```

Now make links to the would-be secondary pages, like so:

```
<P><A HREF="georgian.html">Georgian Styles</A>,
1700 - 1776
<P><A HREF="victorian.html">Victorian Styles</A>,
1850 - 1900
<P><A HREF="revival.html">Revival Styles</A>,
1800 - 1870
<P><A HREF="prairie.html">Prairie Styles</A>,
1900 - 1920
```

Next we'll create victorian.html and incorporate some lists.

3. Open a new document in your HTML editor and call it victorian.html. Replace the four color photos down the left side with the Victorian JPEG files on the CD-ROM (vict1.jpg, vict2.jpg, vict3.jpg, vict4.jpg) in whichever order you like. Use dropv.gif, a large ornate capital on the CD-ROM, to create a header called "Victorian Styles." Then create an introductory description of one of the house types, the Queen Anne, followed by a list of distinctive architectural characteristics. Use a darker color from the informational site individual palette to highlight the house type via the <FONT> tag.

4. The basic text I typed in below is as follows (you can cut and paste, or shorten it to your liking):

"When a real estate listing describes a house as 'Victorian,' you'd better hope there's a photo. American Victorian residential style covers the whole spectrum of architectural design, from the simpler Greek Revivals, Urban Victorians and Italianates, to the wild and whimsical Queen Annes, Gothic Revivals and Victorian Eclectics. (The examples on this page, from top to bottom, are a Queen Anne, an Italianate, an Urban Victorian, and a Gothic Revival.)

"The Queen Anne was most popular in America between 1870 and 1900, as a reflection of the expanding, newly wealthy middle class. The more ornamentation, and the more patterns and materials used, the better. Some Queen Annes, or 'painted ladies' as they are better known today, were painted eight different colors to show off their unique individualities."

Some possible list items are:

- projecting bay windows

- cone-shaped corner towers

- several kinds of shingles in horizontal bands

- dormers

- gables

- decorated porches and gingerbread

I went all-out because historical houses are a particular passion of mine (just exercising a little authorial prerogative). When you're through, the HTML should look something like this:

```
<HTML>
<HEAD>
<TITLE>The Historic House Style Gallery: Victo-
rian Styles</TITLE>
</HEAD>
<BODY TEXT="#666699" BACKGROUND="infoslice.gif"
LINK="#666699" ALINK="#FFFFCC" VLINK="#FF9900">
```

```
<P>
<TABLE BORDER=0 CELLSPACING=0 CELLPADDING=0
WIDTH=600>
<TR>
<TD WIDTH=95 ALIGN=left VALIGN=top>
<P><IMG SRC="vict3.jpg">
<P><IMG SRC="vict1.jpg">
<P><IMG SRC="vict2.jpg">
<P><IMG SRC="vict4.jpg">
</TD>
<TD WIDTH=17>
</TD>
<TD WIDTH=470 ALIGN=left VALIGN=top>
<CENTER>
<P><FONT COLOR="#666699" SIZE="+4">
<IMG SRC="dropv.gif">ictorian Styles
</FONT>
<P><FONT COLOR="#999999" SIZE="+3">
1850 - 1900
</FONT>
</CENTER>
<IMG SRC="pixel.gif" HEIGHT=25 WIDTH=1>
<FONT FACE="georgia" COLOR="#999966"
SIZE="+1"><B>
<P>When a real estate listing describes a house
as "Victorian," you'd better hope there's a
photo. American Victorian residential style cov-
ers the whole spectrum of architectural design,
from the simpler Greek Revivals, Urban Victorians
and Italianates, to the wild and whimsical Queen
Annes, Gothic Revivals and Victorian Eclectics.
(The examples on this page, from top to bottom,
are a Queen Anne, an Italianate, an Urban Victo-
rian, and a Gothic Revival.)<BR>
<P>The <FONT COLOR="#666699">Queen Anne</FONT>
was most popular in America between 1870 and
1900, as a reflection of the expanding, newly
wealthy middle class. The more ornamentation, and
the more patterns and materials used, the better.
```

```
Some Queen Annes, or "painted ladies" as they are
better known today, were painted eight different
colors to show off their unique individuali-
ties.<BR>
<P>The Queen Anne's distinguishing characteris-
tics are:
<UL TYPE=circle>
<LI>projecting bay windows
<LI>cone-shaped corner towers
<LI>several kinds of shingles in horizontal bands
<LI>dormers, gables, and other irregular roofline
extensions
<LI>decorated porches and gingerbread
</UL>
</B>
</FONT>
</TD>
</TABLE>
</BODY>
</HTML>
```

The page victorian.html in your browser will look something like Figure 9.42 or 9.43.

A few final notes: we changed the name of the slice GIF for this page from infoslice.gif to islice.gif, because it was more than eight characters long. The PC automatically places an exclamation point (!) in front of such files, so the browser couldn't locate the slice GIF and reverted to a default gray background instead.

Aesthetically, we were forced to design around black-and-white images because that's how we found them on the Web, but they do lend themselves well to our color palette. The highly desaturated text and graphics look entirely readable against the vivid yellow slice GIF, which is what you want for a site such as this, where your visitors will have to sit and study its contents. Careful use of subtle color to highlight a few keywords—one per paragraph at the most—will help the reader who skims, but will not distract the reader who takes his or her time.

Amy: I think this is a great example of the need to plan ahead in site design. Rebecca's islice.gif background looks great with the black-

FIGURE 9.42. victorian.html in Internet Explorer 4 for the PC

and-white JPEGs of the Victorian homes. The homeslice.gif (which you could rename hslice.gif or islice2.gif so that the name is fewer than eight characters long) that I designed does not look as good with this secondary page. Granted, I could change the background for every secondary page based on its images and elements, but it's nice for continuity's sake to have the same background on every (or nearly every) page in the site, I think.

Rebecca: Sometimes changing the background or slice GIF for each secondary page isn't such a bad idea. All of the secondary pages in The Pyramid, for example (this is the Egyptian site I showed you in Chapter 6) have slightly different slice GIF backgrounds. I used the same monkey but a different hieroglyphic letter in the parchment area to the left, so the GIF design still ties in to the rest of the site but has a little individuality, too. Amy can easily do something like this with her slice GIF just by changing the color of either the narrower, solid stripe on the left or the sandstonelike texture on the right.

FIGURE 9.43. victorian.html in Netscape Navigator 4 for the Macintosh

Notice, also, how much larger the text is in IE4 for the PC than in NN4 for the Macintosh; we couldn't fit in a list on the PC screen shot even though the whole thing fit into the one taken on the Mac. This is the significant discrepancy you have to contend with when you design for both platforms. Also, remember that IE4 for the PC does not recognize any other value for <UL TYPE> than the default, disc. So the hollow circular bullets on the Mac are smaller, and/or solid circular bullets on the PC.

> **Amy:** I also notice a difference in the bullets between NN4 and IE4 on the PC. NN4 displays them as hollow square shapes, while IE4 displays hollow circle shapes.

Designing with Forms

When we began designing the main, home page for the sample business site in the last chapter, we put an item on the menu called Are You Fiscally Fit? Now let's create that quiz with forms on its own new page called quiz.html, and link it appropriately to the main, home page.

If you've closed your HTML editor and your browser, open them again. You won't need the CD-ROM for this exercise.

1. Create a new document and call it quiz.html. We're going to create a short fiscal-fitness quiz for online visitors to determine if they are saving enough money for retirement—but remember, this is only the HTML for the web page itself. We are not going to write a CGI script, or any other kind of gateway program, which is the other necessary part of a forms page that actually makes it work online.

2. First, create two one-line text boxes asking for the visitors' full names and email addresses. Then create a series of checkboxes asking visitors to select their age from a range: are they in their late teens or twenties, their thirties, their forties, or their fifties?

3. Now create a pulldown menu asking the visitors to choose their salaries from ranges beginning with $15,000 a year to $200,000 and over—there must be five or more ranges, but you can assign them as you please.

4. Next, create a text field for any additional comments, a yes-or-no pair of radio buttons asking if they'd like to be contacted by the first with yes as a default choice, and then a Reset and a Submit button.

5. When you're finished, your HTML should look something like this:

```
<HTML>
<HEAD>
<TITLE>Are You Fiscally Fit?</TITLE>
</HEAD>
<BODY>
<FORM action="http://www.mdc.com/cgiscript"
method="post">
```

```
<P>Your full name:
<INPUT maxlength="25" name="namebox" type="text">
<BR>
<P>Your email address:
<INPUT maxlength="25" name="emailbox"
type="text">
<BR>
<P>I am in my:
<P><INPUT name="check1" type="checkbox">
late teens or twenties
<INPUT name="check2" type="checkbox">
thirties
<INPUT name="check3" type="checkbox">
forties
<INPUT name="check4" type="checkbox">
fifties
<BR>
<P>My (or our) yearly income is:
<SELECT multiple name="salmenu" size="4">
<OPTION value="1">under $15,000
<OPTION value="2">$15-$30K
<OPTION value="3">$31-$40K
<OPTION value="4">$41-$50K
<OPTION value="5">$51-$60K
<OPTION value="6">$61-$70K
<OPTION value="7">$71-$80K
<OPTION value="8">$81-$90K
<OPTION value="9">$91-$100K
<OPTION value="10">$101-$200K
<OPTION value="11">$200K and up
</SELECT>
<BR>
<P>Additional comments: <BR>
<TEXTAREA cols="40" rows="5" name="feedback"
wrap="virtual">
</TEXTAREA>
<P>Would you like to be contacted by MDC?
<INPUT checked name="checkyes" type="radio"
value="yes">
```

```
Yes
<INPUT name="checkno" type="radio" value="no">
No
<BR>
<INPUT name="reset" type="reset" value="Reset">
<INPUT name="submit" type="submit" value="Sub-
mit">
</FORM>
</BODY>
</HTML>
```

Now let's link it to the menu in the sample business site, so visitors can click on the Fiscally Fit link and open the forms quiz in the main viewing window, the largest frame in the lower right corner.

6. Open menu.html in your HTML editor. Look for the <A> tag that specifies survey.html and change it to look like this:

```
<P><A HREF="quiz.html" TARGET="rbottom">Are You
Fiscally Fit?</A>
```

These instructions tell the browser that when someone clicks on the Fiscally Fit link in the menu page, the Fiscally Fit quiz itself should be loaded up in the frame called "rbottom."

Save your changes. Let's establish the other half of the connection and name the correct frame so that quiz.html will be uploaded in the proper place on the main frames page.

7. Open bhome.html in your HTML editor. Look for the <FRAME> tag that specifies menu.html and change it to look like this:

```
<FRAME SRC="info.html" NAME="rbottom">
```

These instructions identify the large, viewing frame in the lower right corner of the frames page as "rbottom," so that when someone clicks the Fiscally Fit link in the menu frame, the actual Fiscally Fit forms quiz will appear here.

Save your changes. The final HTML for bhome.html will look like this:

```
<HTML>
<HEAD>
```

```
<TITLE>Mula Dinero & Cash, Accountants</TITLE>
<META NAME="keywords" CONTENT="mula, dinero,
cash, accountants, accounting, taxes, IRAs,
retirement, financial planning, estate planning,
wills, bequests, inheritance, stocks, bonds,
futures, investments, investors, investing">
</HEAD>
<FRAMESET COLS="23%, 77%">
<FRAME SRC="menu.html">
<FRAMESET ROWS="18%, 82%">
<FRAME SRC="lhead.html" SCROLLING="no">
<FRAME SRC="info.html" NAME="rbottom">
</FRAMESET>
<NOFRAMES>
<BODY BGCOLOR="#ccffcc" TEXT="#006600"
LINK="#0000FF" ALINK="#ccffcc" VLINK="FF0000">
<P>This web page requires frames, but your
browser can't read them. Call MDC
instead at (101) 555-2345 or email us at
<A HREF="mailto:info@mdc.com">info@mdc.com</A>.
</BODY>
</NOFRAMES>
</FRAMESET>
</HTML>
```

8. To save time later on, go back to menu.html and use
   TARGET="rbottom" to connect the services, staff, Fiscally Fit
   quiz, and links hyperlinks to the intro.html frame. Save your
   changes, and menu.html will look like this when you're finished:

```
<HTML>
<BODY BGCOLOR="#ccffcc" TEXT="#006600"
LINK="#0000FF" ALINK="#ccffcc" VLINK="FF0000">
<IMG SRC="blogo2.gif">
<FONT FACE="arial, helvetica" SIZE="+1">
<P><A HREF="bhome.html">Home</A>
<P><A HREF="services.html" TARGET="rbottom">Ser-
vices</A>
<P><A HREF="staff.html" TARGET="rbottom">Meet Our
Staff</A>
```

```
<P><A HREF="quiz.html" TARGET="rbottom">Are You
Fiscally Fit?</A>
<P><A HREF="links.html" TARGET="rbottom">Links</A>
</FONT>
</BODY>
</HTML>
```

9. Now to test the HTML you've just written, load bhome.html in your browser (make sure all the graphics and individual frames pages are in the same folder with it). When you click the link in the menu frame called Are You Fiscally Fit?, the forms-based quiz you just wrote should appear in the largest, lower right corner frame.

Figures 9.44 and 9.45 show what bhome.html looks like with this new frames page included.

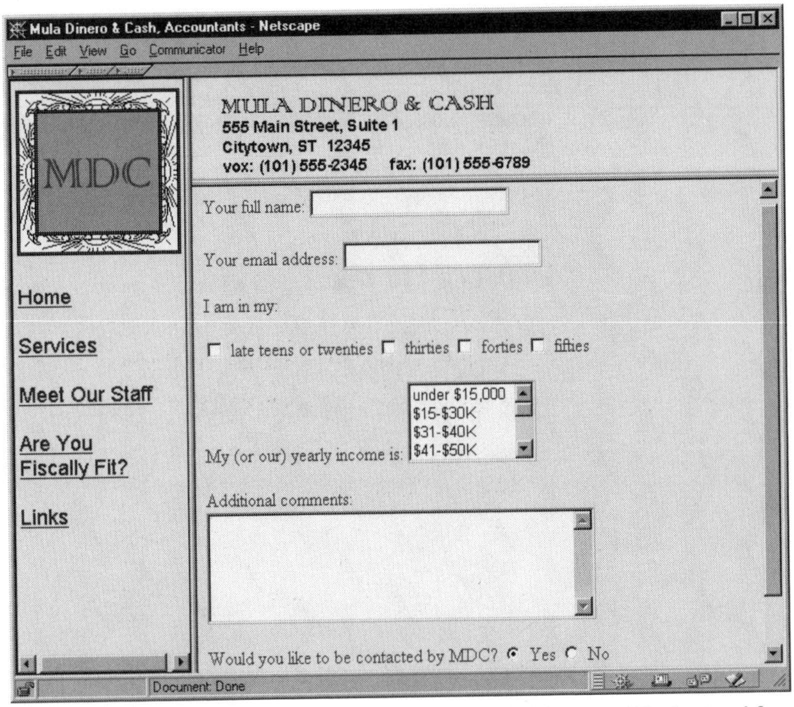

FIGURE 9.44. The forms quiz in bhome.html in Netscape Navigator 4 for the PC

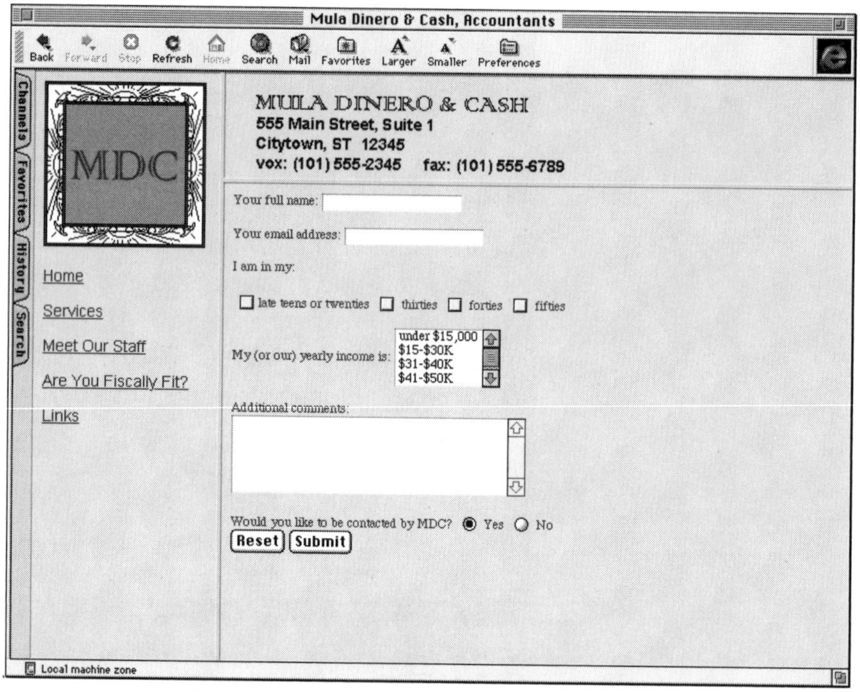

FIGURE 9.45. The forms quiz in bhome.html in Internet Explorer 4 for the Macintosh

"Answers" to the Exercises

Here's what the final HTML for all three sites should look like now that we've completed the exercises:

The personal site main page, doe2.html:

```
<HTML>
<HEAD>
<TITLE>Meet John Doe</TITLE>
</HEAD>
<BODY BACKGROUND="oswirl.gif">
<BR>
<IMG SRC="pixel.gif" ALIGN=bottom HEIGHT=55
WIDTH=1>
<P ALIGN=center>
<A HREF="john.html"><IMG SRC="eye1.gif"  BORDER=0
HSPACE=6 VSPACE=1></A>
```

```
<A HREF="jane.html"><IMG SRC="eye2.gif" BORDER=0
HSPACE=6 VSPACE=1></A>
<A HREF="jack.html"><P ALIGN=center><IMG
SRC="eye3.gif" BORDER=0 HSPACE=6 VSPACE=1></A>
<A HREF="jill.html"><IMG SRC="eye4.gif" BORDER=0
HSPACE=6 VSPACE=1></A>
<BR>
</BODY>
</HTML>
```

The personal site secondary page, john.html:

```
<HTML>
<HEAD>
<TITLE>Meet John Doe</TITLE>
</HEAD>
<BODY BGCOLOR="#FFCC99" TEXT="#996666"
LINK="#663366" ALINK="#FF6699" VLINK="#FF6666">
<FONT FACE="Verdana, Georgia, Helvetica">
<BR>
<P><FONT SIZE="+1"><B>John</B></FONT> is a pro-
grammer at <A HREF="http://www.acmetech.com">Acme
Technology Inc.</A> where he does plenty of tech-
nogeek stuff.
<P>His hobbies include <FONT SIZE="+1"><B>rac-
quetball</B></FONT>, microbrewing, and collecting
<FONT SIZE="+1"><B>Buddy Holly</B></FONT>
records.
<P>Email John at <A HREF="mailto:jdoe@acme-
tech.com">jdoe@acmetech.com</A>.
</BODY>
</HTML>
```

The informational site main page, gallery.html:

```
<HTML>
<HEAD>
<TITLE>The Historic House Style Gallery</TITLE>
<META NAME="description" CONTENT="A gallery of
American residential architectural styles popular
between 1750 and 1950.">
</HEAD>
```

```
<BODY TEXT="#666699" BACKGROUND="infoslice.gif"
LINK="#666699" ALINK="#FFFFCC" VLINK="#FF9900">
<P>
<TABLE BORDER=0 CELLSPACING=0 CELLPADDING=0
WIDTH=600>
<TR>
<TD WIDTH=95 ALIGN=left VALIGN=top>
<P><IMG SRC="salem1s.jpg"><BR>
<P><IMG SRC="salem4s.jpg"><BR>
<P><IMG SRC="salem5s.jpg"><BR>
<P><IMG SRC="salem2s.jpg"><BR>
<P><IMG SRC="salem6s.jpg"><BR>
</TD>
<TD WIDTH=17>
</TD>
<TD WIDTH=470 ALIGN=left VALIGN=top>
<CENTER>
<P><FONT COLOR="#666699" SIZE="+3">The Historic
House Style Gallery</FONT>
<P><FONT COLOR="#999966" SIZE="+2">A gallery of
American historical residential styles<BR></FONT>
</CENTER>
<IMG SRC="pixel.gif" HEIGHT=25 WIDTH=1>
<FONT FACE="georgia" COLOR="#666666" SIZE="+2">
<P><A HREF="georgian.html">Georgian Styles</A>,
1700 - 1776
<P><A HREF="victorian.html">Victorian Styles</A>,
1850 - 1900
<P><A HREF="revival.html">Revival Styles</A>,
1800 - 1870
<P><A HREF="prairie.html">Prairie Styles</A>,
1900 - 1920
</FONT>
<BR>
<FONT FACE="georgia" COLOR="#999966" SIZE="+2">
<P>More Styles Coming Soon
<IMG SRC="pixel.gif" HEIGHT=25 WIDTH=1>
<P>Questions? Submissions? Email <A HREF=
"mailto:curator@hhsg.com">curator@hhsg.com</A>.
```

```
</FONT>
</TD>
</TABLE>
</BODY>
</HTML>
```

The informational site secondary page, victorian.html:

```
<HTML>
<HEAD>
<TITLE>The Historic House Style Gallery: Victo-
rian Styles</TITLE>
</HEAD>
<BODY TEXT="#666699" BACKGROUND="islice.gif"
LINK="#666699" ALINK="#FFFFCC" VLINK="#FF9900">
<P>
<TABLE BORDER=0 CELLSPACING=0 CELLPADDING=0
WIDTH=600>
<TR>
<TD WIDTH=95 ALIGN=left VALIGN=top>
<P><IMG SRC="vict3.jpg">
<P><IMG SRC="vict1.jpg">
<P><IMG SRC="vict2.jpg">
<P><IMG SRC="vict4.jpg">
</TD>
<TD WIDTH=17>
</TD>
<TD WIDTH=470 ALIGN=left VALIGN=top>
<CENTER>
<P><FONT COLOR="#666699" SIZE="+4">
<IMG SRC="dropv.gif">ictorian Styles
</FONT>
<P><FONT COLOR="#999999" SIZE="+3">
1850 - 1900
</FONT>
</CENTER>
<IMG SRC="pixel.gif" HEIGHT=25 WIDTH=1>
<FONT FACE="georgia" COLOR="#999966"><B>
<P>When a real estate listing describes a house
as "Victorian," you'd better hope there's a
```

photo. American Victorian residential style covers the whole spectrum of architectural design, from the simpler Greek Revivals, Urban Victorians and Italianates, to the wild and whimsical Queen Annes, Gothic Revivals and Victorian Eclectics. (The examples on this page, from top to bottom, are a Queen Anne, an Italianate, an Urban Victorian, and a Gothic Revival.)
<P>The <FONT COLOR="#666699">Queen Anne</FONT> was most popular in America between 1870 and 1900, as a reflection of the expanding, newly wealthy middle class. The more ornamentation, and the more patterns and materials used, the better. Some Queen Annes, or "painted ladies" as they are better known today, were painted eight different colors to show off their unique individualities.
<P>The Queen Anne's distinguishing characteristics are:
<UL TYPE=circle>
<LI>projecting bay windows
<LI>cone-shaped corner towers
<LI>several kinds of shingles in horizontal bands
<LI>dormers, gables, and other irregular roofline extensions
<LI>decorated porches and gingerbread
</UL>
</B>
</FONT>
</TD>
</TABLE>
</BODY>
</HTML>

The main, home page with frames for the business site, bhome.html:

<HTML>
<HEAD>
<TITLE>Mula Dinero & Cash, Accountants</TITLE>

```
<META NAME="keywords" CONTENT="mula, dinero,
cash, accountants, accounting, taxes,
IRAs, retirement, financial planning, estate
planning, wills, bequests,
inheritance, stocks, bonds, futures, investments,
investors, investing">
</HEAD>
<FRAMESET COLS="23%, 77%">
<FRAME SRC="menu.html">
<FRAMESET ROWS="18%, 82%">
<FRAME SRC="lhead.html" "rtop" SCROLLING="no">
<FRAME SRC="info.html" NAME="rbottom">
</FRAMESET>
<NOFRAMES>
<BODY BGCOLOR="#ccffcc" TEXT="#006600"
LINK="#0000FF" ALINK="#ccffcc" VLINK="FF0000">
<P>This web page requires frames, but your
browser can't read them. Call MDC
instead at (101) 555-2345 or email us at
<A HREF="mailto:info@mdc.com">info@mdc.com</A>.
</BODY>
</NOFRAMES>
</FRAMESET>
</HTML>
<HTML>
<HEAD>
<TITLE>Mula Dinero & Cash, Accountants</TITLE>
<META NAME="keywords" CONTENT="mula, dinero,
cash, accountants, accounting, taxes,
IRAs, retirement, financial planning, estate
planning, wills, bequests,
inheritance, stocks, bonds, futures, investments,
investors, investing">
</HEAD>
<FRAMESET COLS="23%, 77%">
<FRAME SRC="menu.html">
<FRAMESET ROWS="18%, 82%">
<FRAME SRC="lhead.html" NAME="rtop" SCROLL-
ING="no">
<FRAME SRC="info.html" NAME="rbottom">
```

```
</FRAMESET>
<NOFRAMES>
<BODY BGCOLOR="#ccffcc" TEXT="#006600"
LINK="#0000FF" ALINK="#ccffcc" VLINK="FF0000">
<P>This web page requires frames, but your
browser can't read them. Call MDC
instead at (101) 555-2345 or email us at
<A HREF="mailto:info@mdc.com">info@mdc.com</A>.
</BODY>
</NOFRAMES>
</FRAMESET>
</HTML>
```

The individual frame page, menu.html:

```
<HTML>
<BODY BGCOLOR="#ccffcc" TEXT="#006600"
LINK="#0000FF" ALINK="#ccffcc" VLINK="FF0000">
<IMG SRC="blogo2.gif">
<FONT FACE="arial, helvetica" SIZE="+1">
<P><A HREF="bhome.html">Home</A>
<P><A HREF="services.html" TARGET="rbottom">Ser-
vices</A>
<P><A HREF="staff.html" TARGET="rbottom">Meet Our
Staff</A>
<P><A HREF="quiz.html" TARGET="rbottom">Are You
Fiscally Fit?</A>
<P><A HREF="links.html" TARGET="rbottom">Links</A>
</FONT>
</BODY>
</HTML><HTML>
<BODY BGCOLOR="#ccffcc" TEXT="#006600"
LINK="#0000FF" ALINK="#ccffcc" VLINK="FF0000">
<IMG SRC="blogo2.gif">
<FONT FACE="arial, helvetica" SIZE="+1">
<P><A HREF="bhome.html">Home</A>
<P><A HREF="services.html" TARGET="rbottom">Ser-
vices</A>
<P><A HREF="staff.html" TARGET="rbottom">Meet Our
Staff</A>
```

```
<P><A HREF="quiz.html" TARGET="rbottom">Are You
Fiscally Fit?</A>
<P><A HREF="links.html" TARGET="rbottom">Links</A>
</FONT>
</BODY>
</HTML>
```

Review

- As a rule of thumb, PCs display text one increment larger than a Macintosh. This is most easily remembered by the PC and Mac defaults: Times Roman 12 and Times 10, respectively.

- Also a rule, PCs display colors darker than Macintoshes do. This affects a page's text in particular because of how some fonts are designed—if the letters have narrow sections, they might disappear against a dark background. In addition, there should be high contrast between a font color and a background color, so the contrast can be preserved no matter which platform a visitor is using.

- Use lists sparingly and only for short, plain text items. Plenty of web pages out there use them too often and for lists of links, but these design strategies are considered passé.

- Use forms carefully and with a great deal of patience. You cannot customize a form's appearance to any great extent, nor can you significantly change the margins, spacing, or size of a form. Any other design elements on a page with forms, then, should be extremely simple.

On with the Show

It's time now to add multimedia and other advanced elements to our sample sites—video, audio, GIF animations, VRML worlds, JavaScript, and even a little DHTML. Turn the page and we'll get started.

CHAPTER 10

Adding Multimedia and More

In this chapter, we'll learn how to include and design pages with video, audio, VRML worlds, and GIF animations. This is the part of the book, however, where you will need all the plug-ins we discussed in Chapter 2, "RealPlayer, QuickTime, Shockwave, and WorldView." If you didn't download and install them then, do it now. Otherwise you won't be able to see the things we want to point out to you, and incorporating multimedia elements will be very difficult for you.

Definitions

Way back in Chapter 1, we defined **audio** as any way of adding sound to a web page: as a sound effect, as a soundtrack, as a recording of music or some other sound file. We also spoke of **video** as adding motion pictures to a web page, but we separated these two kinds of effects according to the way they work. Audio and video, for our purposes, are sound and motion picture files that can be controlled by the visitor via a **play box**, a set of stereo- or VCR-like buttons. We will discuss controlling audio and video, and letting them run continuously, later on in the chapter and in the exercises.

Animation is another broad term we defined as any short visual effect that plays continuously or is available to the web page visitor anytime. This includes **GIF animations**, a short series of single GIF files or **cells** that play in sequence. **VRML**, on the other hand, falls somewhere in between video and animation. It's virtual reality, a three-dimensional sensory experience, which downloads and can be controlled like a video clip but has the appearance of an animation sequence. Unfortunately, VRML worlds are still relatively crude and very large in terms of file size. Also, we cannot teach you how to create one for yourself (just as we aren't teaching you how to write JavaScripts or CGI programs for your forms) so we'll have to go a-borrowing. But we will show you how to incorporate a VRML world as a regular link.

So, we should clear up the difference between the two main ways you can add multimedia. You can provide a link to a sound file, a video clip, or a VRML world that will cause it and its play box to load up in a new page, or you can **embed** it. When you embed audio, video, and VRML, you make them part of your actual web page, like a GIF or some other graphic. This strategy enables you to use these technologies in more diverse, creative ways, which we will discuss later on in this chapter.

We should also acquaint you with the idea of **file formats**, which are the different ways to save sound, video, and other files. Unlike the reasoning behind GIFs and JPEGs, implementing one kind of multimedia format over another has to do with platform support. We will introduce you to the most popular and/or common audio, video, and other file formats as they are needed throughout the chapter.

Objectives

Our objectives in this chapter focus on the rather plain or simple pages we've created so far with backgrounds and/or colors, plain text, links, and graphics. We are going to spice them up by adding audio and video clips to the personal web site and GIF animations to the business and informational sample sites. This chapter will teach you both how to code and incorporate these cool tricks, and when such extras are appropriate and enhancing, rather than gimmicky or distracting. As always, context matters. Keep that in mind as we go along.

Designing with Multimedia Links

First, let's visit some web pages that were designed around audio, video, and VRML in a functional but practical and interesting way. It's important to understand what the HTML for these elements looks like, because the coding is static and not necessarily reflective of the end result.

Audio Links

We're going to revisit part of Steve Mulder's site now: The Emma Thompson Sanctuary. It's not just a good example of a celebrity informational site; it makes lavish and effective use of video and audio links. (See Figure 10.1.)

Choose the second text link—"Sing no more ditties..."—because it's only 27K. A small Netscape window will open, and eventually a playbox will appear.

Navigator will play the sound for you automatically once, and then you can use the buttons and volume slider to replay it as much as you like. Now let's check the same URL in Internet Explorer 4 for the PC. Explorer opens a whole new browser window and then the playbox. It also gives you the option to open the file now or to save it to disk. If you don't save it, once you close the playbox, the sound file is flushed from your disk cache. This is one way copyright and ownership of these files is maintained on the Web.

> **Amy:** Earlier you said that .AU is Mac, and .WAV is PC; it's unclear to me whether each file format can be played on either platform or not.

> **Rebecca:** The .AU format can be played on both the PC and the Macintosh, but the .WAV format is PC-only. .WAV files are important

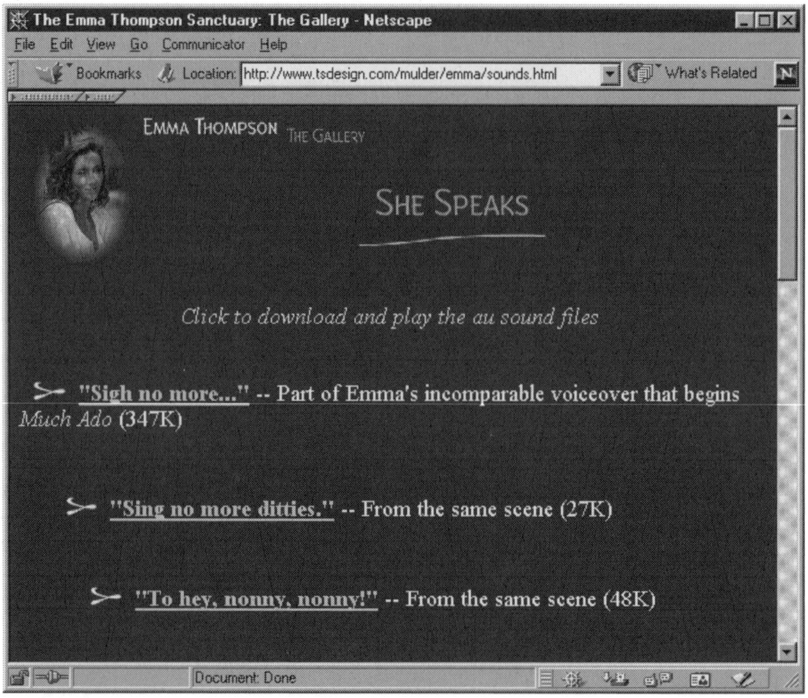

FIGURE 10.1. A collection of sound files: The Emma Thompson Sanctuary, The Gallery (http://www.tsdesign.com/mulder/emma/sounds.html) in Netscape Navigator 4 for the PC

for backward compatibility; we haven't used that term in a while, but it means support or consideration for visitors using older browsers. (In this book, an older browser is version 2.0 or earlier of our two main browsers, Netscape Navigator and Microsoft Internet Explorer, or Mosaic.)

Video Links

There's an excellent collection of movie clips, too, right on this same site. This is Steve Mulder's video clip archive of Emma Thompson's film work. (See Figure 10.2.)

Let's choose the last picture link on the right from *Sense and Sensibility*. Click the small still frame to begin the download.

Navigator will load the movie in a new browser window—eventually. In the meantime, the QuickTime multicolored Q symbol appears, and you can watch the download progress in the text box

FIGURE 10.2. A collection of video clips: The Emma Thompson Sanctuary, The Gallery (http://www.tsdesign.com/mulder/emma/gallery.html) in Netscape Navigator 4 for the Mac

along the bottom edge of the browser window. (Or you can go make yourself some lunch. You have plenty of time.)

As a matter of design, this site is a great example of the way to display a collection of sound and video files for the downloading. It's also another overall site design that contends nicely with lots of color photographs. (The still photo pages are particularly well done.) The overall design of this site is very simple yet distinctive, and it frames the text and photo links without detracting from their purpose.

Amy: You mention that the still photo pages are particularly well done. Why? Because the designer used themes, such as "Magazine and other Poses" and "Biographical Photos"? Because of the layout and color choices? What else?

Rebecca: This goes back, in part, to our earlier discussion of the informational site color palette in Chapter 7. I think it's difficult to design a site that will contain many photographs or multicolored graphics from many different locations, because no palette is going to complement all those colors. The deep teal Mulder uses on his site is a nice choice, though, because it has many yellow, blue, and green hues in it.

I also like his use of themes or categories, in addition to the way the graphics are staggered down the page. You never feel overwhelmed by too many choices, and every graphic looks interesting. This kind of site can easily seem cluttered or endless if you're forced to view too many pictures all packed together, or if you have to scroll down too far to reach the end of the page.

Somehow this site seems elegant and simple, both in execution and usability, even though it contains a staggering number of graphics. That's why I like it and recommend it as a good example of site design.

When the download is complete, click on the Play button (next to last on the left) to play the video. As long as your current browsing session lasts, you can return to this "page" in your viewing history and see the clip. But once you end your session, it gets flushed out of Navigator's system along with other items in your disk cache.

> **Amy:**   Here's a warning to readers: IE4 for the PC didn't tell me it was loading anything or give me an estimate for the download time remaining. I saw the QuickTime Q icon and was left guessing as to whether the download was happening or not.

VRML Worlds

Before we embark upon a tour of various VRML worlds, it's important that we state a few disclaimers up front. (No, most people don't dislike VRML the way they dislike frames!)

First, audio and video are far more accessible and learnable for the average web page designer than VRML is. A handful of VRML software applications enable users to make VRML worlds, but with lots of patience, setbacks, and a big-time investment. You can make an audio clip in a minute if you have the right shareware, and a video clip in about fifteen minutes if you've got a desktop camera. But with current VRML technology, it can take weeks or months just to create one room in one house with VRML. That's the reason why there's so little VRML on the web—it's a barrier of technology, not public disinterest.

Second, there's nothing close to a plug-in or file format consensus—and you think the file format situation with audio and video files is confusing! There were several other VRML pages and galleries we wanted to show you, but *each* of them required a new, different VRML plug-in. It's a pain. And for our purposes, it would have been a waste of time.

Third, VRML is hard to experience as it was designed if you have a "slow" connection, slow being anything less than a cable modem, an ISDN, a T1, or any other kind of dedicated Internet linkup. That leaves the vast majority of Web users—those of us with mundane modems—in the dust. We can view and participate in VRML environments, but our movements are slow or jerky, and it's very hard to have immediate control over crucial orientation. On a slow connection with a mouse, you can easily find yourself in the air when you thought you were walking forward.

It's also necessary for the reader to understand that we will not be working with an actual VRML world in the exercises. Why? Because VRML worlds are enormous files, even the small demonstration worlds we found when we scoured the Internet. I (Rebecca) don't even have the room on my hard disk to download and keep one. But this situation will undoubtedly change, as the Web moves closer and closer to becoming a real three-dimensional environment. It's what people ultimately expect, and the technology is coming.

> **Amy:**   I can definitely see the possibilities in VRML if you have a good connection and the interaction isn't slow.

> **Rebecca:**   You just reminded me to remind the reader of something: If you're using a "high-speed" modem, don't expect to reach top connection speed every time you log on to the Internet. If there's lots of line traffic, if your ISP makes you use the same phone line as everyone else with 14.4 or 28.8 modems, if the weather is bad in your area, you're going to have slower connections. Most of the time you're on the net, this isn't terribly evident. But if you're trying to navigate a VRML world, you're going to notice the difference.

From this point forward in this section, we are wandering into complicated territory, with browser compatibility issues and strange workaround HTML. So let's explore other HTML tags which support multimedia, both individually and in combination with the <A> tag: <BGSOUND>, <EMBED>, and <IMG>.

Now let's talk about implementing these multimedia elements.

Multimedia HTML

The <BGSOUND> Tag

<BGSOUND> is an Internet Explorer-only tag used to incorporate sound clips or background, embedded sound into a web page. Its rough equivalent for Netscape Navigator is the <EMBED> tag, which we will cover in the next section.

Here's the basic HTML:

```
<BGSOUND SRC="sound.au" LOOP=3>
```

with SRC specifying the name of the sound file and LOOP specifying the number of times the file will play (use -1 or infinite to make the sound loop continuously).

> **NOTE:** It is easy to record your own sounds if you have the shareware/freeware and the microphone that comes standard with all new personal computers.
>
> If you're using a PC, GoldWave is good for both recording and editing sound files. If you're using a Macintosh, SoundHandle is good for recording sounds and SoundMover is a simple, intuitive sound editor. You can find all these tools (plus many others) at the TUCOWS repository:
>
> http://www.tucows.com

You can use the <EMBED> tag to provide background sound for visitors using Navigator, though, so let's address how to do that.

The <EMBED> Tag

The <EMBED> tag is, in some ways, God's gift to the web page designer. It enables you to place any kind of multimedia file into your web page with one catch: Your visitors must have an appropriate plug-in installed to hear, see, or experience the embedded feature.

Amy: To clarify, does the <EMBED> tag work only with Navigator (which versions)?

Rebecca: No; both Navigator and Explorer support it. In this particular instance (we're talking about audio files) <EMBED> is most commonly used to supplement the <BGSOUND> tag, which is not supported by Explorer. We'll get to the proper syntax involved in using these two tags together in just a little bit.

It has several useful and/or necessary attributes, depending upon which kind of media you're embedding:

ALIGN   Specifies the alignment of the embedded object's play box.

   bottom   The play box is aligned with the bottom horizontal edge of the browser window.

   center   The play box is aligned with the center point of the browser window.

   left   The play box is aligned with the left vertical side of the browser window. (This is the default setting.)

   top   The play box is aligned with the top horizontal edge of the browser window.

   right   The play box is aligned with the right vertical side of the browser window.

AUTOSTART   Specifies automatic startup of a sound file. Used with one value, true, to disable the play box and run the file immediately upon completion of download. Must be used with PLAYBACK.

BORDER   Specifies a black border around the play box in pixels.

HEIGHT   Specifies the overall height of the embedded object. Must be used with WIDTH.

> **en**   Renders the embedded object in increments equal to half the point size of the page text. (The default point size for the Macintosh is 10, and the default for the PC is 12.
>
> **pixels**   Renders the embedded object in pixels. (This is the default value.)

WIDTH   Specifies the overall width of the embedded object. Must be used with HEIGHT.

There's another attribute, PALETTE, which you can use like this to specify the background and foreground colors for the play box:

```
PALETTE="blue/brown"
```

or

```
PALETTE="#FFCC00/#336699"
```

but at this writing it is not supported by Navigator or Explorer for the Macintosh. However, this may change as new versions of these two browsers come along, so keep this attribute in mind for future reference.

There are also <EMBED> tag attributes, oddly enough, that are recognized only by certain plug-ins. A seldom-used video player plug-in for the PC, for example, recognizes the ONCURSOR attribute, which prompts an embedded video clip to start playing when the cursor touches it. But this attribute is worthless to the more popular, standardized plug-ins, even those that already come installed with Navigator and Explorer.

However, some of these plug-ins, such as LiveVideo, which is included with Netscape Navigator, also have their own attributes. LiveVideo supports an attribute called AUTOPLAY that prompts Navigator to immediately open and play the specified video clip if the value is specified. However, do not interpret this situation to mean that AUTOPLAY and its like have true *browser* support, like that of the attributes listed above. If visitors to your web site prefer some other kind of video plug-in, such as RealPlayer, and have adjusted their browser Preferences to reflect this fact, then AUTOPLAY will not work even though LiveVideo is present and installed.

Now, back to the puzzle of multimedia. To embed a sound file with the <EMBED> tag, write your HTML like this:

```
<EMBED SRC="sound.au" ALIGN=center HEIGHT=115
WIDTH=150>
```

The HEIGHT and WIDTH measurements should always be as precise as you can manage, no matter what kind of file you've embedded. These two attributes will prompt the browser to display a play box immediately, even before the sound file is finished loading up, which is especially kind to your visitor if the sound file is rather large.

You can, and arguably should, use <BGSOUND> and <EMBED> together in the same HTML document for crossbrowser support, and here's what that HTML would look like:

```
<EMBED SRC="sound.au">
<NOEMBED>
<BGSOUND = "sound.au" LOOP=infinite>
</NOEMBED>
```

The <NOEMBED> tag isolates an alternate snippet of HTML for people who don't have a certain browser or other requisite <EMBED> technology, the same way <NOFRAMES> isolates a text message for people using non-frames-enabled browsers. This is how you add continuous, soundtrack-like sound to a web page so that both browsers can read it reliably.

To embed a video file with the <EMBED> tag, write your HTML like this:

```
<EMBED SRC="video.avi" ALIGN=center HEIGHT=115
WIDTH=150 AUTOSTART=true PLAYBACK=3>
```

Remember that you can use the <EMBED> tag for video much as you use the <A> tag just by leaving out the AUTOSTART attribute. Without AUTOSTART, only a play box will load up with the web page, but with it, the video clip itself will load up and repeat (in this example, because PLAYBACK=3) three times before quitting.

You can also use the <EMBED> tag to implement a VRML world file like this:

```
<EMBED SRC="vrml.wrl" HEIGHT=95 WIDTH=130>
```

but only Netscape browsers will see it; hence the need again for the <NOEMBED> tag, and the <IMG> tag, so Explorer users can see your VRML world. Using these tags together looks roughly like this:

```
<EMBED SRC="vrml.wrl" HEIGHT=95 WIDTH=130>
<NOEMBED>
<IMG DYNASRC="vrml.wrl">
</NOEMBED>
```

Amy: The concept here is similar to the one behind the HTML for the sound files, right? <EMBED> for Netscape and <IMG DYNASRC> for Internet Explorer.

Rebecca: Yes, but not because of limited browser support (we use <EMBED> for background sound together with <BGSOUND> because <BGSOUND> is not supported by Navigator). The wrinkle here is that Navigator *can* recognize both the <EMBED> and <IMG> tags, so you use <NOEMBED> to prevent Navigator from becoming confused.

This HTML will help any visitor to your page using a VRML-enabled browser, which is version 3 or 4 of Navigator or Explorer. (People using Mosaic or an earlier version of Navigator or Explorer are just plain out of luck.)

NOTE: You can help visitors to your page who don't have the right plug-ins for the embedded content you've used. You can warn them in your entryway and provide a link to the right URL where they can get the plug-in. Or you can rely on Navigator or Explorer to provide this warning in a separate dialog box, but either way, the <EMBED> tag is not as much of an obstacle as the <BGSOUND> tag or other tags that are not crossplatform.

The <A> Tag

The <A> tag is the choice for dropping in simple links to audio, video, and VRML. This is not necessarily your design choice of preference, but it can work well.

Here's the basic <A> tag HTML:

```
<A HREF="sound.au">
<A HREF="movie.mov">
<A HREF="vrml.wrl.">
```

There are two attributes to address. HREF, naturally, specifies the file name of the multimedia element to be displayed, as shown above. TARGET, however, specifies where the multimedia element play box will be loaded up. This gives you a couple of design options, so you can allow space and environment for the play box in the same page where the link is located, or for the opening of a new blank browser window.

TARGET's three possible values are:

blank   The play box will appear in a new, unnamed, blank browser window.

self   The play box will appear in the same browser window where the link is located.

top   The play box will appear alone, taking up the entire open browser window.

As a rule of thumb, you can almost always allow room in a web page for video and audio play boxes that tend to be small. By the same token, you'll want to display VRML worlds in their own new, blank browser windows, because they need to be somewhat large. With frames, you can mix and match "new" browser windows, with one side narrow frame retaining the actual links and a large main frame acting as the viewscreen. This is perhaps the only design environment in which you could incorporate even the largest VRML world into the "same page," although your design is completely up to you.

The <IMG> Tag

Finally, here's the <IMG> tag. The basic <IMG> HTML is the same as if you were dropping in a GIF:

```
<IMG SRC="movie.mov">
```

unless you're putting in a VRML world, per the last example in the <EMBED> section, in which case it looks like this:

```
<IMG DYNASRC="vrml.wrl">
```

but there are many required, useful attributes to be implemented, too. Let's cover them briefly and then go into detail.

ALIGN   Specifies the alignment of an embedded object in relation to any text surrounding it.

   bottom   The bottom edge of the object and the baseline of the first line of text are aligned.

   left   The left side of the embedded image lies flush against the browser window edge and the text flows around it.

   middle   The middle points of the object and of the surrounding text block are aligned.

   right   The right side of the embedded image lies flush against the browser window edge and the text flows around it.

   top   Text is aligned with and flowed around the top edge of the embedded object. (This is Navigator's and Explorer's default.)

ALT   Used to specify a text message for visitors using text-only browsers, or who are browsing with image downloading disabled.

BORDER   Specifies the presence and width, or the absence, of a border.

CONTROLS   Specifies the presence or absence of a play box for video and audio. (This attribute is not recognized by Netscape Navigator.)

DYNSRC   Used instead of SRC to specify a video clip or a VRML world. (This attribute is not recognized by Netscape Navigator.)

HEIGHT   Specifies the overall height of the object display area in pixels. Without HEIGHT and its corresponding attribute, WIDTH, the embedded object will not appear at all until the entire web page is loaded up.

HSPACE   Specifies a pixel-based amount of horizontal space between the embedded object and any text surrounding it.

LOOP   Specifies the number of times a video clip will play before shutting off. A value of -1 or infinite will make the clip play continuously.

LOOPDELAY   Specifies the number of milliseconds between iterations of a video clip.

SRC   Specifies the file name of the video or audio clip to be embedded.

START   Specifies when and how an embedded video clip will begin playing.

    fileopen   The video clip will begin playing continuously as soon as it is downloaded and the web page is fully downloaded.

    mouseover   The video clip will be playing when and if the visitor rolls the cursor over it.

VRML   Embeds a VRML world into a web page and tells the browser to provide a VRML play box. (This attribute is not recognized by Netscape Navigator.)

VSPACE   Specifies a pixel-based amount of vertical space between the embedded object and any text surrounding it.

WIDTH   Specifies the overall width of the object display area in pixels. Without WIDTH and its corresponding attribute, HEIGHT, the embedded object will not appear at all until the entire web page is loaded up.

Let's apply these attributes in each situation, but let's do VRML first since we left the <A> tag hanging in the last <EMBED> example, which looked like this:

```
<EMBED SRC="vrml.wrl" HEIGHT=95 WIDTH=130>
<NOEMBED>
<IMG ALIGN=center ALT="You're using a browser
that doesn't support VRML. Go get Netscape Navi-
gator or Internet Explorer!" DYNASRC="vrml.wrl"
HEIGHT=120 SRC="vrml.gif" START=mouseover
VRML="vrml.wrl" WIDTH=210">
</NOEMBED>
```

First of all, because there are so many attributes to be used (eight in total), I wrote them into the HTML alphabetically for easy reference. This is an optional technique, but I for one find it easier to maintain and update HTML if I sort a large number of attributes in this fashion.

Back to the coding itself: ALT, DYNASRC, SRC, and VRML are all related to how the VRML world is displayed, or not displayed, on the web page. ALT and SRC are safeguards for visitors who don't have VRML-enabled browsers. SRC presents them with a GIF image—preferably a tantalizing still from the cool VRML world they're missing—while ALT gives them the message: Go get Navigator or Explorer! DYNASRC and VRML, respectively, are used to cover the needs of Navigator and Explorer both; DYNASRC is an Explorer-only attribute that specifies a VRML world, while VRML serves two functions. Like DYNASRC, it specifies the VRML world file name, but it also tells both Navigator and Explorer to display the play box controls.

ALIGN, HEIGHT, and WIDTH work the same way as they do with other <IMG> tag elements, as placement and display instructions for the browser. START, in this cast, is context-specific—the VRML world won't commence until the visitor rolls the cursor over it.

Amy: Are the ALIGN, HEIGHT and WIDTH values for the play box or the actual VRML? It seems that the VRML dimensions would be written into the VRML itself.

Rebecca: They are, but in some instances the browser functions better if you let it know how big the play box should be ahead of time. That's the purpose of HEIGHT and WIDTH, while ALIGN (or alignment) is not intrinsic to the VRML world. You, the web page designer, use ALIGN to decide where the world play box should appear.

Now, to use the <IMG> tag, your basic HTML should look like this:

```
<IMG SRC="movie.mov" ALIGN=center HEIGHT=120
WIDTH=210 START=fileopen LOOP=6 LOOPDELAY=4000>
```

Amy: Why would you use the <IMG> tag to embed video (or anything else) for Navigator users? Doesn't Netscape support the <EMBED> tag in all cases? Is there a difference in using <IMG> instead?

Rebecca: First of all, yes, <EMBED> is supported by Netscape Navigator. To answer the rest of your question, though, here's what I suspect about the <IMG> and <EMBED> situation.

Remember that we talked about the different generations of web pages? There are also different generations of HTML tags, and <IMG> was one of the first HTML tags that allowed designers to put something other than text on a web page. At that point in Web history, programmers used existing tags to stretch HTML's capabilities to the limit, successfully and unsuccessfully, when it came to interactivity. So I believe this is why the <IMG> tag can be used to put multimedia on a web page. It was intended, I believe, only to put GIFs and JPEGs in a page, but desperate programmers might have tweaked it into doing a little more.

However, <EMBED> is the better option by far. But that's exactly what it is: an option. At minimum, <IMG> is the more reliable of the two precisely because it is a first- or second-generation tag and you know earlier browsers will recognize it. But <EMBED> was arguably created from scratch to do the same kinds of things, so it will just work better.

This sequencing represents the other way I choose to write a long string of attributes: first the name of the file (SRC), then everything associated with its size and placement (ALIGN, HEIGHT, and WIDTH), then anything concerning its display or movement on the page (START, LOOP, and LOOPDELAY).

But let's stick to the HTML protocol. We've already covered SRC, ALIGN, HEIGHT, and WIDTH, so we'll concentrate on the last three attributes. In this example, we used fileopen as the START value so that the video clip would open immediately as soon as it's downloaded. LOOP represents the number of times the video clip will play (we could specify -1 or infinite if we wanted it to play continuously) while LOOPDELAY counts off the number of milliseconds between playbacks. There are 1000 milliseconds in every second, so this measurement represents a delay of 4 seconds.

So, here's how you embed video:

```
<EMBED SRC="movie.avi" ALIGN=center HEIGHT=120
WIDTH=210 AUTOSTART=true PLAYBACK=6>
<NOEMBED>
<IMG SRC="movie.mov" ALIGN=center HEIGHT=120
WIDTH=210 START=fileopen LOOP=6 LOOPDELAY=4000>
</NOEMBED>
```

Notice the different video file formats, with the Explorer-friendly version specified in the <EMBED> tag and the Navigator-friendly version specified in the <IMG> tag. However, look at the absence of a LOOPDELAY equivalent in the <EMBED> tag and remember that Explorer users will see your video clip played over and over without the short pause that Navigator users will experience. That should strongly affect the way you decide to use continuous video in your overall page design.

NOTE: The downside of embedding audio, video, and even VRML is the download time. If you think an oversized GIF or richly colored JPEG will make a visitor wait too long, imagine a movie trailer, or a VRML house tour.

GIF Animations

If you want movement on your page without the hassle of plug-ins or browser problems, then a GIF animation might be the more practical solution than fussing with <A>, <IMG>, and <EMBED> all together. Here's what a GIF animation is and how it works.

Remember when we introduced the idea of layers in connection with Photoshop in Chapter 6? A collection of layers is like a stack of transparent films, with one graphic element on each layer only, so that the stack looks like a complete image. One layer is the background, the next is an object, the third is the object's shadow, and so on.

GIF animations work on a very similar principle, only the layers or cells are loaded up and dropped out in a sequence you establish. For example, the first cell might be a traffic light with the green light on, the second would be the same light with green off but yellow on, and the last would be the yellow light off and the red light on. When you ran the sequence of those cells, the effect would mimic a traffic light changing.

The benefits of using a GIF animation are many. A GIF animation cell is saved as a plain, ordinary GIF and written into your HTML code using the <A> tag. There are no browser or platform support issues, no special or potentially uncommon plug-ins needed, and even very early browsers that don't support animation will still display the first "layer" rather than a broken graphic symbol. Better yet, GIF animations are handled solely by the browser, unlike a video clip, which relies upon your ISP's server for a long download.

The drawbacks are few but significant. You can't add sound to a GIF animation, and there's no special interaction with the visitor. They don't get a different effect when they click it, or roll the cursor over it, as can happen with a JavaScript, although you can make a link of the whole thing as you can with a plain GIF. (That's the basic construction of most banner ads, actually.) So while GIF animations are very user-friendly, you have to use them carefully, simply, and specifically. Let's talk about how to do that after we run through the process of making GIF animations.

Before you actually open GIF animation software and begin constructing the actual sequence of cells, you have to make the cells themselves. This is by far the most time-consuming part of creating GIF animations; the individual cell GIFs provided for you on the CD-ROM took a couple of hours to create and optimize in a graphics program. So don't be fooled by how easy the GIF animation software is to use; it merely assembles artwork that's already been crafted elsewhere.

Using GIF Animator (Windows)

Ulead's GIF Animator is superior GIF animation demoware, but it is still demoware. That means that you can only use it for a specific period of time before you have to uninstall and download another trial version or pay the fee to purchase it outright.

To get started here, you'll need GIF Animator, your HTML editor, your browser of choice, and the CD-ROM. We'll be creating a simple flashing GIF animation.

1. Open GIF Animator. The Startup Wizard dialog box will appear. We're creating a new GIF animation, so click on the icon for Blank Animation. The main GIF Animator window will open.

2. Choose Open Images from the main toolbar—roll the cursor over the buttons and descriptions will appear—and the Add Images dialog box will open. On the CD, there is a folder called "flash." Open all four of the GIFs inside it (flash1.gif, flash2.gif, and so on) by holding down the Control key as you click with the mouse.

3. To begin with, click the Start Preview button to view the animation as it stands. It moves too slowly from animation frame to animation frame, so let's speed it up.

4. In the sequence window on the left side, click flash1.gif to highlight it. Use the Delay window to change the increment from 10/100th of a second to 5/100th of a second.

Click on all four flash GIFs, and repeat the process. Click Start Preview to view the results; now these four dots look more like flashing lights.

5. Now let's make certain this GIF animation is the right file size. Choose Optimization Wizard from the File pulldown menu, and the Optimization Wizard will start up.

6. In this first window, the Wizard asks if you want to optimize all the GIFs colors the same way, creating a "super-palette." The right answer, Yes, is already selected, so click Next to continue.

7. In the second window, you get to choose the number of colors in the super-palette. The GIF animation we're working with is extremely simple, so we can afford to greatly reduce it. Use the Number of Colors window to select 8 rather than 64. Also, we don't want GIF Animator to dither these colors, so leave the bottom radio button selected at No, and click Next.

8. In the third window, again, the right answers are already selected for you. You do want the Wizard to remove any redundant pixels, and you also want it to remove comment blocks. So Yes is the correct answer to both questions, and you can click Next.

9. In the fourth window, you are given the option to use these settings as a default optimization scheme. You should leave this box unchecked because each GIF animation will require different settings. Click Finish to finish.

10. The optimization will proceed—you can watch in the progress window—and then the Wizard will present you with the results in the GIF Optimization dialog box.

11. Click Save As to finish, and the standard Windows Save As dialog box will appear. Name this new animation flash.gif, and click Save.

12. Finally, use the Preview in Explorer or Preview in Navigator buttons on the main button bar to view the animation in a browser, or Close the program altogether.

Using GIFBuilder (Macintosh)

To begin, you'll need GIFBuilder, your HTML editor, and the CD-ROM that accompanies the book.

1. First, open the CD-ROM on your desktop so you can see all the files. There's a folder called "meow," containing twelve GIFs called meow1.gif through meow12.gif. This is a more sophisticated GIF animation than the first one we did in the GIF Construction Set, so it has many more individual GIF files.

2. Now open GIFBuilder. A window called Frames will open. Use the mouse to highlight all twelve of the meow GIF files in the open exercise file folder and drag-and-drop them into the GIFBuilder window.

   You should name your individual GIF cells in numerical order, so GIFBuilder will know which file comes first, second, and so on in the animation sequence.

3. GIFBuilder has loaded the GIFs numerically, which means that there are three GIF cells out of sequence: meow10.gif, meow11.gif, and meow12.gif. Click meow10.gif, hold down the Apple key, and you can drag this cell to the end of the list to reposition it properly. Repeat the process with the other two.

4. You need to save this GIFBuilder file, so choose Save from the Edit pulldown menu or press Control+S. The standard Save dialog box will appear; save this GIF animation as meow.gif and click OK. GIFBuilder will take a minute to think, but that's it. The animation sequence is constructed.

5. Now open your HTML editor and create a new HTML document called anim2.html. The minimal HTML you need without the GIF animation code looks like this:

```
<HTML>
<HEAD>
<TITLE>Meow Animation</TITLE>
</HEAD>
```

```
<BODY>
</BODY>
</HTML>
```

6. Put in the GIF animation code in the blank line between the <BODY> opening and closing tags (the meow.gif cells are 398 pixels wide and 98 pixels tall). Save the changes, and your HTML should look something like this:

```
<HTML>
<HEAD>
<TITLE>Meow Animation</TITLE>
</HEAD>
<BODY>
<IMG SRC="meow.gif" WIDTH=398 HEIGHT=98>
</BODY>
</HTML>
```

7. Now choose Start from the Animation pulldown menu to test the animation. It moves too fast for you to really see what's going on, so let's change the timing between GIF animation frames. Click on the frame that displays *before* the affected change, and choose Interframe Delay from the Options pulldown menu. The Interframe Delay dialog box will open.

8. Type a new delay time (we chose 20) in the available text box, and click OK. You should change all the delays to the presets we chose, and then choose Save. All the new delays are shown in the Delay column.

Notice, though, that there is another option in the Interframe Delay dialog box: as fast as possible. This is the setting you want to choose if you're trying for true animation, such as a butterfly flying or a human figure running, though you should remember that a GIF animation will only move from cell to cell as quickly as the visitor's connection speed will permit. This is why GIF animations should be kept simple; you need to "design down" to the lowest (slowest) common denominator.

9. When you're relatively satisfied, open your browser and upload anim2.html. The white background of the animation will look a little funny against the default gray background, but the animation should work without a hitch. (You can always make the background transparent—it's just a set of GIFs, remember?)

Amy: When I did this exercise in GIF Animator, I decided to make the delay times different for part of the sequence. I used 40 for most of the frames, but for meow5.gif through meow9.gif, I used 20. That gave me time to read the words "Eliot sez, repeat after me," but helped smooth out the extended ME—OW animation. I ended with a 60/100-second delay for the last frame for emphasis on the "MEOW!" I don't know if the change in rhythm would be distracting when this was actually loaded on a web page. Any ideas on that?

Rebecca: Good plan! You can and should change the delay times between different kinds of cells, depending upon where you want the visitors' focus. We'll experiment with different delay times in one of the exercises, actually.

Exercises

In these exercises, we are going to add audio and video to the personal site, and GIF animations to all three sample sites.

First, the audio and video. Open your HTML editor, your browser of choice, and put in the CD-ROM.

Adding Video and Audio Links

1. We're going to create another secondary page for Jill Doe, John Doe's daughter. To save yourself some typing, open john.html that we created in chapter 9 (or open john1.html on the CD) in your HTML editor. Plug in the following changes:

```
<HTML>
<HEAD>
```

```
<TITLE>Meet Jill Doe</TITLE>
</HEAD>
<BODY BGCOLOR="#FFCC99" TEXT="#996666"
LINK="#663366" ALINK="#FF6699" VLINK="#FF6666">
<FONT FACE="Verdana, Georgia, Helvetica">
<BR>
<P><FONT SIZE="+1"><B>Jill</B></FONT> is ---
<P>Email Jill at <A
HREF="mailto:jill@doe.com">jill@doe.com</A>.
</BODY>
</HTML>
```

Save this new page as jill.html.

2. Jill is, of course, a child prodigy. She attends a school for budding adolescent brains (you think of an appropriate name), she makes cutting-edge independent films, she designs VRML worlds, and she composes poetry. Add some text to her page to this effect, so that the final result looks something like this:

```
<HTML>
<HEAD>
<TITLE>Meet Jill Doe</TITLE>
</HEAD>
<BODY BGCOLOR="#FFCC99" TEXT="#996666"
LINK="#663366" ALINK="#FF6699" VLINK="#FF6666">
<FONT FACE="Verdana, Georgia, Helvetica">
<BR>
<P><FONT SIZE="+1"><B>Jill</B></FONT> attends the
prestigious <A HREF="http://www.tate-
heads.edu">Little Man Tate Academy for the Gifted
and Talented</A>. <FONT SIZE=+1>Her last film
</FONT> was well-received at Sundance and Cannes,
her <FONT SIZE=+1>poetry</FONT> has been nomi-
nated for the <FONT SIZE=+1>Nobel Prize</FONT>,
and her <FONT SIZE=+1>VRML worlds</FONT> are fre-
quently mistaken for the real thing.
<P>Email Jill at <A
HREF="mailto:jill@doe.com">jill@doe.com</A>.
</BODY>
</HTML>
```

3. Now let's add <A> tag links to a poem, a video clip, and a VRML world. The poem is available as both ode.au and ode.wav, so you should provide links for Windows and Mac users. The movie clip is also available as both life.mov and life.au. The VRML world file is vrml.wrl. (Note: These audio, video, and VRML files do not exist on the CD. We are focusing just on writing the correct HTML.)

```
<HTML>
<HEAD>
<TITLE>Meet Jill Doe</TITLE>
</HEAD>
<BODY BGCOLOR="#FFCC99" TEXT="#996666"
LINK="#663366" ALINK="#FF6699" VLINK="#FF6666">
<FONT FACE="Verdana, Georgia, Helvetica">
<BR>
<P><FONT SIZE="+1"><B>Jill</B></FONT> attends the
prestigious <A HREF="http://www.tate-
heads.edu">Little Man Tate Academy for the Gifted
and Talented</A>. <FONT SIZE=+1>Her last film
</FONT> was well-received at Sundance and Cannes,
her <FONT SIZE=+1>poetry</FONT> has been nomi-
nated for the <FONT SIZE=+1>Nobel Prize</FONT>,
and her <FONT SIZE=+1>VRML worlds</FONT> are fre-
quently mistaken for the real thing.
<P>Listen to "Ode" for <A HREF="ode.wav">Win-
dows</A> (.WAV) or for the  <A HREF="ode.au">Mac-
intosh</A> (.AU) — 20KB
<P>View a pivotal scene in "The Meaning of Life"
for <A HREF="life.mov">Windows</A> (.MOV) or for
the <A HREF="life.avi">Macintosh</A> (.AVI) — 320KB
<P>Interact with Jill's latest <A
HREF="vrml.wrl">VRML world</A> — 6MB
<P>Email Jill at <A
HREF="mailto:jill@doe.com">jill@doe.com</A>.
</BODY>
</HTML>
```

Now let's experiment some more with GIF animations.

GIF Animation #1: The Tax Time Marquee

We're going to add a GIF animation marquee to the sample business web site, so get your HTML editor, your browser, your GIF animation software, and the CD-ROM handy. We'll be alternating between GIF animation programs, so this exercise will be done in GIFBuilder. Remember, though, that GIFBuilder and GIF Animator are very similar, so you PC users should be able to follow along very easily.

1. First, open info.html in your HTML editor. Then let's build the GIF animation. Open GIFBuilder and import the tax GIF files in the Chapter 10 folder. We're going to make a flashing marquee advertising MDC's tax season services.

2. View the animation as it is by choosing Start from the Animation pulldown menu, or by pressing Control+R. The timing is a little too fast, so change the delay between cells by choosing Interframe Delay from the Options menu, and change the delay from 10 to 18.

3. We're going to place this GIF animation at the bottom of the main menu page in the viewing frame on the MDC business site (info.html). So we want it to loop (play continuously). Ordinarily, this would not be the strategy for a GIF animation unless you were creating a banner ad, but visitors to the MDC site will not stay on the main menu page for very long.

   Choose Loop from the Options pulldown menu, and the Loop dialog box will appear. Choose forever to make the animation play continuously, and click OK.

4. Check the animation again by pressing Control+R to start it and Control+. (the period key) to stop. The animation should be readable but not obnoxious, and the pause between each iteration, or the end of one loop and the beginning of the next, should be long enough to convey a brief ending. This sounds tricky, but you'll know the right tempo when you see it.

5. Save this animation as tax.gif when you're satisfied. Then choose Copy HTML Image Tag from the Edit pulldown menu. Now switch to info.html in your HTML editor, and let's drop in the animation. Here's what the HTML should look like when you're finished:

```
<HTML>
<BODY BGCOLOR="#ccffcc" TEXT="#006600"
LINK="#0000FF" ALINK="#ccffcc" VLINK="FF0000">
<FONT FACE="arial, helvetica" SIZE="+1">
<P>Explore the <A HREF="services.html" TAR-
GET="rbottom">services</A> we have to offer,
including tax preparation, estate planning, and
investment advice.
<P><A HREF="staff.html" TARGET="rbottom">Meet Our
Staff</A>, who are always here to serve you.
<P>Got enough invested to make your retirement
comfortable? Take our <A HREF="quiz.html" TAR-
GET="rbottom">Fiscally Fit Quiz</A>.
<P>Check out other useful <A HREF="links.html"
TARGET="rbottom">links</A> including mortgage and
college tuition calculators, the latest on the
Dow Jones, and more money management.
<BR>
<P><CENTER><IMG SRC="tax.gif" WIDTH=377
HEIGHT=75></CENTER>
<BR>
</FONT>
</BODY>
</HTML>
```

NOTE: I made the seven individual cells for the tax-time marquee in Photoshop using the Layers feature to position each cell's elements where I wanted them. But first, I wrote out the animation like so:

1: There are only (red)
2: 42 days left (yellow)
3: till tax time. (red)

4: - blank - (yellow)
5: Are you ready? (red)
6: - blank - (yellow)
7: Get help from MDC. (red)
8: - blank - (yellow)

Making a simple list of individual animation cells in this manner helped me visualize which part of the message would fall where, and which color "light" would be on when each bit of the message would be revealed. I put in blank cells, with only the "lighted" edge but no text, (steps 6 and 8). It only takes a minute to sketch a GIF animation out with paper and pencil, but it can save you some editing later if you forget something.

GIF Animation #2: The Gallery Entryway

We're going to make a slide show GIF animation for the sample informational site (the Historic House Style Gallery), so open your HTML editor, your GIF animation software (we're using GIF Animator on the PC for this example), and your browser of choice, and have the CD-ROM handy.

1. Open GIF Animator and the CD-ROM. On the CD, there's a folder within the Graphics folder called "houses." Click-and-drag all 21 GIFs in this folder (housesa.gif through housesq.gif) into the GIF Animator cell window on the left side.

2. Here, GIF Animator has automatically placed the individual GIF files in the proper order because the files are alphabetically (housesa.gif) rather than numerically (houses1.gif). So we can proceed right toward customizing the animation—click on Global Information at the top of the stack.

3. First, click on the Global Information frame at the top of the cell stack. This will allow you to customize certain aspects of all the cells in the animation at once.

4. Change the size of the Logical Screen so it will be flush with the edges of the cells—the width setting should be 175 and the height setting should be 111.

5. Next, uncheck the Infinite setting in the Looping area, and choose 0 (zero) to make sure the animation will only play once.

6. Then establish the delay between cells as follows (click on the slide named here before typing its corresponding number in the Delay window):

housesa.gif	80
housesb.gif	75
housesc.gif	80
housesd.gif	75
housese.gif	80
housesf.gif	75
housesg.gif	80
housesh.gif	75
housesi.gif	80
housesj.gif	75
housesk.gif	80
housesl.gif	75
housesm.gif	80
housesn.gif	75
houseso.gif	80
housesp.gif	75
housesq.gif	80

7. Click the Save button, or press Control+S, and the Optimization Wizard opens automatically. Follow the steps just as we did earlier in this chapter, with the exception of specifying 128 colors, and click Finish. The Wizard will do its thing, and give you the results.

8. This animation will take 32 seconds to download! Can we do significantly better and still preserve image quality? Click Preview to see how the quality looks.

9. Click the Play button and view the animation. The quality looks very good, so perhaps you can safely reduce the number of colors in the super-palette. Close the preview window by clicking the X

in the upper right corner, and click Another Try. (If Another Try doesn't appear in the GIF Optimization dialog box, you can click Optimization Wizard in the File menu.)

10. This time, when you run the Optimization Wizard, accept the 64-color default setting. Finish the Wizard, let it do its work, and click Preview in the final Wizard window to view the animation again.

11. Look at the numbers in the GIF optimization window; the download time has been cut in half! But, unfortunately, you've reduced the animation too far—look at the sky in the eighth cell. (It's the square house with double porches and a small square construction on the roof. There's always one cell in an animation that gives overreduction away.) The sky is banded like a rainbow rather than smoothly monochromatic, so 64 colors will not do. Close the Preview window, click Another Try, and let's have one last stab at optimization.

12. After some tinkering (we tried 96 colors and 128 colors again, respectively) we left the reduced color palette at 128. Why? Because 96 colors is as low as we could comfortably go and this put the download time at 31 seconds. If we increased the number of colors to 128, the image quality was greatly improved, but download time only increased by one second. That tradeoff is too good to pass up.

13. Click Save As, click Cancel in the Optimization Wizard, and save the animation as houses.gif. Now you can click the Preview in Explorer or Preview in Navigator buttons to get a real look at the animation in situ, but we're moving on. Let's create the actual entryway page.

14. Open your HTML editor and open gallery1.html from the CD. You'll notice that for this entry page we've replaced the slice GIF background with a deep mustard solid color.

This is your starting HTML:

```
<HTML>
<HEAD>
<TITLE>The Historic House Style Gallery</TITLE>
<META NAME="description" CONTENT="A gallery of
American residential architectural styles popular
between 1750 and 1950.">
</HEAD>
<BODY TEXT="#666699" BGCOLOR="#FFCCOO"
LINK="#666699" ALINK="#FFFFCC" VLINK="#FF9900">
<FONT FACE="georgia, verdana, helvetica"
SIZE="+1">

</FONT>
</BODY>
</HTML>
```

15. Now drop in the GIF animation. First, use the pixel.gif trick to push the GIF animation toward the middle of the page (a HEIGHT value of 155 is what we came up with). Then enter the GIF HTML itself; the cells measure 175 pixels wide and 111 pixels tall. Center it all on the page, and this is what you have:

```
<HTML>
<HEAD>
<TITLE>The Historic House Style Gallery</TITLE>
<META NAME="description" CONTENT="A gallery of
American residential architectural styles popular
between 1750 and 1950.">
</HEAD>
<BODY TEXT="#666699" BGCOLOR="#FFCCOO"
LINK="#666699" ALINK="#FFFFCC" VLINK="#FF9900">
<FONT FACE="georgia, verdana, helvetica"
SIZE="+1">
<CENTER>
<P><IMG SRC="pixel.gif" HEIGHT=155 WIDTH=1>
<BR>
<P><IMG SRC="houses.gif" WIDTH=175 HEIGHT=111>
<BR>
```

Who's Afraid of Web Page Design?

```
<P>Click <A HREF="gallery.html">here</A> at any
time to enter the Gallery.
</CENTER>
<BR>
</FONT>
</BODY>
</HTML>
```

16. Because a GIF animation is just a GIF, you can make it a link to another page. Make houses.gif a link to the menu page for this site, gallery.html. The HTML for that line alone will look like this:

```
<P><A HREF="gallery.html"><IMG SRC="houses.gif"
WIDTH=175 HEIGHT=111></A>
```

17. Save this new HTML page as galentry.html, and view it in your browser of choice to finish.

"Answers" to the Exercises

The "answers," such as they are, have already been shown to you. But here they are again just in case.

The final HTML for Jill Doe's page, jill.html, should look like this:

```
<HTML>
<HEAD>
<TITLE>Meet Jill Doe</TITLE>
</HEAD>
<BODY BGCOLOR="#FFCC99" TEXT="#996666"
LINK="#663366" ALINK="#FF6699" VLINK="#FF6666">
<FONT FACE="Verdana, Georgia, Helvetica">
<BR>
<P><FONT SIZE="+1"><B>Jill</B></FONT> attends the
prestigious <A HREF="http://www.tate-
heads.edu">Little Man Tate Academy for the Gifted
and Talented</A>. <FONT SIZE=+1>Her last film</
FONT> was well-received at Sundance and Cannes, her
<FONT SIZE=+1>poetry</FONT> has been nominated for
```

```
the <FONT SIZE=+1>Nobel Prize</FONT>, and her <FONT
SIZE=+1>VRML worlds</FONT> are frequently mistaken
for the real thing.
<P>Listen to "Ode" for <A HREF="ode.wav">Win-
dows</A> (.WAV) or for the  <A HREF="ode.au">Mac-
intosh</A> (.AU) — 20KB
<P>View a pivotal scene in "The Meaning of Life"
for <A HREF="life.mov">Windows</A> (.MOV) or for
the  <A HREF="life.avi">Macintosh</A> (.AVI) —
320KB
<P>Interact with Jill's latest <A
HREF="vrml.wrl">VRML world</A> — 6MB
<P>Email Jill at <A
HREF="mailto:jill@doe.com">jill@doe.com</A>.
</BODY>
</HTML>
```

The final HTML for the MDC business page, including the tax time marquee GIF animation, should look like this:

```
<HTML>
<BODY BGCOLOR="#ccffcc" TEXT="#006600"
LINK="#0000FF" ALINK="#ccffcc" VLINK="FF0000">
<FONT FACE="arial, helvetica" SIZE="+1">
<P>Explore the <A HREF="services.html" TAR-
GET="rbottom">services</A> we have to offer,
including tax preparation, estate planning, and
investment advice.
<P><A HREF="staff.html" TARGET="rbottom">Meet Our
Staff</A>, who are always here to serve you.
<P>Got enough invested to make your retirement
comfortable? Take our <A HREF="quiz.html" TAR-
GET="rbottom">Fiscally Fit Quiz</A>.
<P>Check out other useful <A HREF="links.html"
TARGET="rbottom">links</A> including mortgage and
college tuition calculators, the latest on the
Dow Jones, and more money management.
<BR>
<P><CENTER><IMG SRC="tax.gif" WIDTH=377
HEIGHT=75></CENTER>
```

```
<BR>
</FONT>
</BODY>
</HTML>
```

The final HTML for the gallery entryway page, galentry.html, should look like this:

```
<HTML>
<HEAD>
<TITLE>The Historic House Style Gallery</TITLE>
<META NAME="description" CONTENT="A gallery of
American residential architectural styles popular
between 1750 and 1950.">
</HEAD>
<BODY TEXT="#666699" BGCOLOR="#FFCCOO"
LINK="#666699" ALINK="#FFFFCC" VLINK="#FF9900">
<FONT FACE="georgia, verdana, helvetica"
SIZE="+1">
<CENTER>
<P><IMG SRC="pixel.gif" HEIGHT=155 WIDTH=1>
<BR>
<P><A HREF="gallery.html"><IMG SRC="houses.gif"
WIDTH=175 HEIGHT=111></A>
<BR>
<P>Click <A HREF="gallery.html">here</A> at any
time to enter the Gallery.
</CENTER>
<BR>
</FONT>
</BODY>
</HTML>
```

Review

- Make multimedia optional. The HTML, the plug-ins, and the browser support for audio, video, and VRML at this writing is not collectively reliable enough for designers to depend upon. Visitors to your site should not need its multimedia elements in order to navigate or understand how your site works—and neither should multimedia make or break your overall page design.

- You can include audio, video, and VRML to a web page by creating either a regular text or image link, or you can embed it. Embedding multimedia makes it part of the actual web page, so the file gets downloaded as the page downloads and discarded with the web page when the viewer is finished.

- A GIF animation is like a slide show, or an old-fashioned cartoon, made from a series of still GIFS cycled through a particular sequence. The results you get are dependent upon a visitor's connection speed, which is typically very slow or full of interruptions, so it's tough to make true animation effects this way.

- VRML, particularly, means working with very large and cumbersome files. Try to keep the limitations of your hard disk, your ISP's server, and your visitor's patience in mind when implementing it (this also applies to audio and video, but to a lesser extent).

On with the Show

From this point forward, we go into Chapter 11, which is a wrap-up of all the basic, general concepts we've discussed throughout this book. We provide some additional exercises, an overview of the summary bulleted lists at the end of Chapters 1 through 10, and some FAQs.

We hope you'll continue to come back to this book as a point of reference for your future design work, and we wish you good luck.

Epilogue

Welcome to the end of your web design journey. You fell through the rabbit's hole into the Wonderland of the Web and immersed yourself, hoping to learn more than you knew before you set out.

This chapter serves two purposes in the scheme of the book: to offer a few more suggestions for practice, since our three sample sites aren't technically finished, and to provide some insight into web site maintenance. So let's run through the list of suggestions first, and then talk a little bit about long-term site management.

Additional "Exercises"

These really aren't exercises, per se, because we won't be putting you through any steps or showing you any code. This is strictly optional stuff we have included as a springboard for your next big assignment: designing pages on your own. Here are some optional tasks you can try to round out missing parts of our three sample web sites:

The Personal Site: Meet the Does

- Create jack.html and jane.html, the personal pages for the other two members of the Doe family. Practice simple and complex positioning, both with the pixel.gif and with tables.

- Can you make the background of the main page (doe.html) swirl around? How about the eyeballs? Why not both? Determine which would be the best way to accomplish this kind of movement: GIF animations, or JavaScript?

- Use style sheets to achieve really wacky text effects, with colors, fonts, and more—remember personal sites can be the furthest out there on the cutting edge designwise.

- Commit to creating more visual interest on all of the pages without adding any more normal GIFs or JPGs. What can text "say" about a web site all on its own? How about audio? Video?

The Informational Site: The Historic House Style Gallery

- Create the remaining style pages. Practice writing clear, brief blocks of text and using lists effectively.

- Make an imagemap from a floor plan for the main page, gallery.html, instead of a list of plain text links.

- If you're feeling extremely ambitious, find some VRML software and create your own three-dimensional examples of these historic house styles.

- Research the different kinds of music that were popular when certain house styles were in vogue, find some appropriate audio files on the Web, and make a soundtrack for each style page.

The Business Site: Mula Dinero & Cash, Accountants

- Create the remaining pages in the site to practice using the frame tag and linking individual frames pages together.

- Establish a link archive of important tax forms and other common paperwork used for creating wills, contracts, and other money-related documents.

- In order to entice customers, design an online contest. It could feature tax trivia or could just be a form that visitors fill out to enter a drawing. Don't forget the JPGs of prizes!

- Create a simple online calculator that will help people, say, figure their deduction for interest on their mortgage or a form that will help them figure which tax bracket they are in.

Site Maintenance Q&A

How Often Should I Update Information on My Web Site?

When you come to the end of designing a web site, you arrive at the beginning of the site maintenance process. Even if all your code is perfect and you find no problems after uploading your pages to your server, something can become outdated on your site within the hour. People switch ISPs and don't leave a "forwarding" link after they move their pages. People also move, or change jobs, rendering their email addresses obsolete. New browsers, or new versions of existing browsers, arrive in beta before all the bugs are worked out. So how often do you retest your pages or change your site content? It depends.

Let's refer to our sample sites one last time. The personal page, for example, is the least likely to change significantly or require major updating within a short period of time. Maybe the Does will get a dog, or have another child. Maybe John or Jane will get promoted and the family will move to San Francisco. These are big life changes but they will happen only occasionally, if they ever happen at all. So updating the personal page is almost strictly a matter of choice.

> **Amy:** I would think there's one more consideration in updating a personal page: how many links you have and how current they are. It seems like you should visit your own site once every month or two to make sure.

Rebecca: You're definitely right—dead links are the most common reason to update a web page, and they happen unexpectedly. But we designed the personal site so that it contains very few links, and some designers might choose that strategy. The gallery you talked about creating, for example, might work very well as a nearly linkless web site. And in that case, you would only update your site if you had new artwork to display or if you sold something on "display."

The Historic House Style Gallery, our informational page, is somewhat likely to need frequent updating. By its very nature, this web site is limited in scope as something doesn't become "antique" or "historical" until it's been around for fifty years. (That makes the seventies trilevel a historic house style, by the way.) But even though there may be a limited number of style pages to be created, there's a practically unlimited number of historic houses. People who maintain this kind of web site might very well find themselves flooded with photos and other graphics; think about a celebrity site like the Emma Thompson Sanctuary, for example. Every time she does a movie, she also does interviews and TV appearances and publicity shoots. That's a lot of web site maintenance, adding all those clips and photos and sounds bites, but in brief concentrated amounts.

On the other hand, there's the MDC page, our business web site. The nature of a business site calls for frequent, if not constant, updating. You might have inventory listings, new products or services to offer or withdraw, press releases, legal or procedural changes, and so on. Think about some of the business sites we've seen, like eBay or NetGrocer. They've undoubtedly hired a whole team of webmasters solely dedicated to keeping those web sites current and running smoothly.

How Often Should I Add New Technologies to My Web Site?

If you decide to read Appendix A, you will be introduced to some of the things new technologies such as DHTML can do, and you might feel either excited or pressured about keeping up. Maybe you feel it's a continuation of your Web education to keep abreast of everything new and hot in the online world. Then again, maybe you haven't been paying attention!

Adding every new and trendy doodad to your web site is probably the worst thing you can do design-wise. Remember, very often on the Web, *less is more*. Or, as Amy said early on, just because you *can* do something doesn't mean you *should*, right? Exactly! Believe it or not, the goal of all these new technologies is to make some aspect of web design easier, or to make up for some problem or obstacle in HTML that already exists. They don't *mean* to intimidate you, or drive you and your visitors crazy by crashing sensitive browsers or requiring new plug-ins, but that's what's happened. You might make yourself stand out from the crowd by *not* using new technologies right away. Common sense, after all, is a pretty rare commodity in both the real and the virtual world.

The good news is that HTML and its ancillary technologies have developed so that you can create a relatively elegant and useful web site without many worries. Maybe you don't get to use style sheets or VRML exactly as you would if all things were equal. But if you can convey the information you want to send out, in a way that's savvy but won't bother or frustrate version 3 browsers, then you've done a good design job. Then, when version 5 browsers start appearing on the scene, you can "scale back" to designing for version 4 browsers.

How Often Should I Redesign My Site Entirely?

This is the toughest question. Part of it depends upon your audience; part of it depends on why you chose to design a site in the first place. Most of it depends upon the flexibility and pertinence of your existing site; have you outgrown it, or do you just need to sit down for an afternoon and do some tweaking? Or have you been struck by some incredible inspiration that makes your old design look downright first-generation?

Ideally, you design a web site so it will last a long, long time with only occasional light maintenance work. This means you don't use anything dated or ultratrendy in your color scheme, cultural references, or other contextual markers. Ideally. In the real world, though, your site is a reflection of some need or want on your part, so you're going to get tired of it.

The problem is that a redesign takes lots of time. Redesigning really means tossing out your previous site structure and content and making something utterly new. Who has time for that, unless your job is to design web sites? Probably not the recreational web page designer. So the best answer, again ideally, is to avoid having to ask the question. The fact that you're reading this book shows that you're probably at a design crossroads in terms of your own site, if you have one. The best and first resolution you can make at this point is to design something as open-ended, as elegant, and as simple as possible. Don't take on a tough technology like JavaScript unless you think you'll enjoy it. Don't bother with style sheets yet unless you have a high tolerance for disappointment. Design something you can live with well beyond your first idle thoughts about redesigning it—because chances are, you'll still be having those not-so-idle thoughts six or ten months down the road without having done anything about them.

Review

To recap the best of what we've shown you throughout the book, here are the highlights:

Planning a Site

- You should ask yourself five basic questions when you plan the content of your web site: *Who* is the site for, *what* belongs on this site, *when* do I want to launch it, *where* will this site be seen, and *why* create this particular site at all? Decide whether you'd like a temporary or UC page to advertise your web site ahead of time. Apply these same questions and answers to its design, create it, test it, and upload it to the Web as quickly as possible.

- Your site's *framework* should be either a literal map on paper or a visualization in your head—a flow chart, if you will—detailing how all your pages relate to one another. Sketch it out with a pencil or try to see it in your mind's eye, but establish it concretely. You should have an entryway, a main page, secondary and even tertiary pages, and an exit mechanism.

- *Content* is the material and information that will appear on your site. *Form* encompasses everything about the way your web site is organized on the page.

Graphics

- There are two universally acceptable graphics formats, the GIF and the JPG. (The PNG is far superior but isn't reliably supported by many browsers yet.) The JPG format is best for photos or photorealistic graphics, and the GIF is best for everything else.

- The ultimate goal in preparing graphics for the Web is to make each graphic as small as possible without sacrificing overall sharpness, brilliance, and quality. Sometimes this means leaving a graphic (particularly a JPG) larger than you may like, but this can be better than saving it at a lower resolution and making it look ugly.

- Never make an important graphic too large, period. Imagemaps, menus, logos, and other crucial elements should load quickly and easily if your visitors cannot navigate or understand your site without them. It is better to change a graphic's overall design to make it simpler or less colorful (and therefore smaller) than to leave it too large.

- Texture and noise involve how the human eyes and brain perceive grouped colors. If you combine too many colors and patterns to create texture on a page, visitors will not know where to focus—the page will have too much noise—and they will move on.

Color

- It's good to combine like colors in a background pattern, for example, lighter and darker shades of red. It's not good to choose a text or link color that's similar to a background, such as light blue on white.

- Similarly, it's not good to combine dissimilar colors such as light yellow and dark purple in a background pattern, or visitors will have difficulty reading your text. But it *is* good to choose a dark text color for a light background color, or a light text color for a dark background color.

- Try to use a blend of hues and saturations in your web site palette. Combine light, medium, bright, and dark colors imaginatively and in balance, so visitors will know where you want them to look and what's most important.

HTML

- *Syntax* is synonymous with grammar in HTML. It tells you how and where to locate a tag, how to write out its attributes and values, and what other tags can be placed within it. But unlike with real grammar, there are no shortcuts or slang in HTML—you cannot even add or forget one single space or your code will not work.

- Make a rough sketch of your UC page—graphics, text, any logos or identities, any backgrounds or other artistic renderings. Then translate this sketch into basic (repeat, *basic*) HTML and test it on each of the three browsers you downloaded. If you like how your page looks, upload it to your ISP and view it on the Web.

- Arrange your opening and closing tags in corresponding ascending and descending order. This will help you read it more easily, so you can discover whether or not you've left something out. Also, arrange a tag's attributes alphabetically if you're using more than six for one tag, for the same reasons. Otherwise, group attributes by their functions so they're arranged logically.

- Get comfortable with experimentation. The best way to learn HTML is to play around with your code, make mistakes, and then get yourself out of them.

Frames

- Consider both the pros and the cons of a frames-based web site. There are legitimate reasons for both opinions. If you do decide to use frames, give your visitors a warning in your entryway, and/or provide a nonframes version of your web site as an alternative.

Crossplatform Issues

- PCs usually display text one increment larger than a Macintosh. This is most easily remembered by the PC and Mac defaults: Times Roman 12 and Times 10, respectively.

- As a rule, PCs display colors darker than Macintoshes do. This affects a page's text in particular, because of how some fonts are designed—if the letters have narrow sections, they might disappear against a dark background. Also, there should be high contrast between a font color and a background color, so the contrast can be preserved no matter which platform a visitor is using.

Forms

- Use forms carefully and with a great deal of patience. You cannot customize a form's appearance to any great extent, nor can you significantly change the margins, spacing, or size of a form. Any other design elements on a page with forms, then, should be extremely simple.

Multimedia

- Make multimedia optional. The HTML, the plug-ins, and the browser support for audio, video, and VRML at this writing is not collectively reliable enough for designers to depend upon. Visitors to your site should not need its multimedia elements in order to navigate or understand how your site works—and neither should multimedia make or break your overall page design.

- You can include audio, video, and VRML on a web page by creating either a regular text or image link, or you can embed it. Embedding multimedia makes it part of the actual web page, so the file gets downloaded as the page downloads and is discarded with the web page when the viewer is finished.

- Working with VRML means working with particularly large and cumbersome files. Try to keep the limitations of your hard disk, your ISP's server, and your visitor's patience in mind when implementing it (this also applies to audio and video, but to a lesser extent).

- Use newer technologies such as JavaScript or style sheets with caution, and never depend upon them to make or break the overall design of your page.

- On the Web, very often less is more. Present your information as elegantly and (if only on the surface) as simply as possible. Don't let technology get in the way.

What's Left?

There are still a few more resources for you to explore in this book, even though we're done with the formal chapters. The CD-ROM contains the Gallery, featuring full-color images and descriptions of more excellent sites we recommend you visit for inspiration, and a color-chip chart of all 216 browser-safe colors. Also, if you skipped Chapter 6 (about advanced graphic design) the first time around, now might be a good time to have a look.

Amy: Some final questions: Will the sites and gallery be available on the Web anywhere for further study?

Rebecca: Yes, it's my intention to put these three sites up on my own personal page. The URL is:

http://users.rcn.com/rtapley

Amy: How about some kind of discussion board in which readers can share ideas and discuss concerns?

Rebecca: Readers can always email me with questions: rtapley@rcn.com. If this book becomes a best-seller, I'll make a guestbook page so people can see each other's comments and questions.

Amy: Any further recommendations for sites or books for further study? What is your opinion of *Web Pages that Suck* by Vincent Flanders and Michael Willis? Their web site is at:

www.webpagesthatsuck.com/home.html.

Their focus seems to be on fewer gimmicks, more content.

Rebecca: I really liked that site—some of their humor made me laugh out loud. As for other recommendations, hotWIRED's Webmonkey site features many quality tutorials on HTML topics such as forms, JavaScript, and style sheets just to name a few. Their URL again is:

http://www.hotwired.com/webmonkey

Let me also remind people again of David Siegel's site about web design principles at:

http://www.killersites.com

and Lynda Weinman's site about color issues (you can also download the browser-safe color palette here) at:

http://www.lynda.com

Some other useful URLs are:

http://www.tucows.com

http://www.shareware.com

for utilities, shareware, demoware, and other free or nearly free Web tools.

http://www.essex1.com/people/timothy/js-index.htm

http://www.developer.com

For cut-and-pastable scripts including JavaScripts (ask first!)

http://www.w3.org

The World Wide Web Consortium, the people who create the world-wide HTML standards and post the very latest on browser and platform support issues.

Here's more recommended reading on various topics we've covered:

Who's Afraid of HTML? (Morgan Kaufmann), the "beginner's" book in the Who's Afraid of series, designed as a "prequel" to this book.

The Web Authoring Desk Reference (Hayden Books), an encyclopedic reference of JavaScript properties and methods, and HTML tags.

hotWIRED Style by Jeff Veen (HardWired), as a nice general dos and don'ts approach to total web design.

Photoshop Studio Skills and *Teach Yourself Paint Shop Pro in 24 Hours* (Macmillan), for people who want to dig more deeply into the graphics software we used.

Photoshop Web Magic, *HTML Web Magic*, and *JavaScript Web Magic* (Hayden Books) to learn more graphical doodads for spicing up your web pages.

HTML Artistry: More than Code (New Riders), *GIF Animation Studio* (O'Reilly), and *Designing with JavaScript* (O'Reilly) for more information on advanced HTML, GIF animation, and JavaScripts.

The Web Designer's Guide to Style Sheets (Hayden) is technically outdated with the release of the version 5 browsers, but it is the best introduction on the basics of style sheets.

From this point, you can check out one or all of the Appendices, or be satisfied you've completed a basic course in web page design. Appendix A shows you how to modify existing DHTML (including JavaScripts and style sheets) to add more interactivity and interest to your web pages. Appendix B is a color preview of the extended gallery section included on the CD-ROM.

Adding DHTML: JavaScript, Style Sheets, and More

This appendix shows you how to include and design pages with some DHTML, namely a little JavaScript, a little style sheets, and a little something extra. This is another part of the book, however, where you will need all the plug-ins we discussed in Chapter 2. If you didn't download and install them then, do it now. Otherwise you won't be able to see the things we want to point out to you, and incorporating multimedia elements will be very difficult.

Definitions

First, here's a reminder of what **HTML** is: It's a shorthand version of a larger markup language specifically designed for putting text on the World Wide Web. This definition is a little more specific than the one we gave you in Chapter 1, but we've come a long way since then. We've explored the outer limits of what HTML can and cannot do by itself. This is where DHTML comes in.

DHTML, or dynamic HTML, is a third-generation language with the ability to script (with JavaScript) and position (with style sheets) any HTML element on a web page. It was created by Netscape in 1995 in response to people who were trying to make regular HTML more interactive with "add-on" technology. The two operative words in that last sentence are "add-on" and "trying." Page designers tried to add motion, color, and precise placement into their web sites using CGI scripts or other gateway programs (as with forms, for example) and other technologies that required either cooperation from a server or a dizzying array of plug-ins.

As we've already recognized, the Web is a wild world. Servers get swamped, and/or parts of the Internet get zapped by lightning and go temporarily offline. Visitors cannot be expected to download and install every hot new plug-in before they stumble across a web page that requires it. So a patchwork approach to solving web page interactivity is not the answer. What designers *really* needed, then, was a new aspect of regular HTML that could incorporate interactivity without relying on something else outside the web page. That, in a nutshell, is DHTML's purpose.

To understand how DHTML works, you must first understand how DHTML "sees" your web page. In this context, everything concrete within the environment of your web site is called an **object**: the browser window itself or the web page loaded up within the browser window, just to name two examples. **JavaScript**, perhaps the most popular and widely used aspect of DHTML at this writing, makes objects **scriptable**, or able to be manipulated, both interactively *and* individually. JavaScript is not a true programming language such as Java, the language used to create it, because it cannot function without HTML tags. But this relative simplicity makes JavaScript much more accessible to people without programming experience. We'll rely on that in the exercises as we customize existing JavaScripts to enhance our web pages.

Amy: I have a question about objects: Besides seeing the browser window and the web page as objects, DHTML also sees each block of text and each image as an object, right? How exactly is this different from HTML? (See also my comment in the review section.)

Rebecca: The difference between HTML and DHTML is like the difference between nouns alone, and nouns with verbs. Remember that HTML is part of a bigger, parent language called SGML? Well, HTML was written with the intention of simply putting text and graphics (period) in one place, stagnant, on the web page. That was good enough for the founders of the Internet, if you remember, because they saw the Web only as a means of exchanging reports and technical papers. So they incorporated only the "nouns" they needed for first-generation, non-dynamic web pages.

DHTML, on the other hand, recognizes every single object as interactive because it contains, so to speak, nouns and verbs together. This really means two things. First, any object can be situated anywhere on the web page with absolute reliability. No more messing with pixel.gifs or <TABLE> tags to force objects into place against HTML's will. It also means, though, that an object on the web page can be made to move without needing an unreliable intermediary, like a plug-in. The "verbs" in DHTML make all these workarounds unecessary.

Style sheets, on the other hand, makes all objects **positionable** on a web page. In other words, you don't have to take a stab in the dark at arranging text, graphics, and other elements using <P>, <BR>, and <ALIGN>. Style sheets allows you to be precise, and to be more flexible, in your decisions about where various page elements can go. We should clear one thing up immediately, though: We are not going to teach you how to write your own original scripts. Those tasks are way beyond the scope of this book and also require some proficiency and familiarity with basic programming. Instead, we're going to show you where to find existing scripts, how to customize them for your own purposes, and how to incorporate them into your HTML documents. This is a talent and skill quite sufficient enough for most web page designers who have no programming background, so don't feel you're being cheated.

We *will*, however, introduce you to writing style sheets information into HTML from scratch, as style sheets is more like HTML than like an entirely new language. There still isn't room in this book, though, to cover all the existing possibilities—and much of style sheets is still relegated to the realm of possibility, as browser and platform support for style sheets is spotty at best. Look for reading recommendations, useful URLs, and other resources throughout this appendix to extend your understanding beyond what this book can supply.

Objectives

Our objectives here are to use JavaScripts to create subtle rollover effects in our sample business site and in our informational site. Then we'll use style sheets in the personal site to produce some way-cool text and color effects. Finally, we'll implement a complicated DHTML rollover menu in the personal site to demonstrate a little cutting-edge animation. This chapter is also meant (again) to show you when such elements are appropriate. Context still matters as it did in the last chapter, as well as in this entire book.

JavaScript

JavaScript was invented by Netscape in 1995 to pick up where regular HTML leaves off. HTML was written solely with printed pages and written words in mind. It does not easily adapt itself to the demands of the Web today, with all kinds of multimedia, animation, and other nonlinear features. JavaScript fills in the gaps, so to speak, by making interactivity easier. It also links HTML more efficiently to technologies such as Java, Shockwave, and ActiveX, to name just a few.

JavaScript is *un*like programming languages such as Perl or C++ because you can write it right into your web page. It works in tandem with HTML because the instructions for interpreting it are written right into your browser (well, versions 3 and later of Navigator and Explorer only). You don't have to force the browser to look elsewhere on your own site, or on your ISP's server, to make JavaScript work. This saves time for the visitor to your site and for you if and when you do a site update. You might have to ask a programmer to write a new gateway program for forms, but you can update the JavaScript yourself using your HTML editor alone. No computer science degree required.

To understand JavaScript more thoroughly, you have to understand its individual components. An **event**, in this context, is some action that happens on your web page, such as a visitor rolling the cursor over a graphic. An **event handler**, by extension, is a bit of JavaScript code that starts to run when an event occurs. Also, within JavaScript, different objects have different **properties**, such as the location of a web page or the size of a browser window. JavaScript also enables us to better control the various properties of an object by means of **methods** and **functions**. Let's expand on these ideas a little more so you'll understand the basics of how JavaScript works.

> **NOTE:** Do *not* rely upon this extremely bare-bones description of JavaScript if you want to write it from scratch. We recommend two sources for beginning JavaScripters: *Designing with JavaScript* by Nick Heinle, and Webmonkey's JavaScript tutorial at http://www.hotwired.com/webmonkey.

Events and Event Handlers

An event, as we just said, is an action taken by the visitor on a web page: clicking a link, rolling the cursor over a graphic, and so on. An event handler, therefore, is a bit of JavaScript code that makes something happen when a specified event occurs. Here are the five most popular JavaScript events on the Web:

onMouseOver   The visitor rolls the cursor over a link or graphic.

onMouseOut   The visitor rolls the cursor off a link or graphic.

onChange   The visitor selects an option from an imagemap or menu.

onLoad   A document is finished loading up within the <BODY>, <FRAMESET>, or <IMG> tag.

onUnload   A document is cleared out in favor of another within the <BODY> or <FRAMESET> tags.

An event handler is written into the relevant HTML like so:

```
<A HREF="links.html" onMouseOver="window.status =
```

```
'Other Frasier fan sites'; return true;"><IMG
SRC="links.gif" HEIGHT=35 WIDTH=50 BORDER=0></A>
```

As you can see, this is a simple graphical link specified by the <IMG> and <A> tags, with a little extra something special. This use of onMouseOver tells the browser to display the phrase "Other Frasier fan sites" along the bottom edge of the browser window when a visitor rolls the cursor over the graphic links.gif. Other aspects of ways of using JavaScript are not so simple.

The Object Model

An object, as we already established, is something literal within the environment of your web site, such as the browser window or the page loaded up within it. However, there is a hierarchy, or pecking order, to all the different objects in terms of how JavaScript and DHTML in general affect them.

Think of it sort of as the <BODY> tag; <BODY> and its attributes define and describe almost everything on the web page to the browser. Similarly, the object document defines and describes something more specific, like the <P> tag. Then the object forms gets even more specific, like the <FONT> tag. Yet in JavaScript, you can focus down even one "level" further, with the other six objects at the bottom of the diagram: location, history, select menu, text input, applets, and images.

This is where any similarity between HTML and JavaScript objects ends. Where HTML only has attributes, JavaScript objects have **properties** and **methods**. What's the difference? Let's explain it in more mundane terms.

A bike, for example, can represent a JavaScript object. In JavaScript we would introduce it as:

```
var mybike
```

This bike's properties could be described in literal terms: its color, type, manufacturer, and so on. In JavaScript we would add one of these property descriptions as:

```
mybike.color = "blue";
```

In English, this "sentence" says, "Make the color of my bike blue." The object `mybike` is separated from the property `color` by a period, which enables you to finish the "sentence" with the equal sign and the value "blue" completing this bit of JavaScript.

We can also use JavaScript to make objects do something by using methods. In other words, a possible method of the object mybike could be:

```
mybike.accelerate( );
```

The first three parts of the "sentence" use the same syntax as in the first example: the object, the period, and then the method, "Make my bike accelerate." But the method logically asks for something more, between those parentheses: a speed. We then give the method accelerate a value of 20 like so:

```
mybike.accelerate(20);
```

and it "reads" as, "Make my bike accelerate 20 miles per hour."

Get it? Properties affect how the object appears, and methods affect what the object can do. That's the extremely short version of how JavaScript objects, properties, and methods work; now let's tie them together.

> **Amy:**   Just to clarify—this is an analogy, right? These are not supposed to be real JavaScript commands, but instead a breakdown of how the language works.

> **Rebecca:**   No, these aren't real commands. If you put them in your web page, nothing will happen. But it was the best way I could think of to describe the difference between properties and methods.

if Statements

if statements tie two specific ideas together: cause and effect. In JavaScript this is written out, very loosely, as:

```
if ( this happens ) { then run this code }
```

All if statements are made up of the word "if" followed by a statement in parentheses, separated from a string of code instructions in braces (those curly brackets, { and }). The visitor's browser reads the statement and sees if the condition or action it describes occurs. Then, at the appropriate time, the browser translates the relevant bit of code and whatever its instructions it might contain. Cause and effect in action.

There's also the cause-effect-otherwise way of writing JavaScript, which loosely looks like this:

```
if ( this happens ) { then run this code } else {
run this code instead }.
```

This way of specifying an alternate to the bracketed instructions helps you allow for all kinds of wrinkles. You can modify this basic scenario to solve many platform or browser support problems, even to the extent of "sniffing" out which browser the visitor is using and telling the browser to load up a Navigator- or Explorer-specific web page. We'll do a little more iffing and elseing later on in the Exercises as we modify existing JavaScripts to make our sample sites more interactive.

While this is certainly not a complete explanation of how JavaScript works, it should be enough for you to understand how we will import and customize an exisiting JavaScript. That is the focus of the exercises you'll be doing later on; for now, let's proceed to a discussion of style sheets.

Style Sheets

Style sheets (more formally known as **cascading** style sheets) is the hottest part of DHTML at this writing, so it's received more attention, and more books, tutorials, and other resources are available on it. However, style sheets is one of the least supported aspects of DHTML browser-wise—only versions 4 of Navigator and Explorer even *partly* support style sheets instructions. (Versions 5 of Navigator and Explorer do an even better job, but still not best.) But the allure of being able to absolutely position an object on a web page practically down to a single pixel, and to make it stick as well, is just too great. We predict that style sheets is certainly the wave of the future here in the present, even if it's currently not much more than the proverbial dangling carrot. We're also going to go into more detail with style sheets than we did with JavaScript, so let's hit the highlights.

The advantages to using style sheets are similar to the advantages for using JavaScript; it allows you to separate the form of an object on a web page from its appearance, and to create customized instructions on how those objects should be displayed by a browser. Style sheets also allows you to write these instructions only once—*once*—in shorthand and in one place, rather than having to repeat them over and over. Remember how we made John and Jill Doe's pages look interesting with all those instances of the <FONT> tag? Forget it— this time around, we'll specify all those colors and font faces and sizes in one place, and let the browser do all the work.

> **NOTE:** As with JavaScript, we want to give you only the simple basics of style sheets here, so you should explore other sources if style sheets really intrigues you. Steve Mulder, the rabid Emma Thompson fan we visited earlier, wrote a good reference called *The Web Designer's Guide to Style Sheets*, but his Webmonkey style sheets tutorial at http://www.hotwired.com/webmonkey is also excellent.

Syntax, Grouping, and Inheritance

Style sheets is made up of two parts: the **selector** and the **declaration**. The selector is more or less like an HTML tag; it tells the browser which objects will be affected by the instructions that follow it. Similarly, the declaration tells the browser how to implement the instructions in its two parts, the **property** and the **value**. Properties in style sheets are like properties in JavaScripts; they allow the declaration to be extra-specific. Properties tell the browser what part of the object to change while the value spells those changes out. HTML doesn't permit you to have that much control. Hence the beauty, and the necessity, of style sheets.

Here's some basic style sheets syntax:

```
blockquote {  font-family: arial  }
```

Amy: Why this particular layout and spacing? I'm referring specifically to the spaces within the braces.

Rebecca: It's just the way it's done, I suppose. With JavaScript, however, every little space counts. So go ahead and try to remove the "extra" spaces here and see what happens, but do *not* remove them from the JavaScripts or the DHTML later on in this appendix.

In this example, called a **rule**, blockquote is the selector, and the rest enclosed in brackets is the declaration—font-family is the property and arial is the value. Altogether, this rule tells the browser that all text coded with the <BLOCKQUOTE> tag should be displayed using Arial. It's no coincidence that blockquote is also an HTML tag; you can use any HTML tag as a selector in this fashion. However, you should remember one important change if you're using style sheets to specify plain text with the <P> tag: You must close it with a </P>, which is usually just implied.

Selectors and declarations can also be **grouped** to work together, as in this example:

```
blockquote    { font-family: verdana ;
                font-weight: italic ;
                font-size: 18pt }
```

Amy: I found it surprising that what I know as "font style" is called "font weight" here; it's something I'll note for future reference.

Rebecca: I know; it's one of those strange discrepancies that says—to me, at least—that a designer wasn't in on the process, or else we'd have continuity of terms!

Amy: Also, I'm wondering about the spacing above; it looks like you've inserted a tab between "blockquote" and the rest of the rule. Why, and is it a tab or what?

Rebecca: Yes, there's a tab between the selector blockquote and the opening bracket {. Why? Beats me. Again, I'm just teaching you to do things the way I learned to do them myself. If you remove it and add only a single space and the style sheets still works, then you don't need it.

According to this HTML, everything written within the <BLOCK-QUOTE> tag should be displayed in 18-point, italicized Verdana. Note that you must separate these declarations with semi-colons to make them work.

NOTE: There is a property, color, of almost every declaration we mention in the book, but because this is a black-and-white book, we'll be using it sparingly in our examples. We will use them normally in the exercises, but you'll have to rely on your own monitor to determine if color is working properly.

What happens when two different rules seemingly contradict each other? Look at this example:

```
p          { font-size: 24pt ;
               font-family: helvetica }
```

This rule establishes everything inside the <P> tag displayed in Helvetica at a size of 24 points. But, consider the following HTML:

```
<P>Four out of five dentists recommend <B>sugar-
less gum</B> for their patients who chew gum.</P>
```

What happens to that <B>-specified text? It is also displayed in Helvetica at a size of 24 points because it is written inside a <P> tag. It has **inherited** the declarations of the "parent" tag (in this case, the <P> tag), which sounds useful until you pause and consider the potential problems. Almost every tag on your web page is the "child" of some other tag, with <HTML> being the ultimate parental authority. In other words, if you use style sheets to create a selector called html, everything in the <HEAD> tag, the <BODY> tag, and/or the <FRAMESET> tag (to use three examples we've used in this book) will be affected. Once you start specifying selectors and declarations at the top level, you must consider how these changes will trickle down, or you can have a real mess on your hands.

Classes

Now let's talk about even easier ways to implement style sheets changes—classes, IDs, and contextual selectors—as they represent the cutting-edge of style sheets technology at this writing; first, classes.

What if you want to make your main body text three different colors and three different font faces on different areas of the same page? You can create three **classes** of the <P> tag, like so:

```
p.textA        { color: red;
                 font-family: arial }
p.textB        { color: green
                 font-family: kino MT }
p.textC        { color: purple
                 font-family: courier }
```

You can name the classes anything you like after the period, using whatever logic or description makes the most sense to you, although Navigator doesn't like numbers, for some inexplicable reason. So to carry on with our example, when you want to apply these classes you use the CLASS attribute like this:

```
<P CLASS="textA">This little piggy went to
market.</P>
<P CLASS="textB">This little piggy stayed home.</P>
<P CLASS="textC">This little piggy ate roast
beef.</P>
<P>Mmm, roast beef.</P>
```

The CLASS attribute specifies which declaration applies to each line of <P>-specified text. Yet the fourth, last line will be displayed according to whatever instructions you might assign to p, or in standard default mode.

Adding Style Sheets to Web Pages

There are two practical ways you can insert style sheets instructions into a web page once you've written them out. You can either embed them, or link to an external style sheets document. There are two other ways that are not so practical: importing one style sheet into another, or adding the styles inline in your HTML document. We're not really discussing the third option, because it isn't supported by either Netscape Navigator 4 or Internet Explorer 4 (in effect, it's useless). The fourth option, also, is merely for changing a single tag or group of tags in one document without disturbing the rest of the page; this makes for very messy code and an extremely time-consuming editing process. We want to present you with the most simple and useful options, so it's options one and two only.

If you want to add style sheets to only one page in a web site, you should embed your style sheets like so:

```
<HTML>
<STYLE TYPE="text/css">
<!--
body            { background: yellow ;
                   font-family: georgia }
p               { font-size: 14pt }
li              { font-color: orange }
-->
</STYLE>

the rest of the page goes here
</HTML>
```

Amy: So you insert the <STYLE> tags before the <HEAD> tags, correct?

Rebecca: Yes, that's correct. The <STYLE> information goes inside the <HTML> tag before the contents of the <HEAD> tag, right at the top of the document.

In this scenario, all the style sheets information goes inside the <STYLE> tag with the attribute TYPE and a value of text/css. This simply alerts the browser that style sheets instructions are included in the page, so the browser can interpret or ignore these instructions at its leisure. However, you also want to use the comment tag—the funny-looking <!--> thing that's separated in half like any other tag. This hides your style sheets instructions from older browsers, which would interpret style sheets as regular text because they aren't surrounded by $<$ and $>$ brackets.

If you want to add style sheets to many pages, an external style sheet is best for long-term site maintenance. This way, if you want to change one small thing in your style sheets instructions, you only have to change it in one place.

To borrow from the previous example, you'd first cut-and-paste all the style sheets information:

```
body            { background: yellow ;
                   font-family: georgia }
p               { font-size: 14pt }
li              { font-color: orange }
```

and save it in your HTML editor as something like ssheet1.css (just as an example, though; the three-letter suffix should always be .css). Don't add any tags; just save the instructions. Then open an existing page in your web site and add this HTML at the top like so:

```
<HTML>
<HEAD>
<LINK REL=stylesheet HREF="ssheet1.css"
TYPE="text/css">
</HEAD>
```

The $<$LINK$>$ tag tells the browser it needs to look for style sheets information elsewhere and gives it the proper location. You can also specify the location using a relative path if you sort your web page files into different folders (HREF="../styles/ssheet1.css" for example) or as a complete URL (HREF="http://www.provider.com/~mysite/ ssheet1.css" for another example). You don't have to put this HTML inside a comment tag, because earlier browsers will just ignore the $<$LINK$>$ tag as something they don't understand.

The Downside of Style Sheets

We've touched on the problem of browser and platform support (or lack thereof) in previous chapters, but you ain't seen *nothing* like the support problems currently involved with using style sheets. It is enough to make a web designer weep, but this book doesn't come with tissues so we'll try to help you cope.

One problem you *can* do something about is cascading, which is more a feature than a drawback, even though it can cause big headaches. Let's look at an intricate—well, a messy—example of how cascading works:

```
<HTML>
<STYLE TYPE="text/css">
<!--
body          { color: maroon;
                font-family: geneva }
em            { color: green ;
                font-family: arial }
h2            { color: blue ;
                font-family: georgia }
- -->
</STYLE>
<HEAD>
<TITLE>Style Sheets Cascade Test</TITLE>
<LINK REL="ssheets2.css" TYPE="text/css">
</HEAD>
<BODY>
<H2>
<EM>
<FONT FACE="verdana">
What the heck is this text and which rule affects
it??
</FONT>
</EM>
</H2>
</BODY>
</HTML>
```

The style sheet referred to by the <LINK> tag looks like this:

```
em        { color: orange ;
            font-family: courier }
```

So what in the world would a browser do now? Which rule applies to that single line of text when there are five instructions for the browser to follow? There's an imported style sheet specified by the <LINK> tag, three rules written in at the top with the <STYLE> and <!--> tags, as well as a <FONT FACE> specification. Let's load this page up and see what happens.

The heart of the conflict here is the cascading order of rules. When a browser is faced with conflicting instructions from too many rules and/or too many style sheets and/or HTML tags, it decides which rule to follow based on this cascading order. The winner in this instance is the <EM> tag rule, which instructs the browser to display all <EM>-specified text in Arial as green. How did it get italicized, though? That's the effect of the <EM> tag alone, because it instructs the browser to display all <EM>-specified text in italics. So style sheets is far from perfect, and not always predictable.

Speaking of predictability, there is one last style sheets issue we should cover before going ahead with some exercises. We have briefly mentioned in previous chapters how web pages should degrade gracefully, when we were talking about designing for visitors with early-version browsers. **Degrading** is what happens when a visitor to your site uses a browser that cannot interpret all the bells and whistles properly. If your site relies even slightly on advanced technologies (like style sheets), it must also somehow be designed to look good without these technologies.

At this writing, the vast majority of people on the Web are using browsers that do not properly interpret style sheets—and many of them still using version 3 browsers may have difficulty with JavaScript as well. So in theory, you should still be making allowances for visitors to your site who can really only see text and graphics. Sound challenging? It is. We'll cover this problem in the exercises.

Exercises

In these exercises, we're going to show you how to paste in and customize three of the most popular JavaScripts: the browser message bar rollover, the illuminating rollover, and the pop-up text box rollover. Then we'll play with style sheets, and finally put both these technologies together with a little extra DHTML to make a flying menu banner.

Let us repeat these disclaimers, though: You will *not* learn how to write JavaScript from scratch here, and *all* of these DHTML-based web page effects are quite difficult to customize and implement.

JavaScript #1: The Message Window Rollover

To get started, open your HTML editor and your browser of choice, and get the CD-ROM that accompanies this book. We'll be adding this rollover effect to the personal site menu page, doe2.html.

This rollover effect is most popularly used on a page like doe2.html, with a non-text-based menu of links to other parts of the web site. It will make the browser load a text description of the link in the message bar—this is the small horizontal text window along the bottom edge of the browser window. You saw text messages there when we looked at the Homewrecker and Riven Journal sites back in Chapter 4, "More Basics of Site Creation."

1. Open doe2.html in your HTML editor. The HTML should look like this before we begin:

```
<HTML>
<HEAD>
<TITLE>Meet John Doe</TITLE>
</HEAD>
<BODY BACKGROUND="oswirl.gif">
<BR>
<IMG SRC="pixel.gif" ALIGN=bottom HEIGHT=155
WIDTH=1>
<P ALIGN=center>
<A HREF="john.html"><IMG SRC="eye1.gif" BORDER=0
HSPACE=6 VSPACE=1></A>
<A HREF="jane.html"><IMG SRC="eye2.gif" BORDER=0
HSPACE=6 VSPACE=1></A>
<A HREF="jack.html"><P ALIGN=center><IMG
SRC="eye3.gif" BORDER=0 HSPACE=6 VSPACE=1></A>
```

```
<A HREF="jill.html"><IMG SRC="eye4.gif" BORDER=0
HSPACE=6 VSPACE=1></A>
<BR>
</BODY>
</HTML>
```

If you're not confident in your page-editing abilities, it might be a good idea to save another copy of this page and work with it in this exercise instead. That way, you'll always have a version of this page that works properly, and you'll always have an easy way to start over if you really get tangled up later on.

2. Next, let's add the JavaScript instructions at the top of the document inside the <HEAD> tag.

```
<SCRIPT LANGUAGE='JavaScript'>
<!--
function wordage (txt) {
window.status=txt;
setTimeout("clear()",99000)
}
function clear () {
window.status= "";
}

-->
</SCRIPT>
```

JavaScript is more sensitive to line breaks, extra spaces, and other extraneous things in its code than HTML, so type in this <SCRIPT> tag information *precisely*.

3. Now let's tie these JavaScript instructions in to the objects on the web page they will affect: the eyeball links. The tie-in instructions should be written within the <A> tag like so:

```
<A HREF="linkedpage.html" onMouseOver = "word-
age('the message window text goes here');
return true;"  >
```

so that the HTML for the first eyeball link on doe2.html, john.html, will look something like this:

```
<A HREF="john.html" onMouseOver = "wordage('John
Doe, Master of his Domain');
return true;"><IMG SRC="eye1.gif"  BORDER=0
HSPACE=6 VSPACE=1></A>
```

You can describe John Doe with whatever value you like—
"John Doe, Master of his Domain" is sufficient for us, though, so
we'll continue.

4. Add the tie-in information to the remaining three eyeball links on
the page, creating whatever descriptive values you like. In the end,
the finished HTML for this page will look something like this,
with the descriptive values being the only part that should look
different:

```
<HTML>
<HEAD>
<TITLE>Meet John Doe</TITLE>
</HEAD>
<BODY BACKGROUND="oswirl.gif">
<BR>
<IMG SRC="pixel.gif" ALIGN=bottom HEIGHT=155
WIDTH=1>
<P ALIGN=center>
<A HREF="john.html" onMouseOver = "wordage('John
Doe, Master of his Domain');
return true;"><IMG SRC="eye1.gif"  BORDER=0
HSPACE=6 VSPACE=1></A>
<A HREF="jane.html" onMouseOver = "wordage('Jane
Doe, A Woman of Endless Talents'); return
true;"><IMG SRC="eye2.gif"  BORDER=0 HSPACE=6
VSPACE=1></A>
<A HREF="jack.html" onMouseOver = "wordage('Jack
Doe, Wonder Boy');
return true;"><P ALIGN=center><IMG SRC="eye3.gif"
BORDER=0 HSPACE=6 VSPACE=1></A>
<A HREF="jill.html" onMouseOver = "wordage('Jill
Doe, Child Prodigy');
return true;"><IMG SRC="eye4.gif"  BORDER=0
HSPACE=6 VSPACE=1></A>
```

```
<BR>
</BODY>
</HTML>
```

5. Save the final version of this code in doe2.html, regardless of whether or not you created an alternate copy to play with, to preserve continuity in these exercises.

You get a little extra surprise in Navigator on the PC—pop-up text box descriptions containing the same phrases that appear in the message bar. This is actually a platform-based feature (meaning the same thing happens in Explorer on the PC), and you can make this happen without the JavaScript by means of the <IMG> tag's ALT attribute:

```
<IMG SRC="linkedgraphic.gif" ALT="Contents of the
pop-up text box go here.">
```

Many web page designers disdain this approach, though, because the pop-up text box is not customizable and it hides the page area beneath. It's also considered a "dumbing down" technique, particularly in instances such as our personal site's main page where there is no text. After all, or so the logic goes, what's the incentive for visitors to go exploring if you spell out all their options with text?

JavaScript #2: The Button Bar Rollover

This second JavaScript is another simple, visual trick that can be useful or merely decorative. It's also a rollover, only it is commonly used for special effects such as a color change, as with the graphic menu buttons on the Byte It! site, or the glass 3DVR button on the Cybertown site. We'll customize it to be both decorative *and* useful as part of the Historic House Style Gallery, our informational site.

The rollover trick works by prompting the browser to load up an entirely new GIF in the exact location of the first one. This replacement trick fools the eye into thinking it sees only the effect because the transformation is so fast. Unfortunately, the JavaScript code needed to make this simple switch work is very long and *very* complicated. So we highly recommend you work with a copy of gallery.html rather than the original.

1. Open gallery.html in your HTML editor; this is the page we created in Chapter 10. This is what the HTML should look like before we begin:

```
<HTML>
<HEAD>
<TITLE>The Historic House Style Gallery</TITLE>
<META NAME="description" CONTENT="A gallery of
American residential architectural styles popular
between 1750 and 1950.">
</HEAD>
<BODY TEXT="#666699" BACKGROUND="infoslice.gif"
LINK="#666699" ALINK="#FFFFCC" VLINK="#FF9900">
<P>
<TABLE BORDER=0 CELLSPACING=0 CELLPADDING=0
WIDTH=600>
<TR>
<TD WIDTH=95 ALIGN=left VALIGN=top>
<P><IMG SRC="salem1s.jpg"><BR>
<P><IMG SRC="salem4s.jpg"><BR>
<P><IMG SRC="salem5s.jpg"><BR>
<P><IMG SRC="salem2s.jpg"><BR>
<P><IMG SRC="salem6s.jpg"><BR>
</TD>
<TD WIDTH=17>
</TD>
<TD WIDTH=470 ALIGN=left VALIGN=top>
<CENTER>
<P><FONT COLOR="#666699" SIZE="+3">The Historic
House Style Gallery</FONT>
<P><FONT COLOR="#999966" SIZE="+2">A gallery of
American historical residential styles<BR></FONT>
</CENTER>
<IMG SRC="pixel.gif" HEIGHT=25 WIDTH=1>
<FONT FACE="georgia" COLOR="#666666" SIZE="+2">
<P><A HREF="georgian.html">Georgian Styles</A>,
1700 - 1776
```

```
<P><A HREF="victorian.html">Victorian Styles</A>,
1850 - 1900
<P><A HREF="revival.html">Revival Styles</A>,
1800 - 1870
<P><A HREF="prairie.html">Prairie Styles</A>,
1900 - 1920
</FONT>
<BR>
<FONT FACE="georgia" COLOR="#999966" SIZE="+2">
<P>More Styles Coming Soon
<IMG SRC="pixel.gif" HEIGHT=25 WIDTH=1>
<P>Questions? Submissions? Email <A
HREF="mailto:curator@hhsg.com">curator@hhsg.com</
A>.
</FONT>
</TD>
</TABLE>
</BODY>
</HTML>
```

2. We're going to be adding rollover effects to the six house JPGs along the left side of the page—a halo of color for visual emphasis, and a text description of the house's architectural style. Unfortunately the code to do this is extremely long and involved, so we're going to cut you a break: the final HTML for this entire exercise is available on the CD-ROM as a rich-text Word document called js2.rtf.

   Here's what js2.rtf, the finished product, looks like:

```
<HTML>
<HEAD>
<TITLE>The Historic House Style Gallery</TITLE>
<META NAME="description" CONTENT="A gallery of
American residential architectural styles popular
between 1750 and 1950.">

<script language="JavaScript">
<!--
function MM_preloadImages() { //v1.2
```

Colony City

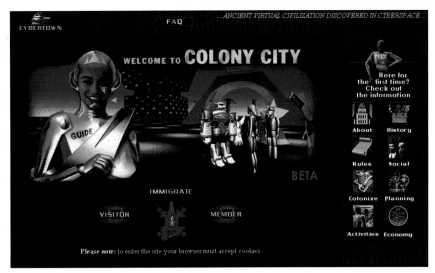

FIGURE B.1. An online VRML community, Colony City
(http://www.colonycity.html)

Virgin Records America

FIGURE B.2. Marketing music online, Virgin Records America
(http://www.virginrecords.com)

Abulafia/Dennett's Dream

FIGURE B.3. An online gallery of interesting artwork, Dennett's Dream (http://www.cgrg.ohio-state.edu/~mlewis/Gallery/gallery.html). Copyright 1995, Matthew Lewis.

Äda'web

FIGURE B.4. A whole collection of fascinating pages, Äda'web (http://www.adaweb.com)

glassdog

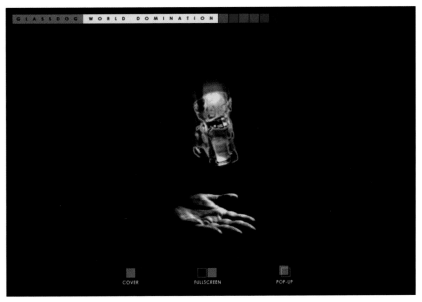

FIGURE B.5. Frames within frames, glassdog.com
(http://www.glassdog.com)

HighFive.com

FIGURE B.6. An archive of the "best" of the Web, HighFive.com
(http://www.highfive.com)

dELiAs.com

FIGURE B.7. For the 12 to 24 crowd, dELiAs.com (http://www.delias.com)

Guthrie Bowron

FIGURE B.8. Gorgeous color palette, in more ways than one, Guthrie
Bowron (http://www.guthriebowron.co.nz)

FUSE98

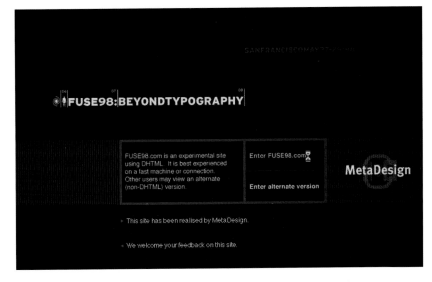

FIGURE B.9. An online experiment with DHTML, FUSE98 (http://www.fuse98.com/net4M)

<typospace>

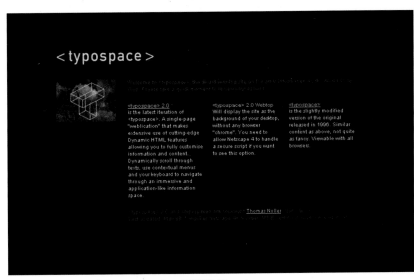

FIGURE B.10. More superior DHTML, <typospace> (http://typospace.drikka.net)

TSDesign

FIGURE B.11. Nice layered menus, TSDesign (http://www.tsdesign.com)

counterspace

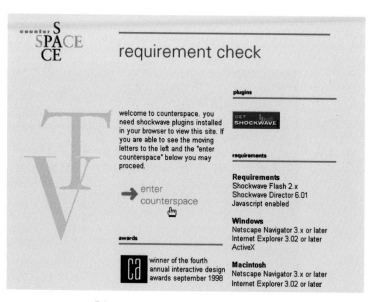

FIGURE B.12. More web page experimentation, counterspace (http://www.studiomotiv.com/counterspace)

Wert & Company

FIGURE B.13. Makes other business sites jealous, Wert & Company (http://www.wertco.com)

BRNR Labs

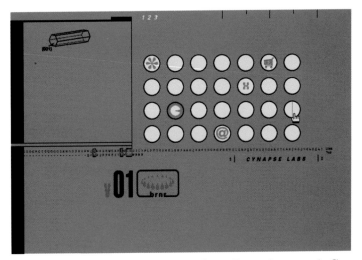

FIGURE B.14. A cohesive theme (http://www.brnr.com). Copyright Brnr New Media.

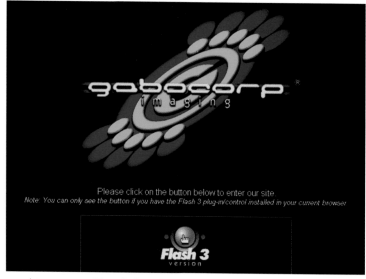

FIGURE B.15. Text infused with interactivity, Gabocorp X (http://www.gabocorp.com)

```
    if (document.images) {
      var imgFiles = MM_preloadImages.arguments;
      var preloadArray = new Array();
      for (var i=0; i<imgFiles.length; i++) {
        preloadArray[i] = new Image;
        preloadArray[i].src = imgFiles[i];
      }
    }
}
//-->
</script>
  <script language="JavaScript">
<!--
function MM_swapImage() { //v1.2
  var i,j=0,objStr,obj,swapArray=new Array,oldAr-
ray=document.MM_swapImgData;
  for (i=0; i < (MM_swapImage.arguments.length-
2); i+=3) {
    objStr = MM_swapImage.arguments[(naviga-
tor.appName == 'Netscape')?i:i+1];
    if ((objStr.indexOf('document.layers[')==0 &&
document.layers==null) ||
        (objStr.indexOf('document.all[')   ==0 &&
document.all    ==null))
      objStr = 'document'+objStr.sub-
string(objStr.lastIndexOf('.'),objStr.length);
    obj = eval(objStr);
    if (obj != null) {
      swapArray[j++] = obj;
      swapArray[j++] = (oldArray==null || oldAr-
ray[j-1]!=obj)?obj.src:oldArray[j];
      obj.src = MM_swapImage.arguments[i+2];
  } }
  document.MM_swapImgData = swapArray; //used for
restore
}
//-->
</script>
  <script language="JavaScript">
```

```
<!--
function MM_displayStatusMsg(msgStr) { //v1.2
  status=msgStr;
  document.MM_returnValue = true;
}
//-->
</script>
  <script language="JavaScript">
<!--
function MM_swapImgRestore() { //v1.2
  if (document.MM_swapImgData != null)
    for (var i=0; i<(docu-
ment.MM_swapImgData.length-1); i+=2)
      document.MM_swapImgData[i].src = docu-
ment.MM_swapImgData[i+1];
}
//-->
</script>

<!-- #BeginBehavior MM_swapImage5 -->
<script language='JavaScript'>
  MM_preloadImages('salem1s2.jpg');
</script>
<!-- #EndBehavior MM_swapImage5 -->
<!-- #BeginBehavior MM_swapImage4 -->
<script language='JavaScript'>
  MM_preloadImages(' salem4s2.jpg');
</script>
<!-- #EndBehavior MM_swapImage4 -->
 <!-- #BeginBehavior MM_swapImage3 -->
<script language='JavaScript'>
  MM_preloadImages(' salem5s2.jpg');
</script>
<!-- #EndBehavior MM_swapImage3 -->
<!-- #BeginBehavior MM_swapImage2 -->
<script language='JavaScript'>
  MM_preloadImages(' salem2s2.jpg');
</script>
<!-- #EndBehavior MM_swapImage2 -->
```

```
<!-- #BeginBehavior MM_swapImage1 -->
<script language='JavaScript'>
  MM_preloadImages(' salem6s2.jpg');
</script>
<!-- #EndBehavior MM_swapImage1 -->
</HEAD>
<BODY TEXT="#666699" BACKGROUND="infoslice.gif"
LINK="#666699" ALINK="#FFFFCC" VLINK="#FF9900">
<P>
<TABLE BORDER=0 CELLSPACING=0 CELLPADDING=0
WIDTH=600>
<TR>
<TD WIDTH=95 ALIGN=left VALIGN=top>
<P>
<A HREF="victorian.html"
onMou-
seOver="MM_preloadImages('salem1s.jpg','salem1s2.
jpg');MM_swapImage('document.salem1','docu-
ment.salem1','salem1s2.jpg','MM_swapImage5');MM_d
isplayStatusMsg('This is a Mansard Victo-
rian.');return document.MM_returnValue" onMouse-
Out="MM_swapImgRestore()">
<IMG SRC="salem1s.jpg" NAME="salem1"><BR>
<P>
<A HREF="revival.html"
onMou-
seOver="MM_preloadImages('salem4s.jpg','salem4s2.
jpg');MM_swapImage('document.salem4','docu-
ment.salem4','salem4s2.jpg','MM_swapImage4');MM_d
isplayStatusMsg('This is a Greek Revival');return
document.MM_returnValue" onMouse-
Out="MM_swapImgRestore()">
<IMG SRC="salem4s.jpg" NAME="salem4"><BR>
<P>
<A HREF="georgian.html"
onMou-
seOver="MM_preloadImages('salem5s.jpg','salem5s2.
jpg ');MM_swapImage('document.salem5','docu-
ment.salem5','salem5s2.jpg
```

```
','MM_swapImage3');MM_displayStatusMsg('A Geor-
gian.');return document.MM_returnValue" onMouse-
Out="MM_swapImgRestore()">
<IMG SRC="salem5s.jpg" NAME="salem5"></A><BR>
<P>
<A HREF="victorian.html"
onMou-
seOver="MM_preloadImages('salem2s.jpg','salem2s2.
jpg');MM_swapImage('document.salem2','docu-
ment.salem2','
salem2s2.jpg','MM_swapImage2');MM_displayStatusMs
g('An Italianate.');return docu-
ment.MM_returnValue" onMouse-
Out="MM_swapImgRestore()">
<IMG SRC="salem2s.jpg" NAME="salem2"></A><BR>
<P>
<A HREF="victorian.html" onMou-
seOver="MM_preloadImages('salem6s.jpg','salem6s2.
jpg');MM_swapImage('document.salem6','docu-
ment.salem6','salem6s2.jpg','MM_swapImage1');MM_d
isplayStatusMsg('A Queen Anne.');return docu-
ment.MM_returnValue" onMouse-
Out="MM_swapImgRestore()"><IMG SRC="salem6s.jpg"
NAME="salem6"></A>
<BR>
<TD WIDTH=17>
</TD>
<TD WIDTH=470 ALIGN=left VALIGN=top>
<CENTER>
<P><FONT COLOR="#666699" SIZE="+3">The Historic
House Style Gallery</FONT>
<P><FONT COLOR="#999966" SIZE="+2">A gallery of
American historical residential styles<BR></FONT>
</CENTER>
<IMG SRC="pixel.gif" HEIGHT=25 WIDTH=1>
<FONT FACE="georgia" COLOR="#666666" SIZE="+2">
<P><A HREF="georgian.html">Georgian Styles</A>,
1700 - 1776
<P><A HREF="victorian.html">Victorian Styles</A>,
1850 - 1900
```

```
<P><A HREF="revival.html">Revival Styles</A>,
1800 - 1870
<P><A HREF="prairie.html">Prairie Styles</A>,
1900 - 1920
</FONT>
<BR>
<FONT FACE="georgia" COLOR="#999966" SIZE="+2">
<P>More Styles Coming Soon
<IMG SRC="pixel.gif" HEIGHT=25 WIDTH=1>
<P>Questions? Submissions? Email <A
HREF="mailto:curator@hhsg.com">curator@hhsg.com</
A>.
</FONT>
</TD>
</TABLE>
</BODY>
</HTML>
```

If any of this cryptic stuff makes the slightest bit of sense to you, congratulations—you're getting the hang of JavaScript. Let us interpret this code, though, just in case.

There are actually ten separate JavaScripts that makes this trick work—count the number of <SCRIPT> tags—but they work quickly. They specify which graphics are affected by the rollover, which graphics should be removed, which graphics should replace the ones that have been removed, and how the removal should take place. They also create a message box description as we saw in the previous exercise, although the first way we showed you is much easier. And truly, that's all you need to know because we're not coding this stuff from scratch. Truly. Don't strain your brain.

The rest of this exercise shows you how we pasted in and customized this JavaScript from another web page. So let's get started.

3. First, we customized the last bit JavaScript near the closing </HEAD> tag, the part that looks like this:

```
<!-- #BeginBehavior MM_swapImage5 -->
<script language='JavaScript'>
   MM_preloadImages('salem1s2.jpg');
```

```
</script>
<!-- #EndBehavior MM_swapImage5 -->
<!-- #BeginBehavior MM_swapImage4 -->
<script language='JavaScript'>
  MM_preloadImages('salem4s2.jpg');
</script>
<!-- #EndBehavior MM_swapImage4 -->
 <!-- #BeginBehavior MM_swapImage3 -->
<script language='JavaScript'>
  MM_preloadImages('salem5s2.jpg');
</script>
<!-- #EndBehavior MM_swapImage3 -->
<!-- #BeginBehavior MM_swapImage2 -->
<script language='JavaScript'>
  MM_preloadImages('salem2s2.jpg');
</script>
<!-- #EndBehavior MM_swapImage2 -->
<!-- #BeginBehavior MM_swapImage1 -->
<script language='JavaScript'>
  MM_preloadImages('salem6s2.jpg');
</script>
<!-- #EndBehavior MM_swapImage1 -->
```

If you take a closer look, you'll see why: this code tells the browser to preload the replacement JPGs (salem1s2.jpg and so forth) so they'll be readily available when the visitor sets the rollover in motion. Without this code, the browser would not download these JPGs from your server because they aren't specified on the web page the way normal graphics are.

Next we tied these instructions to the actual house JPGs to complete the circle.

4. In gallery.html, we took the bit of HTML that reads like this:

```
<P><IMG SRC="salem6s.jpg"><BR>
```

and enclosed the <IMG> tag with these <A> tag and requisite JavaScript instructions like so:

```
<A HREF="victorian.html" onMou-
seOver="MM_preloadImages('salem6s.jpg','salem6s2.
jpg');MM_swapImage('document.salem6','docu-
ment.salem6','salem6s2.jpg','MM_swapImage1');MM_d
isplayStatusMsg('A Queen Anne.');return docu-
ment.MM_returnValue" onMouse-
Out="MM_swapImgRestore()"><IMG SRC="salem6s.jpg"
NAME="salem6"></A>
```

What does all this code mean, and what did we change or add? We'll take it one bit at a time.

- The HREF value in the <A> tag links the JPG to another page in the Gallery site, in this case, victorian.html because this house style is a Victorian style.

- The preloadImages value is established as salem6s.jpg and salem6s2.jpg, respectively, so the browser will recognize both the original graphic and the one that will replace it during the "switch."

- The swapImage value is established as

  ```
  'document.salem6','document.salem6',
  'salem6s2.jpg','MM_swapImage1'
  ```

- to physically tie the original JPG graphic to its replacement in the JavaScript, because the replacement does not appear in the regular HTML on the page.

- The DisplayStatusMsg value reads "A Queen Anne." so that this phrase will appear in the message bar purely for the visitor's benefit.

- Finally, we added NAME="salem6" in this particular example to identify the original house JPG to the browser. This is what will make the swapImage function work, and guarantee that the browser will replace salem6s.jpg with salem6s2.jpg when the visitor rolls the cursor away.

5. Then we applied the changes described above to all five house JPGs in gallery.html so the code looked like this:

```
<P>
<A HREF="victorian.html"
onMou-
seOver="MM_preloadImages('salem1s.jpg','salem1s2.
jpg');MM_swapImage('document.salem1','docu-
ment.salem1','salem1s2.jpg','MM_swapImage5');MM_d
isplayStatusMsg('This is a Mansard Victo-
rian.');return document.MM_returnValue" onMouse-
Out="MM_swapImgRestore()">
<IMG SRC="salem1s.jpg" NAME="salem1"><BR>
<P>
<A HREF="revival.html"
onMou-
seOver="MM_preloadImages('salem4s.jpg','salem4s2.
jpg');MM_swapImage('document.salem4','docu-
ment.salem4','salem4s2.jpg','MM_swapImage4');MM_d
isplayStatusMsg('This is a Greek Revival');return
document.MM_returnValue" onMouse-
Out="MM_swapImgRestore()">
<IMG SRC="salem4s.jpg" NAME="salem4"><BR>
<P>
<A HREF="georgian.html"
onMou-
seOver="MM_preloadImages('salem5s.jpg','salem5s2.
jpg ');MM_swapImage('document.salem5','docu-
ment.salem5','salem5s2.jpg
','MM_swapImage3');MM_displayStatusMsg('A Geor-
gian.');return document.MM_returnValue" onMouse-
Out="MM_swapImgRestore()">
<IMG SRC="salem5s.jpg" NAME="salem5"></A><BR>
<P>
<A HREF="victorian.html"
onMou-
seOver="MM_preloadImages('salem2s.jpg','salem2s2.
jpg');MM_swapImage('document.salem2','docu-
ment.salem2','
salem2s2.jpg','MM_swapImage2');MM_displayStatusMs
g('An Italianate.');return docu-
```

```
ment.MM_returnValue" onMouse-
Out="MM_swapImgRestore()">
<IMG SRC="salem2s.jpg" NAME="salem2"></A><BR>
<P>
<A HREF="victorian.html" onMou-
seOver="MM_preloadImages('salem6s.jpg','salem6s2.
jpg');MM_swapImage('document.salem6','docu-
ment.salem6','salem6s2.jpg','MM_swapImage1');MM_d
isplayStatusMsg('A Queen Anne.');return docu-
ment.MM_returnValue" onMouse-
Out="MM_swapImgRestore()"><IMG SRC="salem6s.jpg"
NAME="salem6"></A>
```

6. Then, finally (!) we saved all this HTML as jsgallery.html and uploaded it in a browser to test it. When we were certain it worked properly, we saved it as gallery.html.

Style Sheets: Absolute Text Positioning

Now let's have some fun with style sheets on the business site, beginning with our business site.

1. Open info.html in your HTML editor; this is a file that we finished in Chapter 10. The HTML for this page should look like this before we get started:

```
<HTML>
<BODY BGCOLOR="#ccffcc" TEXT="#006600"
LINK="#0000FF" ALINK="#ccffcc" VLINK="FF0000">
<FONT FACE="arial, helvetica" SIZE="+1">
<P>Explore the <A HREF="services.html" TAR-
GET="rbottom">services</A> we have to offer,
including tax preparation, estate planning, and
investment advice.
<P><A HREF="staff.html" TARGET="rbottom">Meet Our
Staff</A>, who are always here to serve you.
<P>Got enough invested to make your retirement
comfortable? Take our <A HREF="quiz.html" TAR-
GET="rbottom">Fiscally Fit Quiz</A>.
```

```
<P>Check out other useful <A HREF="links.html"
TARGET="rbottom">links</A> including mortgage and
college tuition calculators, the latest on the
Dow Jones, and  more money management.
<BR>
<P><CENTER><IMG SRC="tax.gif" WIDTH=377
HEIGHT=75></CENTER>
<BR>
</FONT>
</BODY>
</HTML>
```

2. First, let's establish some style rules at the top within the <HEAD> tag:

```
<HEAD>
<STYLE TYPE="text/css">
<!--
p                { color: #336699 ;
                   font-size: 20pt ;
                   font-family: arial }

p.services       { margin: 5% 20% -10% 5% }

p.staff             { margin: 5% 55% 10% 5% ;
                      float: left }

p.quiz              { margin: 5% 20% -10% 5% }

p.links             { margin: 5% -10% -10% 5% }
                      float: right }

a                   { font-size: 24pt }
-->
</STYLE><HEAD>
```

3. Now let's tie in the HTML like so:

```
<P CLASS="services">Explore the <A HREF="ser-
vices.html" TARGET="rbottom">Services</A> we have
to offer, including tax preparation, estate plan-
ning, and investment advice.
```

Who's Afraid of Web Page Design?

```
<P CLASS="staff"><A HREF="staff.html" TAR-
GET="rbottom">Meet Our Staff</A>, who are always
here to serve you.
<P CLASS="quiz">Got enough invested to make your
retirement comfortable? Take our <A
HREF="quiz.html" TARGET="rbottom">Fiscally Fit
Quiz</A>.
<P CLASS="links">Check out other useful <A
HREF="links.html" TARGET="rbottom">Links</A>
including mortgage and college tuition calcula-
tors, the latest on the Dow Jones, and more money
management.
```

4. To make sure this page degrades well, let's test it in Netscape 3. It's not as interesting, but it works.

5. Save the final HTML as info.html.

Putting It All Together: The Animated Menu Bar

In this exercise, we're going to try something with the personal site (the operative word here being *try*) that's even more complex than the second JavaScript exercise and even buggier than style sheets. This last exercise is true DHTML; it incorporates both scripting and positioning capabilities to make a controllable, moving menu bar that opens and closes on command. Let's get started—you'll need the HTML editor, your browser of choice, and the CD-ROM.

1. Open john.html in your HTML editor. (You may use either the file we created in Chapter 9 or john1.html from the CD-ROM.) Here's what the HTML should look like before we get started:

```
<HTML>
<HEAD>
<TITLE>Meet John Doe</TITLE>
</HEAD>
<BODY BGCOLOR="#FFCC99" TEXT="#996666"
LINK="#663366" ALINK="#FF6699" VLINK="#FF6666">
<FONT FACE="Verdana, Georgia, Helvetica">
<BR>
```

```
<P><FONT SIZE="+1"><B>John</B></FONT> is a pro-
grammer at <A HREF="http://www.acmetech.com">Acme
Technology Inc.</A> where he does plenty of tech-
nogeek stuff.
<P>His hobbies include <FONT SIZE="+1"><B>rac-
quetball</B></FONT>, microbrewing, and collecting
<FONT SIZE="+1"><B>Buddy Holly</B></FONT>
records.
<P>Email John at <A HREF="mailto:jdoe@acme-
tech.com">jdoe@acmetech.com</A>.
</BODY>
</HTML>
```

and here's what it looks like when we're finished—this is another text-only file on the CD, doemenu.txt:

```
<HTML>
<HEAD>
<TITLE>Meet John Doe</TITLE>
<STYLE TYPE="text/css">
<!--
#divMenu  { position: absolute; top: 0; left: -
280; width: 335; height: 50; z-index: 100; }
A:link  { text-decoration: none }
A:alink { text-decoration: none }
A:vlink { text-decoration: none }
A:hover { text-decoration: underline }
-->
</STYLE>

<SCRIPT LANGUAGE="JavaScript">
<!--
/*This script made by www.bratta.com*/
//The speed the menu moves in, in milliseconds
var speed=10
//How many pixels do you want the menu to move
every step
var pix=1
```

```
//The place you want the menu to stop. you will
have to change this if you add or subtract menu
items
var stop=-280
//If you want to the menu to be "out" when you
start, set the top in the stylesheet to the same
value as stop

//browser check
if(document.all){
                var Menu="divMenu.style.pixelLeft"
}else if(document.layers)
                var Menu="document.layers.div-
Menu.left"

//check which way the menu should go
function movemenu(){
                if (eval(Menu+'==stop')){
                     out();
                }else if(eval(Menu+'==0')){
                     inn();
                }
}
//This function moves the menu in
function inn(){
                if(eval(Menu+'!=stop')){
                     eval(Menu+'-=10')
                     setTimeout("inn()",speed)
                }
}
//This function moves the menu out
function out(){
                if(eval(Menu+'!=0')){
                     eval(Menu+'+=10')
                     setTimeout("out()",speed)
                }
}
//-->
</SCRIPT>
```

```
</HEAD>
<BODY BGCOLOR="#FFCC99" TEXT="#996666"
LINK="#663366" ALINK="#FF6699" VLINK="#FF6666">
<FONT FACE="Verdana, Georgia, Helvetica">
<BR>
<DIV ID="divMenu">
<NOBR><IMG SRC="doemenu.gif" WIDTH="270"
HEIGHT="50" BORDER="0" USEMAP="#menu"
ALT="hey!"><A onmouseover="javascript:movemenu()"
HREF="#"><IMG SRC="mswirl.gif" ALT="whoosh!"
WIDTH="50" HEIGHT="50" BORDER="0"></A></NOBR>
<MAP NAME="menu">
<AREA SHAPE="rect" HREF="doe.html"
COORDS="3,3,63,33">
<AREA SHAPE="rect" HREF="john.html"
COORDS="64,3,101,33">
<AREA SHAPE="rect" HREF="jane.html"
COORDS="102,3,151,33">
<AREA SHAPE="rect" HREF="jack.html"
COORDS="152,3,207,33">
<AREA SHAPE="rect" HREF="jill.html"
COORDS="208,3,270,33">
</MAP>
</DIV>
<P><IMG SRC="pixel.gif" HEIGHT=50 WIDTH=1>
<BR>
<P><FONT SIZE="+1"><B>John</B></FONT> is a pro-
grammer at <A HREF="http://www.acmetech.com">Acme
Technology Inc.</A> where he does plenty of tech-
nogeek stuff.
<P>His hobbies include <FONT SIZE="+1"><B>rac-
quetball</B></FONT>, microbrewing, and collecting
<FONT SIZE="+1"><B>Buddy Holly</B></FONT>
records.
<P>Email John at <A HREF="mailto:jdoe@acme-
tech.com">jdoe@acmetech.com</A>.
</BODY>
</HTML>
```

Several parts of this code need explaining, so let's take them one at a time.

Amy: The part of the JavaScript that tells you what it's doing is very cool. That must be written specifically to allow people to adapt the JavaScript to their own pages—how generous!

Rebecca: Yes, Thomas Brattli is a very generous—and talented—soul. I believe there are more nifty DHTML things available on his web site at http://www.bratta.com.

Generally speaking, quite a few freely available scripts come with instructions already written in. You should always leave them in, too, even if you incorporate your own code and understand how it all works, because other people might visit your page and download it for themselves. Also, it's good "netiquette" to let everyone know where the script originated, so the author can get his or her proper credit.

2. This bit of style sheets code at the top does a couple of things:

```
<STYLE TYPE="text/css">
<!--
#divMenu  { position: absolute; top: 0; left: -
280; width: 335; height: 50; z-index: 100; }
A:link  { text-decoration: none }
A:alink { text-decoration: none }
A:vlink { text-decoration: none }
A:hover { text-decoration: underline }
-->
</STYLE>
```

The line that begins with the selector "#divMenu" tells the browser where to position the two graphics that make up the retractable menu. The rest of this line, the declaration, contains six properties—position, top, left, width, height, and z-index—that put the menu graphics squarely in place three-dimensionally. The value of left, even, is a negative number; this demonstrates style sheets's negative margin capability. You can't do that with plain HTML!

The remaining four lines of code are CLASS declarations, similar to those we just used in the style sheets exercise, and they remove the underlining from any links on the page until the visitor rolls over them with the cursor. However, this last little trick, A:hover, only works in Explorer, so don't look for it using Navigator and think you've made an error.

3. This next bit of wonderful script, written by Thomas Brattli of Bratta Design and adapted elsewhere, is notated with the comment< ! > tag and therefore is mostly self-explanatory:

```
<SCRIPT LANGUAGE="JavaScript">
<!--
/*This script made by www.bratta.com*/
//The speed the menu moves in, in milliseconds
var speed=10
//How many pixels do you want the menu to move
every step
var pix=1
//The place you want the menu to stop. you will
have to change this if you add or subtract menu
items
var stop=-280
//If you want to the menu to be "out" when you
start, set the top in the stylesheet to the same
value as stop

//browser check
if(document.all){
                var Menu="divMenu.style.pixelLeft"
}else if(document.layers)
                var Menu="document.layers.div-
Menu.left"

//check which way the menu should go
function movemenu(){
                if (eval(Menu+'==stop')){
                        out();
                }else if(eval(Menu+'==0')){
```

```
                                  inn();
                          }
        }
        //This function moves the menu in
        function inn(){
                    if(eval(Menu+'!=stop')){
                          eval(Menu+'-=10')
                          setTimeout("inn()",speed)
                    }
        }
        //This function moves the menu out
        function out(){
                    if(eval(Menu+'!=0')){
                          eval(Menu+'+=10')
                          setTimeout("out()",speed)
                    }
        }
        //-->
        </SCRIPT>
```

The best scripts are helpfully documented this way, because even if a script's functionality is wonderful, you have to understand every line to make it work.

4. Next, this opening <DIV> tag ties and identifies its contents to the style sheets and JavaScript using the ID attribute:

```
<DIV ID="divMenu">
```

Like the CLASS and NAME attributes we've been using in this appendix, ID creates a specific identifier for some other non-HTML language in your HTML document. Without it, you'd get an error, because the browser would not understand which part of the code is affected by the style sheets and JavaScript. So you do *not* want to change the ID attribute here, or the script won't work.

5. This next bit of code puts the two menu graphics, doemenu.gif and mswirl.gif, on the web page using the <IMG> tag—we broke it up a little so you can read it more clearly:

```
<IMG SRC="doemenu.gif" WIDTH="270" HEIGHT="50"
BORDER="0" USEMAP="#menu" ALT="hey!">
```

```
<A onmouseover="javascript:movemenu()" HREF="#">
<IMG SRC="mswirl.gif" ALT="whoosh!" WIDTH="50"
HEIGHT="50" BORDER="0">
</A>
```

The ALT tag text is pretty much just for fun, but the rest is strictly business. The first graphic, doemenu.gif, is the actual imagemap containing the menu links to other parts of the web site. The USEMAP attributes ties it to the actual imagemap instructions (which we'll explain in the next step) using parentheses, the # symbol, and the identifier map.

The second graphic, mswirl.gif, is a little more complex, because it's the real moving, linked part to this menu. The onmouseover event handler causes the menu to unfurl when the visitor rolls the mouse over it, and the HREF attribute ties it to doemenu.gif so it will move as well. You should change only the names of the graphics in this bit of script, and nothing else.

Now let's explain how the menu works as an imagemap.

6. The next bit of code is a set of imagemap instructions, and it looks like this:

```
<MAP NAME="menu">
<AREA SHAPE="rect" HREF="doe.html"
COORDS="3,3,63,33">
<AREA SHAPE="rect" HREF="john.html"
COORDS="64,3,101,33">
<AREA SHAPE="rect" HREF="jane.html"
COORDS="102,3,151,33">
<AREA SHAPE="rect" HREF="jack.html"
COORDS="152,3,207,33">
<AREA SHAPE="rect" HREF="jill.html"
COORDS="208,3,270,33">
</MAP>
```

The <MAP> tag identifies its contents to the browser as an imagemap, a hidden set of multiple links defined by the attributes of the <AREA> tag. The <MAP> tag's NAME attribute ties this code to the actual graphic that the visitor can see—in this instance, doemenu.html. The <AREA> tag describes what's "below" this graphic; the <SHAPE> tag with the value rect says there are five rectangular link "hotspots," the HREF attribute identifies the pages that are linked to these hotspots, and the COORDS attribute defines the perimeters of these hotspots in pixels.

You want to change only the HREF values, to whatever the names of the other pages in your web site might be.

7. When we were satisfied with the changes and everything worked properly, we saved this code as doemenu1.html.

Amy: I know I haven't made many comments during this chapter. I can't say that I exactly understand JavaScript or DHTML, but I understand what they're supposed to do and a little bit about how they do it. As Rebecca said, that's all we're really supposed to get from this appendix, and I thought that limited content was explained quite clearly.

"Answers" to the Exercises

Here's the final HTML for the first JavaScript exercise, john.html:

```
<HTML>
<HEAD>
<TITLE>Meet John Doe</TITLE>
</HEAD>
<BODY BACKGROUND="oswirl.gif">
<BR>
<IMG SRC="pixel.gif" ALIGN=bottom HEIGHT=155
WIDTH=1>
<P ALIGN=center>
<A HREF="john.html" onMouseOver = "wordage('John
Doe, Master of his Domain');
return true;"><IMG SRC="eye1.gif"  BORDER=0
HSPACE=6 VSPACE=1></A>
<A HREF="jane.html" onMouseOver = "wordage('Jane
Doe, A Woman of Endless Talents'); return
true;"><IMG SRC="eye2.gif"  BORDER=0 HSPACE=6
VSPACE=1></A>
```

```
<A HREF="jack.html" onMouseOver = "wordage('Jack
Doe, Wonder Boy');
return true;"><P ALIGN=center><IMG SRC="eye3.gif"
BORDER=0 HSPACE=6 VSPACE=1></A>
<A HREF="jill.html" onMouseOver = "wordage('Jill
Doe, Child Prodigy');
return true;"><IMG SRC="eye4.gif"  BORDER=0
HSPACE=6 VSPACE=1></A>
<BR>
</BODY>
</HTML>
```

The final HTML for the second JavaScript exercise and the general DHTML exercise are already saved on the CD-ROM as rich text files js2.rtf and dhtml.rtf, respectively. These RTF files should open in Microsoft Word, WordPerfect, or the plain text readers we recommended as HTML editors (SimpleText for Macintosh users and NotePad for PC users).

Review

- Dynamic HTML, or DHTML, is a third-generation language with the ability to script (with JavaScript) and position (with style sheets) any HTML element on a web page. It was created by Netscape in 1995 as a response to people who were trying to make regular HTML more interactive with "add-on" technology.

- DHTML sees everything concrete within the environment of your web site as an object with the potential to be interactive. HTML sees everything in your environment more as an element, to be pushed around and manipulated but not affected.

- HTML has attributes, but JavaScript makes objects interactive by means of properties and methods. Properties affect the appearance of the object; methods affect what the object does.

- Style sheets allows you to separate the form of an object on a web page from its appearance, and to create customized instructions on how those objects should be displayed by a browser.

Who's Afraid of Web Page Design?

- JavaScripts and style sheets are supported—and only in part—by version 4 and version 5 browsers, period. You should not rely on such technologies to make or break the overall design and functionality of your web site.

The Gallery: A Sneak Peek

This section consists of the color insert in this book. It is a quick look at fifteen sites found in the Gallery on the CD-ROM. The Gallery is an extension of Chapter 4, our first tour of the Web and of many sites demonstrating quality, effective web page design. Use this section of the book and CD to get new ideas, to see more high-end web page design technologies at work, and to read more conversation between Amy and myself about advanced web page design topics.

Index

A
<A>, 219–226, 333
ACTION, 282
Adobe
  GoLive, 29
  PageMill, 29
  Photoshop, 30, 311
Aladdin Systems, 31
ALIGN, 223–226, 229, 232, 236, 240, 283,
   329, 334
Allaire, 29, 30
ALT, 334
AltaVista, 5
Animation, 8, 322
  See also GIF animations
Apple Computer, 32
Attributes, 6
Audio
  defined, 8, 321
  links, 323–324, 344–346
.AU format, 323–324
Author, Web page, 4
AUTOPLAY, 330–331
AUTOSTART, 329, 331

B
BACKGROUND, 233
Background color, 188
  HTML used to add, 196–204
Backgrounds, 65–73, 188
Bandwidth, 114–115
Bare Bones Software's BBEdit, 29, 30
<BASEFONT>, 262–263

BGCOLOR, 231, 233
<BGSOUND>, 328, 331
Blur, Gaussian versus normal, 146, 150
<BODY> elements, 219–226
BORDER, 231, 236, 330, 334
BORDERCOLOR, 233
BORDERCOLORDARK, 233
BORDERCOLORLIGHT, 233
BoxTop Software, 92–93

, 219–226, 228
Brightness, 187, 193–194
Browser palette, 186
Browsers
  defined, 3
  Microsoft Internet Explorer 4, 27–28
  Netscape Navigator 3, 26–27
Browsers *(continued)*
  Netscape Navigator 4, 24–26
Browser-safe palette/colors, 119,
   140–141, 186
Business site, 41, 358–359

C
Cable modems, 20–21
CD-ROM, 18
CELLPADDING, 231, 236
Cells, 322
CELLSPACING, 231, 236
Checkbox, 258
CHECKED, 284
CLASS, 283
Clip2GIF, creating transparent GIFs
   with, 132–133

Paint Shop Pro, 30, 31
  creating GIFs with, 128–129
  creating JPEGs with, 130–131
  creating transparent GIFs with, 132
  interlacing in, 133–134
PALETTE, 330
Palettes
  defined, 185–186
  individual, 188
  RGB color and, 118–119
Patterns, creating and altering, 158–163
PC (personal computer), 3, 14–16
Personal site, 40, 358
Photoshop, 30, 31
  See also Scanned artwork
  toolbar and description of, 138–139
Pixel, 115, 117
pixel.gif, 226–229
Plastic looks, creating, 154–158
PLAYBACK, 329, 331
Play box, 321
Plug-ins, 3–4, 32
PNG (Portable Network Graphic), 121–122
<PRE>, 228
Primary colors, 191
Progressive display, 120
Properties, 100
Pulldown menu, 258

Q
QuickTime, 32, 95, 96, 98–100

R
Radio button, 258
RAM (random access memory), 18
RealAudio, 32
RealPlayer, 32, 331
Redesigning, frequency of, 361–362
Reset button, 258
Resolution, 115, 117–118
RGB color, 118–119, 186
Riven, 86–89
Rollovers, 72
ROWS, 241, 285
ROWSPAN, 232

S
Salon magazine, 75, 77, 78
Saturation, 187, 192
Scanned artwork
  assembling extracted elements, 176–182

  extracting textures and other
    elements, 167–176
  prelude, 164–167
Scanners, 22–23
Screen resolution, 115
SCROLLING, 241, 242
Search-and-grab technique, 170
Search engines, 5, 74–75
Secondary colors, 191
Secondary pages, 53–54
<SELECT>, 285, 290
SELECTED, 285
SGML (Standard Generalized Markup
    Language), 6
Shockwave, 32, 95
Siegel, David, 62, 80, 367
SimpleText, 28
SIZE, 263–266, 284, 285, 290
Snapple, 72
Software
  defined, 3
  image, 30–31
  requirements, 23–33
SoundHandle, 328
SoundMover, 328
SRC, 241, 284, 335
START, 335
Structure, 38
StuffIt, 31, 115
Style sheets, 10–11, 100–105
Subject pages, 53–54
Submit button, 258
Surfer, 4
Surfing, 4
Syntax, 210
System requirements, 13–16

T
TABINDEX, 284
<TABLE>, 229–239
</TABLE>, 231
Tables, 7
Tags, 6, 210–211
  See also under type of
TARGET, 282, 283, 333
<TD>, 231, 232
</TD>, 237
Text
  <BASEFONT>, 262–263
  COLOR, 267–271
  defined, 7, 257
  embellishing plain, 291–298